Tony Thorne is an author, columnist and broadcaster, and the director of the Slang and New Language Archive at King's College London. His books include the bestselling *Dictionary of Contemporary Slang*, *Countess Dracula*, *Fads, Fashions & Cults* and his acclaimed guide to buzzwords and jargon, *Shoot the Puppy*. He lives in London with his family.

THE 100 WORDS THAT MAKE THE ENGLISH

Tony Thorne

ABACUS

ABACUS

First published in Great Britain under the title *Jolly Wicked, Actually*
in 2009 by Little, Brown
This paperback edition published in 2011 by Abacus

Grateful acknowledgement is made for permission to quote from
the following material: 'Not the Bermuda Triangle' from *Zoom!*
by Simon Armitage (Bloodaxe Books, 2002).

Every effort has been made to contact all copyright holders.
If notified, the publisher will be pleased to rectify any errors
or omissions at the earliest opportunity.

A CIP catalogue record for this book
is available from the British Library.

ISBN 978-0-349-12103-1

Typeset in Caslon by M Rules
Printed and bound in Great Britain by
Clays Ltd, St Ives plc

For Daisy Diana

Introduction

Man is a creature who lives not upon bread
alone, but primarily by catchwords.

Robert Louis Stevenson, *Virginibus Puerisque*,
1881

What you say is what you are.

Playground taunt, 20th century

The 100 Words that Make the English consists of one hundred of 'our' keywords, each followed by a short essay that typically looks at where the word came from and how it may have changed and evolved; how it has been used, by whom and with what intention; and how it keys into shared ideas of Englishness. Where space permits, exemplifying quotes – 'citations' – are included. These are the hundred words out of the million or so in the available lexicon that I think sum up our understanding of ourselves. They have not been selected according to any 'scientific' criteria, or on the basis of a survey; the choice is based on intuition, on personal encounters with

1

language-users in all sorts of settings and on adventuring in archives and libraries. It's certain that no two people asked to make such a selection would choose the same words, and criticism of these choices is very warmly welcomed. Throughout the process of writing, a host of other candidates have thrust themselves forward. In the last couple of hours I've heard or read: 'kicking off', in the sense of losing one's temper and starting a fight; 'continental', in the phrase 'continental manners and mores'; the adjective 'Pooterish', borrowing the name of the hero of George and Weedon Grossmith's 1892 *Diary of a Nobody* to define someone as comically narrow-minded and fastidious; and 'Middle England' (first used by Lord Salisbury in 1882, but popularised as a political buzzword a hundred years later), a paradigm of what the academics call an 'imagined community'. A case for inclusion in the 'Top 100' could be made for any one of these. Each of them can usefully be unbundled to call into question sub-surface assumptions and implications. Why employ a footballing metaphor for a sudden eruption of ill temper and/or violence? What exactly are the attributes held in common by 'continentals' – and where in Europe do these infuriatingly rational, sybaritic aliens and their noisy extended families reside? What could a contemporary lifestyle have in common with a mundane Victorian existence? Where, apart from in our imagination, is Middle England located and what are its defining features? An oblique sort of answer to this last question has been provided by a Dutch visitor, teacher Pieter Boogaart, in his *A272: An Ode to a Road*. Of the highway that runs through Sussex into Hampshire he said, 'for some reason it always filled me with a sense of nostalgia when we came across it or when I saw it on a map. It's a bit like falling in love . . .' The road has since been nominated as number 545 of the 1,170 'icons of England' featured on the internet.

Introduction

This is not a list of my favourite words – that would include such indulgences as 'hoity-toity', 'raffish', 'cringe-worthy' (Cuthbert of that ilk being a sort of anti-Bash Street Kid) and, if I'm honest, 'arse'. I've tried not to be utterly predictable in the choice of terms to cover, while still taking account of clichés and stereotypes if they are genuinely central to our self-image. Thus, **understatement** is included, because a scan of spoken and written sources shows that we do say it and write it, but 'hypocrisy', though alluded to, does not get its own entry, since it features mainly in outsiders' descriptions of English behaviour (scanning international publications confirms that the global hypocrite label, inevitable for any quasi-imperialist claiming the moral high ground, is more often applied to the USA these days), with one notable exception: the cries of 'humbug' (from 1754, origin unknown) whenever Labour politicians send their children to selective schools. 'Stiff upper lip' crops up once or twice in the following pages, but didn't merit an entry to itself. Apart from being, to my mind, a dodgy (1950s, 'unreliable', from 1860s, 'illegal', 'stolen') metaphor, it's actually American in origin, first attested in 1815: as innumerable **bore**s, echoing actor Michael Caine, have observed, 'not many people know that'.

Technology can be of some help in analysing language in action. 'Corpus-based' or computational linguistics, with its techniques of text-scanning and concordancing (electronically mapping relationships between words), now enables us to establish how frequently a given word occurs in a body of writing or a set of recordings, and the entire works of a writer can be scanned and 'tagged' to discover which words and combinations of words she particularly favours. One problem is that nearly all corpora consist only of *written* language, collected from newspapers and books, and where spoken language has been recorded it is nearly always 'standard' English rather than colloquial or quirky language which is fed into the databases, so that we can't count on electronic sources for a fully comprehensive sampling of varieties, styles and idiosyncrasies. In any case, in a book of this kind there is not space enough to examine regional dialects and localised usages, unless they impact (like cockney rhyming slang, or Afro-Caribbean 'patwa', or Asian-influenced 'Hinglish', for example) on the 'mainstream' tongue. Simply listening in on authentic speech allows us to identify the rituals of English conversation, such as **grumbl**ing ('I've been queuing since eight o'clock this morning: what with one thing and another I'm about done for. I'd like to take that Attlee and all the rest of them and put them on the top of a bonfire in Hyde Park and burn them'), saying **sorry**, excusing oneself and others, veiled criticisms, endless social categorising, along with nonstop banter consisting of teasing and facetiousness, and a pervasive, even corrosive, **irony**.

In tracking the cultural and linguistic transformations of the last two hundred years, what strikes us is that there is a watershed, a relatively recent tipping-point or step-change where we started to use jargon unknown to our grandparents. Social upheavals like the agricultural and industrial revolutions, the two world wars, the advent of the so-called affluent society and **permissive**ness have all resulted in feelings of disjuncture and disorientation, but for my purposes the great transition was from 'Old England' to 'New Britain', and I think it happened very quickly, at the end of the 1970s. There have been numerous Old Englands, as from Victorian Pre-Raphaelite times onwards people have conjured up a purer, cleaner, more honest **society**, bucolic and homogeneous. *My* Old England encompasses everything that preceded the free-market post-industrial multi-culti environment of the twenty-first century: I'm using it as shorthand for a relatively complacent, monoglot, insular, fussy, fusty (fourteenth century, from Latin *fustis*, 'cudgel', which became 'fust', a mouldy-smelling wine cask), obtuse (sixteenth century, from Latin *obtusus*, 'dulled' or 'cudgelled into submission') community, fixated on certain rectitudes and responsibilities. New Britain labels the Americanised-to-some-extent (to use a word we have strenuously avoided, even in the depths of self-loathing), service-oriented, unabashed, glossy, confessional, competitive constituency we have become in the have-it-all noughties. The distinction is artificial, of course, because of the continuities: money-making has been what we are all about for centuries; an unspoken tolerance of inequality persists; if we are white we are likely still to be resolutely monolingual.

Punk was the last *cri de coeur* against the old regime, the Sloane Rangers were its last gasp: a three-hundred-year-old system of embedded hierarchical values and behaviours reduced to a few items of clothing and style accessories. In terms of pop conceptualisations, the vortex known by the shorthand 'Thatcher' may have hijacked the 1980s, but New Britain would have come about had she – it – they not existed. It would have been called into existence by the post-punk stylists on the one hand (the evidence is there, first in the French magazine *Actuel*, then in its English imitation *The Face*), and on the other by the liberated lower middle classes, the once-repressed 'aspirational' majority, now united in common purpose with the more glamorous yuppies and upwardly mobile Essex boys. DIY individualism and bricolage met hedonism and consumerism and begat the hypermarket of style, pick-and-mix value systems, an economics of contingency. If this sounds glib – well, it's meant to: reference books have to be glib. But using that word makes me think of someone who hated it. My mother, who died two years ago, was young in the 1940s, flourished in the fifties, was bemused by the sixties and despaired more and more of the succeeding decades. She managed to be neither **common** nor **posh**, was soignée in a rather puritanical way, yet would never have used any of that string of defining adjectives herself. It was not done to objectify oneself, least of all by such overspecific terms. The suburban matron who dismissed her neighbours as 'vulgar and pushy', the ambassador's wife referring to a couple on the social circuit as 'not quite PLU' (for 'People Like Us') unwittingly categorised themselves, betrayed their own snobbishness. My mother had her favourite words, which she used to excess; **nice** exasperated me, 'kind' – an oddly old-fashioned word, little used these days – sticks in my mind: 'the English school, whose motto puts kindliness above flourishment or learning' (A. G. Macdonell, *England, Their England*, 1933). These anodyne (sixteenth century, from Greek *anodunos*, 'painless') words, evasive substitutes and clichés though they may have been, in a different way defined her and many others of her age. For my mother, as for her contemporaries, kindness, right and wrong, reasonableness and common sense were fundamental aspects of Englishness. These were both her personal touchstones and unquestioned, eternal values held in common. But we now realise that they are in fact, in the words of one linguist, 'unexamined cultural prejudices . . . masquerading as human nature', peculiar not even to all English speakers, but only to some of the inhabitants of Great Britain. Another central tenet of ours, **fair** play, is untranslatable and therefore has to be borrowed by other languages, and the concept of fairness itself (as in the child's protest, 'It's not fair!') is not innate or instinctive, but has existed as a component of our language, and part of our mindset, only since the eighteenth century. In the same way, the English tendency towards endlessly hedging and qualifying – 'I think', 'I suppose', 'probably', 'presumably', 'possibly', 'allegedly', 'arguably', **actually** – is not shared by neighbouring cultures. It seems to have arrived with the Enlightenment and been consolidated by the idea of the unique, autonomous, responsible citizen having to negotiate and justify; in other words, the growing individualism accompanying industrialisation and commercialism. Feeding into the mix is the stuttering diffidence with which the English privileged have masked their unshakeable superiority.

Every language is different, every macro- or microculture is special in its way, but the idea that the English are unfathomable anomalies is an old one, and one that we tend, squirming with delighted false modesty, to endorse. Foreigners such as the Hungarian George Mikes have anatomised us and celebrated our peculiarities ('I expected the British nation to rise in wrath but all they said was: "quite amusing"'), while another Dutch visitor, the academic Dr G. J. Renier, entitled his 1931 treatment *The English: Are They Human?* By the English he meant middle-class or upper-middle-class English men, whom he gratifyingly allowed were human, as well as pragmatic and respectable, but hobbled by inarticulacy and emotional illiteracy. This caricature Englishman can still be found, still reluctant to commit, to enthuse or to offend, but his faint mumblings are drowned by a cacophony of other, harsher voices. The Old–New transition has been accompanied, in the UK more markedly perhaps than in any comparable society, by the rapid relaxation of all linguistic constraints and a retreat by the guardians of propriety (only Dr Johnson's 'harmless drudge', the lexicographer, I'm pleased to think, can still pose as an authority on language, but with a strict remit to record, not to prescribe or proscribe). Fine distinctions have been done away with: 'shall' and 'should' have become 'will' and 'would'. Over the last few years, 'as if' has been ousted by 'like' in sentences such as 'She looked like she was experiencing difficulties' without attracting a single comment. Colloquialisms and slang, once forbidden, then permitted only within quotation marks or in imitation of 'racy' dialogue, are now allowed into the 'quality press' and pepper the conversation of respectable citizens. 'Bad language' in the sense of profanity, though still controversial, is everywhere. A tolerance for the non-standard has become a celebration of the outlandish, and older texts, even from popular publications, look strangely stilted or formal to our eyes.

The 100 Words that Make the English looks back over the centuries, highlighting the twentieth century as a pivotal stage of development, but also reports from today's linguistic front line: what would John Betjeman have made of the idea of 'multi-ethnic youth vernacular' – the very latest thing in linguistic circles – the idea that a slangy teen code consisting of black and Asian patois delivered in a hip-hop intonation is set to oust standard English in a few years' time? How would those, my late mother among them, who once insisted on 'manners' react to the appointment just the other day of a national 'respect tsar' to enforce politeness, or the Channel 4 TV documentary entitled *The Seven Sins of England*, proving that rudeness, **slag**gishness, bigotry, **binge** drinking, hooliganism and violence have been bywords of Englishness for hundreds of years? How did we get from 'The English school . . . lay among its water-meads, and all around was the creator, the inheritor, the ancestor and the descendant of it all, the green and kindly land of England'

(*England, Their England* again) to 'The mass drunkenness every weekend which renders British town centres unendurable to even minimally civilised people goes hand-in-hand with the appallingly crude, violent and shallow relations between the sexes' (Theodore Dalrymple, *Our Culture, What's Left of It*, 2005). Rustic, dyspeptic Old England and urban, shouty New Britain actually coexist, quarrelsomely and querulously at times, each occupying its own psychic zone within the archipelago . . .

. . . But wait, was all talk of a classless society, of meritocracy, in vain? Have campaigns for 'equal opportunities' been a sham (thought to be a seventeenth-century northern dialect version of 'shame')? Is Old England staging a comeback? Private education, private health care, restrictions on immigration, the resurgence of outdated public-school slang, sneering at the lower orders (certainly during the noughties, it was fashionable to laugh at the feckless, bothersome 'chav', from a French dialect word for a young fox, first used as a term of endearment or address by Romanies) all are in the ascendant. The Mayor of London is a character from the pages of P. G. Wodehouse, and there are people on television called things like Hugh Fearnley-Whittingstall. Progressive, leftish north London is out of fashion (though the Wodehousian mayor secretly lives there); instead we have been introduced to the patrician glam-Tory 'Notting Hill Set', something like the Bloomsbury Group but without the painting, writing or thinking. Attempts to resurrect the Sloane Rangers or to rename them 'Hedgies' (after '**hedge**-fund managers') seem mercifully to have foundered, but where old money and new celebrity rub shoulders, the pampered 'yummy mummy' lives on. 'Nothing hardens my resolve to abstain from parenthood', snarled **bloke**ish hack Nirpal Dhaliwal, 'more than the herds of posturing yummy mummies who congregate to slurp lattes and share the tedious details of their offspring's development'; although the mania for discovering new micro-categories to dissect and promote means that she too was reinvented not long ago in a spoof blog in the *Telegraph*, as affluent, brand-literate 'Dulwich Mum'. A reader from East Dulwich wrote, 'Whilst I have not met Dulwich Mum, I have encountered any number of her type; vacuous, self-centred with shrill voices, overdressed and under-talented children, no concept of real work and a husband who pays for everything . . . hardship is a closed shop or the cleaner turning up late.' Snippy, **chippy** class envy or a healthy contempt for pretentious twaddle (eighteenth century, from sixteenth-century 'twattle', an imitation of babbling or silly talk)? I think the latter, as she continues: 'Whilst there is a place for all voices in society this blog, like cable TV, demonstrates that unrestricted opportunity certainly does not improve quality.' The to-and-fro continues. The carnival moves on.

In *The 100 Words that Make the English* I have tried to avoid 'lexicographese', the technical formatting, abbreviations and stylised defining language favoured by dictionaries. One convention, though, has been retained, in that some entries are followed by cross-references to similar or related terms listed elsewhere in the book. Additionally, each time one of the hundred keywords appears in a discussion of another term, or in the preceding introduction, it is highlighted in bold face.

In distilling millions of words into tens of thousands, I'm immensely grateful to Eve Marleau for help in foraging in the archives. I relied upon, among others, the British Library and its press archives; the libraries and archives of King's College London and the Borough of Richmond; and the

Introduction

British National Corpus. For language novelties, exoticisms and slang I could rummage in my own Slang and New Language Archive at King's College London, which can be accessed at www.kcl.ac.uk/schools/humanities/depts/elc/resources/slangresearch.html. I consulted a very wide range of published sources and would advise anyone researching language and popular culture to do the same. The most authoritative titles differ considerably on questions of, for example, etymology, so beware of trusting in any single one, even one so eminent, comprehensive and useful as the *OED*. Beware, too, all information displayed on the internet: in every case it requires careful checking and corroboration.

I would like to thank Professor Keith Hoggart for his support over the years, and Richard Curtis, Ben Elton and Penguin Books for permission to quote from *Blackadder*. For seeing this project into print I would like to thank Richard Beswick, Victoria Pepe and Zoë Hood at Little, Brown, copyeditor Jane Selley, and my agent Julian Alexander. For the BBC audiobook version, thanks to Fiona McKenzie-Williams and to Alec Reid and John Telfer.

Thanks are also due to all those who sent in corrections, comments and suggestions prompted by the first edition of the book. I am particularly grateful in this respect to Henry Hitchings, Adam Macqueen, D. R. Garvey, Lex Craandijk, David S. Miller and Peter Jebell.

Modern authors, at least those who consider themselves techno-literate progressives, are expected to endorse 'connectivity' and 'visibility'. Postmodern texts are supposed to be 'open' and 'interactive', so if you would like to suggest your own keywords, or to question, comment on or criticise what appears in these pages, you can email me at tony.thorne@kcl.ac.uk.

Actually

As the *Daily Mirror* had it in 2003: 'Intellectual, thought-provoking, ground-breaking, incisive, courageously different, fascinating ... actually, Richard Curtis's much talked about movie is none of these things.' They were reviewing the film *Love, Actually*, which trades on the notions of repressed or muted feelings, a reluctance to emote honestly, a supposedly charming reticence. Hesitancy and tentativeness, real or feigned, is indeed an English characteristic, and is recognised as such by foreigners, but to be more accurate, it's indicative not of an English manner, but of a middle- and upper-class English manner, of the mannerisms of Oxbridge and the Home Counties. The adverb actually (it can be described more exactly as a sentence modifier, or as a parenthetical filler) has transited from a meaningful term – the meaning in question being 'truly' or 'currently' – to what is more usually an empty qualification or hesitation. It has actually changed its primary sense several times: first 'by way of deeds, actively', from 1470; 'really', 1587; 'currently' (still its meaning in French, Spanish and German), 1663; 'indeed', 1762. In twentieth-century conversation, it became an almost meaningless marker of diffidence, a timid conveyor of a contradiction, an example of unemphatic emphasis – mocked in the past by North Americans and Australians as an effete Anglicism, but increasingly now used by them too. Sometimes it's employed primarily to play for time – 'mmmm . . . actually . . .' – giving us a few seconds to consider before delivering our (not necessarily earth-shattering) conclusions. Sometimes it signals an apology or excuse, or, as in a *Times* report from 1796, a grudging admission. During the trial of a Mr Stone on charges of high treason, his advocates '. . . admitted that he actually did send information to France, but it is said it was done for the express purpose of averting a great calamity from his country'. The word was still being used in the same way in 1980, when 'Lance Hawker's Diplomatic Diary' recorded an encounter with Foreign Office employees: '. . . an expert on Turkey comes to tell us what's going on in the country. "How big is the Turkish army?" someone inquires. "I'm not sure, actually. But rather big."'

A bizarre word in some ways, actually can be simultaneously both insistent and reticent, querulous and indignant, a passive–aggressive word, in short. In practice it's often used (with a sort of veiled or apologetic aggression) to contradict, to correct, to chide: '. . . actually he's very nice'; 'actually it's Charles, not Hugh', or to preface a change of tone, as in 'actually, sod it, I'll do it myself'. It was entirely fitting that the Pet Shop Boys entitled their 1987 album *Actually*, as the word perfectly reflects both their arch, knowing, affectless pose and that decade's glossy mix of smugness and anxiety.

The quintessentially English a-word is a mainstay both of real conversations and of the conversational tone attempted by the print media, frequently again heralding odd juxtapositions or jarring conclusions: 'Army Surgeon Actually a Woman' (tabloid headline); 'What did the Archbishop actually say about Sharia law?'; 'Who actually does all the work in an internet start-up?'; 'These terrible tactics may actually be working' (journalist Max Hastings on the Iraq conflict).

In translation from other European languages, actually (a fifteenth-century borrowing, via French, of Latin *actualis*, 'relating to acts or actions') is a classic 'false friend', in that it looks like *actualmente*, *actuel* or *aktuelle*, but means something different on this side of the Channel. It's doubly confusing for foreigners when it is employed in the mealy-mouthed obfuscation that English English delights in: what do they make of statements such as (in a business meeting) 'Actually, it's not that I think she isn't capable of doing the job . . .' or (in a university tutorial) 'Actually, it might be an idea to read chapters six and nine'? The first is actually an endorsement, albeit a weak one, the second is probably an order.

Ale

'A glass of your best ale, landlord!' if said at all, will these days be heavily laced with self-conscious irony – perhaps embellished by substituting 'foaming pint' for glass – or desperate cheeriness. In Shakespeare's day the enthusiasm was unforced, if we take at face value the speech by the Boy in *Henry V*: 'Would I were in a alehouse in London: I would give all my fame for a pot of ale and safety.' In *Twelfth Night*, (1601), Sir Toby Belch evoked a life of happy indulgence (anticipating the seventeenth-century synonym 'beer and skittles'): 'Dost thou think, because thou art virtuous, there shall be no more cakes and ale?' The Victorian linguist and travel writer George Henry Borrow, who knew the different cultures of Europe first hand, wrote in *Lavengro* (1851), 'He is not deserving of the name of Englishman who speaketh against ale, that is, good ale' (he didn't much like the Welsh variety). In December 1913, *The Times* reviewed a now-forgotten play about life in rural Wales called *Change*, opining that 'Mr Frank Ridley was amusing as a cockney workman, good-humouredly deploring the emotionalism of his Welsh neighbours, and offering them the Anglo-Saxon remedies of common sense, toleration all round and a pint of ale.' At once a nutritious staple, a comfort food and an enduring symbol of Englishness, again and again in the records ale appears as the key ingredient in an otherwise very limited repertoire of refreshment or sustenance. *The Times* reported on 23 December 1840 on plans for Christmas Day in the workhouses of London. 'In Christchurch, Blackfriars, Christmas Eve is to be kept by the adults having a pint of strong ale, and the children half a pint each; on Christmas day the fare is to be, adults each a pint of ale, six ounces of roast beef, and half a pound of plum-pudding.' In 1876, the *Penny Illustrated* paper, reporting on the intention of a 'sportsman', Mr Weston, to carry out a 450-mile walk, questioned his wisdom in abandoning a well-tried dietary formula: 'The old Oxford and Cambridge system of beefsteaks and half a cup of tea for breakfast, beefsteaks and a pint of ale for dinner, rusks and half a cup of tea at six in the evening, and bread and cheese or bread and cold meat and half a pint of ale for supper, evidently finds little favour in his eyes.'

Ale is the modern form of the Old English *(e)alu*, related to modern Scandinavian *öl*, originating in a prehistoric Indo-European word for 'bitter'. It has a short, light sound, while 'beer' (an equally ancient word common to all west Germanic languages) is more of a hearty boom. Until the early modern period the words beer and ale were used without distinction: ale is now either a technical description (for a drink that is top-fermented and unpasteurised, unlike Pilsner or lager) or, in the Midlands and north, slang for beer or alcohol in general. 'Aled' or 'aled up' is still used to mean drunk, and when sixty-one-year-old Rolling Stone Ronnie Wood ran off (allegedly) with a twenty-year-old Russian barmaid, then entered rehab, the *Sun* newspaper quoted an unnamed family member who opined, 'When he's on the ale, he's a different person.' One sometimes nowadays hears the odd phrase 'a cleansing ale', meaning a healthy beer to round off – or compensate for – a heavy meal. This, though, is an imported concept originating in Australasia. As one Aussie observed, 'No other country in the world would believe ale has cleansing powers. But we do. We must have the cleanest intestines in the universe.' In fact from the 1930s to the 1960s, English pale ale was thought to have medicinal qualities, over and above the diuretic effect that it shared with stronger brews. Weak, fitfully fizzy and sour: it's worth recalling the parlous state of English brewing in the mid-1970s. Folk wisdom maintained that the ubiquitous Watney's Red Barrel was so low in alcohol that it could have been sold in the USA under prohibition. CAMRA, the Campaign for Real Ale, after its eruption in the later 1970s – when its legions of woolly-jumpered, bearded advocates seemed to be taking over our culture, and when it was compared as a populist movement with women's liberation – won most of its battles with the big brands and is still quietly flourishing. Now microbreweries and niche brews have re-refreshed the market: for the millennium celebrations, a thousand-year-old ale containing chicken carcasses, nettles, fruit and honey was revived, but didn't catch on, while in 2004 an ale from a tiny British brewery was voted the best in the world. 'Old Growler' won the top award at an international competition in Chicago with a score of 96 per cent. It was the first time Nethergate Brewery, of Clare, Suffolk, had entered. Despite such small victories in the fightback against globalised, cosmopolitan, gassy, chilly lager, the word ale nowadays has a slightly antique air, recalling Old England with its long-ingrained habits and assumptions. But at least it hasn't suffered the ignominies of its rival, enshrined in the formulations 'small beer', 'beery' or the 'warm beer' infamously invoked by then PM John Major in 1997.

(Reflecting on the greatest Conservative electoral humiliation since 1832, the Centre for Policy Studies observed that 'the Conservatives actively promoted themselves as a party of warm beer and cricket in an age when today's icons favour Diet Coke and Rollerblading'.)

In *Wuthering Heights* (1847), Emily Brontë compared her brooding, dangerous anti-hero, Heathcliff, unfavourably with the placid Englishmen living round about him: '. . . such an individual, seated in his arm-chair, his mug of ale frothing on the round table before him, is to be seen in any circuit of five or six miles along these hills, if you go at the right time, after dinner'. Englishwomen are still immune to ale's image, according to a 2002 survey. Only 23 per cent of women drinkers had tried real cask ale in a pub; 22 per cent had not done so because it was not marketed at them; 29 per cent had not sampled it because their friends shunned it; 17 per cent avoided it in the belief that it would make them fat.

See also **binge**

Anglosphere

W hen writing about language, there's a word I constantly invoke – it's a useful shorthand version of the
cumbersome 'areas where English is the dominant language'. But this expression (apparently first used in writing
by science-fiction author Neal Stephenson in 1995, but still
a novelty for some people) may turn out to be the defining
term of the twenty-first century's global order. The word is
'Anglosphere', denoting not just a group of English-speaking
nations, but a sphere – or set of interconnected spheres – of
influence based on a complex notion of Englishness.

According to US businessman and technologist James C.
Bennett, who began popularising the concept in 2000, it
'implies far more than merely the sum of all persons who
employ English as a first or second language. To be part of
the Anglosphere requires adherence to the fundamental customs and values that form the core of English-speaking
cultures.' Primary among these are individualism, openness
and the honouring of contracts. Just doing business in
English doesn't qualify you; you have to have internalised
the hidden system of behaviours and assumptions that
'Anglos' implicitly embrace, thereby gaining membership in

what Bennett calls a 'network civilization' or 'network commonwealth'. Other fashionable buzzwords associated with the phenomenon are 'collectivity', 'commonality' and 'commensurability'.

At the rarefied level of international politics, the Anglosphere can mean a geopolitical conversation for insiders only; in terms of innovation in technology, law and commerce it encourages what have been dubbed 'pathfinder cultures' to cooperate seamlessly. To some anti-globalisers and multiculturalists, this smacks of ethnocentrism, cultural imperialism and 'linguicism' (language-based racism), or at the very least a shared superiority complex on the part of largely right-wing commentators. Part of the potency of the idea is certainly that it offers Brits, and Canadians, Australians and New Zealanders too, the prospect of world domination, alongside the US, despite the looming presence of China and India (and in a 2005 speech, India's PM was already claiming Anglosphere credentials). Others protest that this is all simply stating the obvious, the fact that English-speakers communicate easily with one another. But perhaps they are missing the essential point: the real potential of the Anglosphere lies not just in instantaneous information-sharing but in the millions of informal, often unnoticed relationships and collaborations that together amount to a much more unified power bloc than any artificially created entity – the EU springs to mind.

As a footnote, there were signs in 2008 that the UK government was co-opting the word and applying a potentially narrower definition than before. PM Gordon Brown announced a bid to 'enlarge the Anglosphere' that amounted to no more than reinforcing the 'special relationship' between Britain and the US. A cosy family conversation or a new world order? The real implication of the term, it is worth reiterating, is inescapably that *English* values, beliefs and behaviours may not only retain a worldwide influence, but remain dominant well into the future – amounting from some perspectives to an **empire** of a very different sort. At the same time, and this is crucial, membership of this community has nothing to do with colour or race.

See also **Brit**

Austerity

Self-sacrifice can be sudden and dramatic, as in the case of the Few, or it can be long-drawn-out, carried out with silent determination or undergone with grumbling resignation. 'Austerity' is a word that, for a dwindling number of us, conjures up the most meaningful, if least comfortable, years of a life, a recollection of scarcity and restraint in an age of hyperconsumption and purchasing porn. For a younger generation the word means perhaps nothing at all, apart from a code for the decorative arts of the 1940s and 1950s. For historians and journalists it has functioned as a trigger in conjuring up the realities of daily life in the forties and fifties, most recently in the case of David Kynaston's *Austerity Britain, 1945–1951*, a surprise bestseller of 2007.

Austerity the word emerged from official discourse around 1943 to lodge itself in the national consciousness as a catch-all label for the system of rationing and for the introduction of utility lines in clothing, footwear, furniture, etc. 'Utility' was the Board of Trade's term, introduced in 1941, for items that met its strict rules about how long production should take, how much material was used and how much, if any, decoration was permitted. The utility symbol showed two stylised 'C's, which stood for 'Civilian Clothing'. These, then, were the more formal companions of the humbler watchwords that summed up the day-to-day imperatives of millions of women and some men: 'making do', or 'make-do-and-mend', even 'going' or 'doing without'. The spirit of austerity was at first generally embraced, and the measures essentially self-imposed, even if managed from above. Mass Observation diaries and private letters testify that by the later 1940s it had come for many to be a dirty word, symbolising the fact that hardship – the hoarding and the **queue**s – had not ended with victory, that rationing was to continue in the case of food until 1954.

Austerity had – and has – a wider reference, of course, denoting not only the threadbare day-to-day of a pre-consumerist society, but restraint, even severity, in design. In June 1958, *The Times* commended Barbara Hepworth's latest sculptures: 'Both the austerity and the unruffled beauty of abstract forms have, in the event, reflected a mind dedicated to the expression of something noble, lasting and ideal.' But in September of the same year, *Queen* magazine challenged its readers with 'When did you last hear the word austerity?', and indeed, beginning around 1955, 'affluence' had steadily supplanted it as a keyword of Englishness. Since the 1960s there have been occasional predictions of a return to puritan values, but it hasn't happened yet. On 25 March 1980, under the heading 'Austerity the order of the day', a *Times* editorial warned, 'Nothing that the Chancellor can do in his budget will prevent a severe recession this year.' However, by November, the same paper was declaring cheerfully, 'When times are hard you have two choices when picking presents – the sublime or the ridiculous: price is immaterial as both categories are available from 50p to £50,000 and austerity, after all, is relative and preferably confined to relatives.'

Presumed to be from the late Latin *austeritatum*, from an earlier Greek word meaning 'dry', giving Old French *auster-ité*, our English word originally meant 'harshness' or 'sourness', either literally or metaphorically; by 1597 it could refer to abstinence or asceticism, and while retaining a Latinate, hence formal, flavour, it was associated with the strain of English Puritanism that infused Bunyan's *Pilgrim's Progress* and Milton's *Paradise Lost*. During the nineteenth century, occurrences of the word were more frequent: it was generally used in connection with religious and political matters, sometimes also of the English climate – the formulation 'gloom and austerity' was frequently heard – but increasingly it denoted not only willing self-denial but a not necessarily welcome lack of luxury.

How far we have come is suggested by the *Telegraph*'s recent feature on wooden bathtubs as typical of the latest 'luxury-austerity item', while during the noughties there have been a number of attempts by style journalists and eco-warriors to float the idea of sober-looking, hard-wearing fabrics and materials, swapping and recycling rather than discarding as a combined fashion statement and lifestyle decision. This they dub 'nu-austerity' or 'conspicuous austerity' – also known as 'thrifting' – but the a-word's inescapable flavour of aridity, self-denial and loftiness is an obstacle to reinstatement in a time of rampant hedonism (and accordingly the adjective austere had, prior to the credit crunch, virtually disappeared from our vocabulary, except when referring to alien cultures and pseudo-zen fashions). Ever inventive, the *Sunday Times Style* magazine came up with a zappier response to the economic turmoils of 2008. Their article promised to teach readers 'how to be a recessionista', while rival *Vogue* was touting a 'new icon for the new austerity, a plucky heroine able to fixate on designer logos even at a time when her house might face foreclosure'. So, as a new decade opens, austerity is once again on the agenda, but this time invariably occuring alongside the word 'chic' and not as a state-sponsored moral and economic imperative, but as a lifestyle option.

Barking

In her 1995 poem 'Mountains out of Small Hills', Sophie Hannah claimed that 'Dogs are objecting to the word dogmatic, / the use of certain phrases . . . barking mad, / dog in the manger.' Sometimes intensified by the addition of 'utterly', 'totally', 'completely' or 'absolutely', barking mad means abjectly, visibly and audibly – and the implication is hopelessly, on a long-term basis – deranged; possessed of an aggressive rather than passive craziness. The term is frequently used in grudging celebration of extreme **eccentric**ity, of those displaying a blithe disregard for society's norms. Hence it is often employed to characterise unrestrained members of the upper classes or celebrities ('the actor Tom Baker is delightfully barking'), or to convey the harrumphing tone of conservative – and Conservative – disapproval ('If we introduce road-use charging, we are barking mad'). The phrase has been borrowed, predictably, for the title of a TV series about problem pets, for dog training schools and for self-consciously wacky creative consultancies.

Probably from nineteenth-century references to the barking of mad or enraged dogs, barking mad was used as long ago as 1927 in an American newspaper, but as the one extant example was an ironic comment on the novelty sport of auto-polo, I suspect it might have been a borrowed Anglicism, or else part of an international pre-jet-set slang, especially as the first British citation is of Christina Packenham, Countess Longford, in 1933. Internet discussions have ascribed the phrase to P.G. Wodehouse, but I can't find a single instance in his works. Nowadays the expression is still occasionally used in the USA, but with mad here meaning apoplectic rather than demented.

The 'clipped' (as linguists say) form of the designation, 'barking' *tout court*, is only heard in the UK, gaining wide currency in the early 1980s, when it was part of the Sloane Ranger's slang repertoire, (reflecting, too, their love of hyperbole). It had first appeared in print in an article by the **posh** journalist Nancy Mitford in 1960. Compare the more innocuous 'potty' (from 'crackpot'), the gentler 'loony' and the Americanism 'wacko' (probably originating in English dialect), and there are subtle differences. Barking implies doggy excess: an individual who may be shaggy, messy – perhaps almost feral. The closest equivalent is probably 'bonkers', which has been popular since the 1960s (enjoying a particular vogue in 1959) although first attested in the 1920s: its etymology is uncertain, but it may have begun as a reference to the result of a 'bonk' on the head.

Among hundreds of examples of barkingness gleefully printed by the tabloids since the eighties have been King George III; a £32,000 lottery grant to teach the homeless to growl ('Phil Minton . . . uses the cash to create so-called "feral choirs" of tramps keen to "find their inner voices"); a bride whose wedding train was carried by pug dogs instead of bridesmaids; and according to the *Sun* in 2007, 'Harry Potter star Daniel Radcliffe has said he would never date an actress because they are all "completely barking".'

Slang terms often undergo elaboration by anonymous wits, and more recently the alternative designation 'Dagenham', or 'distinctly Dagenham' has been fashionable. It means 'beyond barking', as the station of the same name is three stops beyond the inner suburb of Barking (once 'the place of Berica's people') on the District Line of the London Underground. Internet folklore claims that when she was still prime minister, Margaret Thatcher was nicknamed 'Daggers', a familiarisation of Dagenham, because she was thought by some colleagues to be barmy (from 'barm', the froth of fermentation), but I can't find any contemporary evidence for this. 'Becontree' (two stops on from Barking) is a rarer version of the same pun. A different folk etymology claims that there was a medieval lunatic asylum attached to the abbey at Barking, but this is quite coincidental. 'Bark' is Old English, and probably goes back to a common Germanic imitation of the noise dogs make. Much newer and distinctly un-**posh** phrases using the same verb are 'barking at the ants', 'pavement' or 'sidewalk', which means vomiting, while 'barking at the badger' is a fairly obscure UK slang term for cunnilingus, the US equivalent being 'barking at the ape'.

Binge

Alcohol-induced bladder-rupture is on the increase in the UK, unprecedentedly now among women as well as men. Quite unfettered hedonism and consumerism, along with the disappearance of all the old unofficial forms of social and cultural constraint, bring with them, to quote the *Daily Mail*, 'growing levels of drink-fuelled aggression and petty crime in our city centres', 'gangs of young women in their late teens and 20s knocking back alcopops and rounds of "shots", 'a health timebomb'. It seems that it was ever thus. In the eighth century, St Boniface (Wessex-born converter of the Germans and later patron saint of brewers) wrote to the Archbishop of Canterbury complaining of the habitual drunkenness of the English: 'in your diocese, the vice of drunkenness is too frequent. This is an evil peculiar to pagans and to our race. Neither the Franks nor the Gauls nor the Lombards nor the Romans nor the Greeks commit it.' In the twelfth century, too, England was characterised in one Latin text as *Anglia Potatrix* – roughly 'England the Drinker'. Excavations at the sites of Elizabethan taverns have uncovered thousands of shards of glass and pottery, along with shattered clay pipes, suggesting that imbibing routinely ended in an orgy of joyous destruction.

Binge

At the end of 2007, reports claimed that anti-binge-drinking advertisements were not working because they made the practice look enjoyable. The adverts warning of the dangers of booze showed people passing out or being carried home, but research found the scenes could remind youngsters of fun nights out. Professor Christine Griffin of Bath University claimed that young people bonded over tales of alcohol-fuelled disasters, while fellow researcher Professor Chris Hackley said that some anti-binge-drinking ads might be 'catastrophically misconceived'. The media concentrates on bingeing as a rite of passage for adolescents; among university undergraduates, for example, bragging or bemoaning bouts of excess, and masochistically savouring the after-effects, is a standard conversational ritual, regardless of gender. I have collected hundreds of the slang synonyms for intoxicated or hung-over (among current favourites are 'hammered', 'bladdered', 'wreckaged', 'carnaged', 'hamstered', 'mullered', 'wankered' and 'wombled') that are used in this bonding process. It remains to be seen whether the new Alcohol Awareness Certificate, worth half a GCSE, will be more persuasive. The course leading to its award concentrates on the health hazards associated with excessive drinking and the legal penalties incurred by those caught buying or selling alcohol under age. Lessons warn school-age youngsters that drinking to excess could make them fat and lead to impotence.

A binge used to mean a prolonged bout of uncontrolled indulgence, perhaps numbered in days; binge-eating is a condition related to bulimia, and (going on) a cocaine binge is self-explanatory. More often, though, today it tends to refer to a night out characterised by drinking oneself senseless. The word's origins are mysterious: it was first written down in the mid-nineteenth century and is said to come from a Lincolnshire dialect term for 'soak'. Morris Marples in his 1949 compendium *University Slang* says that binge was the Oxbridge student slang for 'alcoholic celebration' from the 1880s and spread from there to the rest of the populace by the 1920s. From the early 1990s, what was typically termed '(going on) a drinking binge' has been replaced by the compound 'binge-drinking', cited in nearly every recent survey as a primary part of the UK's social malaise. 'Liberals' hoped that the introduction of licensed 'continental-style' all-day drinking would bring with it the moderation associated with 'wet' societies, while opponents note that the bouts of excess associated with 'dry' societies don't seem to have lessened – the young-adult menace, the 'lager lout' of the 1980s, has been joined by the 'Saga lout' (a nickname, borrowing the name of a tour operator for older travellers, for pensioners misbehaving on foreign holidays) of the noughties. Meanwhile the middle-aged and middle-class, we are told, are bingeing in the comfort and privacy of their own homes: in a survey of adult drinking habits, eight out of ten of those taking part claimed they drank less than the alcohol misuse limit of 60g of alcohol per day – equivalent to five or six drinks; in reality, 43 per cent of samples showed otherwise.

In 2008, the UK Department of Health, perhaps risking criticism that it was, to use a contemporary cliché, 'stating the bleeding obvious', identified nine different alcohol-fuelled personality types. 'De-stress drinkers' use alcohol to regain control of life and calm down. They include middle-class women and men. 'Conformist drinkers' are driven by the need to belong and seek a structure to their lives. They are typically men aged 45 to 59 in clerical or manual jobs. 'Boredom drinkers' consume alcohol to pass the time, seeking stimulation to relieve the monotony of life. Alcohol helps them to feel comforted and secure. 'Depressed drinkers' may be of any age, gender or socio-economic group. They crave comfort, safety and security. 'Re-bonding drinkers' are driven by a need to keep in touch with people who are close to them. 'Community drinkers' are motivated by the need to belong: they are usually lower-middle-class men and women who drink in large friendship groups. 'Hedonistic drinkers' crave stimulation and want to abandon control. They are often divorced people with grown-up children, who want to stand out from the crowd. 'Macho drinkers' spend most of their spare time in pubs. They are mostly men of all ages who also wish to stand out from the crowd. 'Border dependents' regard the pub as a home from home. They visit it during the day and the evening, on weekdays and at weekends, drinking fast and often. Curiously, perhaps, the targets of most hysteria – under-age or young-adult drinkers – seem to be excluded from this list, unless they are to be placed in the (faintly ludicrous?) re-bonding category.

So, is our boozing just replicating the pattern of drinking seen in other northern areas – Scandinavian student rituals and Russian and Finnish weekend benders come to mind (interestingly, in 2008 the only part of France to report a binge-drinking problem among younger drinkers was the Celtic fringe of Brittany) – or is it in some strange way a prolonged reaction to the end of years of English reticence and restraint? When the repressed let go, abandon and abjectness prevail, conveyed by such quintessentially English phrases as 'hog-whimpering' or the more recent 'rat-arsed'. The press reaction to, or fomenting of, public concern is a textbook example of a 'moral panic', along the lines of the 'gin-craze' of the eighteenth century. In those days an underlying fear was that moral breakdown among the lower orders might lead to social revolution of the French variety; now the moralising is expressed in more clinical terminology, but fly-on-the-wall TV documentaries like *Boozing Britain*, and regular *Daily Mail* exposés, just like their predecessors, the cartoons of Hogarth and Gillray, simultaneously celebrate as they condemn. Combat it as we may, it seems that drunken excess is a trait that transcends age and class, one that may be imprinted in our culture, if not our genetic make-up: Vicki Woods, writing in the *Daily Telegraph* in February 2008, was of the opinion that 'binge-drinking is as British as rain'. As usual it is illuminating to look at the online discussions of the phenomenon by 'ordinary people'. Many postings are defiant or accepting: 'Drink makes millions happy every year and it does wonders for the economy, just look at the stats about when the World Cup's on . . . drink rules!' ('Eric'). 'I enjoy myself and I don't feel anyone out there has the authority to tell me otherwise' ('Adam'). 'How many of you have brought home a traffic cone? or have got so drunk you wee'd yourself laughing? Its what being young is all about!!' ('Danielle'). Just a few are poignant: 'Dont binge drink it destroyed my mums life' ('Kerry').

See also **ale**

Blighty

In 2000, under the headline 'True Brit Cruising', the *Sun* newspaper carried a reassuring message for its readers. 'If you are keen to explore new lands but dread the thought of leaving good old Blighty,' it wrote, 'then step aboard the *Oriana* . . . P&O's mega flagship will whisk you to the world's most exciting and colourful ports of call while still remaining a bit of our green and pleasant land. You may be calling at an exotic destination but on board the officers speak English, the currency is the good old Pound and you can still get a pint in the pub.' True Brits' favourite nickname for the home country, Blighty (nearly always with proud initial capital) was first recorded in 1915 as army slang. A letter from the World War I front to *The Times* newspaper reported, 'It has been a horrible time for them, for although no progress was made, each day took its heavy toll of life, and the only thing they looked forward to was getting back to "Blighty" again.' Ford Madox Ford's poem 'Footsloggers' reads: 'Into the mire and the stress, / Into the seven hundred hells, / Until you come down on your stretcher / To the CCS . . . / And back to Blighty again— / Or until you go under the sod.'

By 1916, London journalists were producing a newspaper

called *Blighty* for free distribution to the troops, while a 'Blighty one' was a wound serious enough to warrant being sent home. In 1917 a young officer, in civilian life still a student, addressed his men as he led them over the top for the last time, saying, 'If you are wounded, there is Blighty, if you are killed, there is Resurrection.' Following the war, 'blighty tweeds' were woven in Scotland by disabled soldiers and sailors.

The word originated as an Anglicisation of the Hindi bilay-ati – 'foreign' – itself a version of *wilayati*, an Arabic word meaning inhabitant of a province' or 'provincial'. The English rendering is a piece of Hobson-Jobson, the colonial-era habit of turning foreign words into homely English-sounding ones. (Other examples include 'plonk', from *vin blanc*, 'doolally', from Deolali, the location of a military sanatorium near Bombay, and Hobson-Jobson itself, which is a mangling of the Islamic cry *Ya Hasan! Ya Hosain!* hailing the grandsons of Muhammad.) Thus, although it has no strictly etymological connection with 'blight' (first recorded in the sixteenth century, but almost certainly much older), Blighty probably does hint at the idea of an imperfect, yet yearned-for homeland.

This folksy term is still in use today, retaining its overtones of wry affection or weary resignation, but often, too, employed to evoke and mock jingoism. In Little Englander mode the *Guardian* lauded the Malverns thus in 2002: 'There's something about these hills that makes you come over all David Niven. They're so old-fashioned and handsome. Stay, and I swear you'll start dreaming of Blighty and Empire, and wearing bay rum. Root deep enough in the area's nooks and crannies, and you're sure to come across a crazed, bayonet-toting colonel who swears the Boer war's not yet over.'

We have travelled a distance from the pathos of the

trenches to the bathos of the motorway, as witness the *Express*'s (premature, thank the Lord) lament for the demise of the Little Chef restaurant chain in 2005: 'Another chunk of old Blighty will be washed away like Ford Cortinas and Opal Fruits and a proper, full football programme on Saturday afternoons.' But post-colonial tristesse is out of fashion and the fightback has begun. In February 2009, UKTV's People Channel was rebranded and Blighty was (re)born. Its programme schedule, marketed with the slogan 'One Nation Under a Channel', targets couples in their thirties and forties who are 'interested in reconnecting with the country they live in', and 'anyone who is secretly proud of Britain's landscape, heritage, music, sense of humour, or who loves the eccentricity of the British themselves'.

Blimey

For much of the twentieth century assumed to be the (very) common man's favourite expostulation, blimey first appears in written form in 1889, but of course the many instances of its use in its more natural context – speech – have mainly gone unrecorded. Blimey is always said to be a shortening of 'Cor blimey!' or (from 1896) 'Gawblimey!', a disguising of an otherwise potentially blasphemous oath, 'God blind me!', itself a shortening of a protestation such as 'May God blind me if I do not speak the truth!'. This last certainly has the flavour of an authentic cry, perhaps from the lips of a Puritan, but I have yet to find an example of it anywhere in the records. 'The Craven', a short story by Harold Weston from 1911 does contain the line, uttered by the cringing humbly born anti-hero, 'I'm no bloomin' good, and blimey if I know wot made me come in after yer.'

For the baby-boom generation and their parents, skiffle star Lonnie Donegan's 1960 novelty hit 'My Old Man's a Dustman' lodged in the collective memory. Among the bumptious proletarian hero's defining characteristics are that ''e wears gorblimey trousers and lives in a council flat'. Apparently Donegan took this line from a lost music-hall

38

song of the 1930s, which also mentioned a 'gorblimey hat'. This was indeed, in some circles, a recognised category of flat cap, either a cloth cap as worn by labourers or a felt cap worn by army officers in place of regulation headgear.

It's entirely possible that true proles really have been peppering their conversations with this mild expletive (it also qualifies as a 'minced oath' or 'pseudo-profanity'): a court report from 1923 has 'Blimey, guvnor, and I took you for a mug' from a thief who tried to sell a 'diamond' ring to an undercover policeman, and I can bear witness that it was heard from the fifties to the end of the seventies. I think part of its attraction may have been that it can be self-deprecating; part of a pose by those who want to project a helpless, hapless humility by affecting innocent gormlessness. Its knockabout comedy potential was exploited by the *Carry On* films, in particular by Sid James's characters. What is unarguable is that almost every example of the word in print – from 'Blimey! There's a skipper still alive! Gawd, wouldn't them perishin' 'Uns give nine pence an inch for 'im!' (from a 1918 tale of marine heroism by 'Bartimeus'), through the late John Diamond's column 'Something for the Weekend': 'the two cabbies started having one of those gor' blimey cabbie chats about diesel and brake lights and lunch . . .' in *The Times* in 1995, and beyond – has been an instance of a middle-class writer using – earnestly, facetiously and/or condescendingly – an easy short cut to conjure up working-class speech and attitudes.

Neighbouring languages have their own colourful/comical/now dated exclamations of astonishment, also in the form of altered or imitated oaths: *sacré bleu!* and *sapristi!* (this was borrowed by *The Goon Show*) in French, *Donnerwetter!* in German among the best known. But like its elaboration in 'Blimey O'Riley!' (or 'O'Reilly'), used to express helpless realisation, and like its fellow euphemisms 'blindin'', 'bloomin'' and 'blimmin'', our own blimey has made a comeback as a staple of mockney conversation (see **estuary**) and of the faux-matey journalese used in red-top headlines and quality-press think-pieces to convey feigned shock or jaunty bemusement. Interestingly, its posher equivalents, 'crikey', 'cripes' and 'crumbs' (also 'minced oaths', as they are deliberate manglings of 'Christ'), have been recycled at the same time, just as class distinctions again become a live issue in our culture and its media. Sadly, some of the old London cries, 'garn!' or 'garn it' (from 'go on', used to express dismissal, defiance or irritation), 'strewth!' (from '(it's) God's truth'), 'gertcha!' (a version of 'get away', 'get out of it' or 'give over', used in commercials for Courage Best Bitter in 1983) and 'swipe me!' (presumed to be from 'strike me dead!'), have quite faded away.

Bloke

When cross-dressing artist Grayson Perry collected the 2003 Turner art prize for his pottery, wearing a pink crinoline dress, the aptly named Tony Allman, a painter and decorator from Bethnal Green, went into overdrive in the *Sun* newspaper. 'I didn't know whether to laugh or cry this week when I saw that bloke – or was it a bird? – win the Turner Prize. What a state!' That little b-word, when looked at in close-up, may contain many more layers of meaning than its dictionary definition as 'an unnamed male'. It has not only appeared in the blokeish *Sun* around 15,000 times in the last decade alone, but has been given special prominence in the long-running features 'A Sun Bloke Speaks' ('This week's Sun Bloke is single 25-year-old IT manager Alex Verrey of Stanmore, Middlesex') and 'Bloke Jokes' (sample: 'Husband: Why don't we try some new positions? Wife: OK. You stand behind this ironing board and I'll lie on the sofa and belch all night').

The true etymology of 'bloke' is not entirely clear, but as it's usually given it is an interesting example of confused trains of thought presented as authoritative. First attested in 1851 by Henry Mayhew as London street slang in *London*

Labour and the London Poor, by 1862 the term seems to have become fashionable, or at least understood, in politer company. That year saw the first reference in *The Times*, and a year later Charles Kingsley wrote in *The Water Babies* that 'Epimetheus was a very slow fellow, certainly, and went among men [being taken] for a clod, and a muff, and a milksop, and a slowcoach, and a bloke, and a boodle, and so forth.' A crude rule of thumb in offering derivations for old slang is 'when in doubt, opt for Romany', and accordingly the shared Gypsy and Hindu *loke* (man) is the origin given by many sources. But there is a problem: *loke* does not occur in Roma language, and *lok* in Hindi means people collectively, not an individual. I'm more inclined towards Celtic *ploc*, defined as 'a large, stubborn fellow', in fact a nickname, as the word means literally a large lump of turf, a clod or a club . . . still to be heard in French slang as *plouc*, a bumpkin. *Gloak, gloach* in Shelta, a secret language used in the nineteenth century by Irish and Welsh tinkers and travellers, was used in British slang, but the shift from 'gl-' to 'bl-' is an unlikely one. Middle Dutch *blok*, meaning 'lump of wood', has also been proposed; both this and *ploc* are related to the English 'block' (therefore also to 'blockhead') and I can't see why a dialect pronunciation of this could not be the real antecedent. ('A chip off the old block', by the way, is dated to the 1620s.) The term travelled to Australia and New Zealand in the later 1800s and was occasionally heard in the USA until the 1930s. *The Songs of a Sentimental Bloke*, a verse novel written in 'strine' slang, was a huge hit in Australasia in 1915. Today, as a **Brit** friend of mine put it, 'of course *all* Australians are blokes', forgetting that they, unlike us, had until recently a female counterpart, the Sheila. In Quebec today bloke is (invariably derogatory) French Canadian slang for an English-speaker. (Female) Vancouver writer Meredith

Quartermain opines that Anglo Canada should import the word to describe those 'heavy-set, sheepish-looking males, relentlessly external to the internet in a world of electronic signs'.

From the sixties onwards, bloke acquired such sub-connotations as uncomplicated/unaffected, sound, bluff, perhaps unpolished. In real conversations the word is usually deployed with some element of fellow feeling – 'as one bloke to another', to quote the same friend – therefore not by the genteel, unless said pointedly or condescendingly, as blokes are by definition not genteel. It has usually referred to a mature, at least in years, man, hence the need to specify 'a younger bloke'. It denotes 'a man's man', hence is often used dismissively by women – denoting a tiresomely stereotypical male. From the 1990s, and as uttered, for instance, in imitation of yoof-speak by the comic wigga Ali G ('I seen some bloke chattin' up his sister'), the overtones of gormlessness, gaucheness or lack of sophistication – on the part of the speaker as well as the one described – have come to the fore.

From the 1960s, bloke kept company with 'chap' and 'fellow', though these are a little classier, if not rather dated nowadays: when the late Anthony Buckeridge's Jennings books, stories of public school life from the 1950s, were updated in 1980s, 'chap' was changed to 'bloke', and sounded a jarring note. The gruffly approving 'good bloke' is the demotic successor to the posher 'good sort' and the Wodehousian 'good egg', now partly supplanted by the American and global-English 'good guy', though there was never such a thing as a 'bad bloke'. Though bloke for most of its history denoted an essentially likeable male, 'blokeish' and the rarer 'blokey', terms that gained currency from the later 1980s, imply someone who is intentionally or unintentionally boorish, crass, unreconstructed – not a metrosexual at all, let alone an übersexual. Accordingly voiceover agencies now list 'blokeish' as a style category. Girls can be guys, but not blokes, they may qualify as 'laddish' (even 'ladettes') but never blokeish.

Significantly, neighbouring European languages, though they all have some sort of equivalent, usually have only one universally recognised colloquial term (like American English 'guy'), not several denoting nuances of class. French does, however, use two, *type* and *mec*, the latter being noticeably less respectable. Completists may like to note that bloke does exist in contemporary US slang, but with a seemingly quite unrelated sense; it can mean a portable glass pipe for distilling and inhaling crystal methamphetamine, or, in Chicago, a cigarette, perhaps deriving from some combination of the sounds of blow, smoke and/or toke.

Bon Viveur

With multi-ethnic cuisine on every high street and **Brits** at large in Florida, Spain and Tuscany, the association of good living with Frenchness is no longer so automatic or so exclusive (but note that *cuisine*). As evidenced by the self-mockery of the phrase 'Pretentious? *Moi?*', the use of French, or some semblance of French, in high-flown conversation is thought comical where once it was the mark of sophistication. The nineteenth-century lingua franca of cosmopolitans has been eclipsed by the **Anglosphere**, leaving just a few traces behind. One of these seems particularly evocative of a land of garrulous, bibulous, portly males, overindulging and holding forth in private and in public, resolutely and iredeemably English but appreciative of the finer aspects of a 'continental' way of life. The phrase in question is 'bon viveur', which once kept company – and, significantly, rhymed – with 'racon-teur', a skilled spinner of yarns, a recounter of after-dinner anecdotes. Bon viveur became widespread around 1930 – the year in which a *Times* article about the ideal gift listed 'people of varied tastes – the high brow, the low brow, the week-end cottager, bright young people, the sluggard, the motorist, the bon viveur, and many others'. From then until the 1950s, its flavour was largely appreciative, though since the 1960s, tinges of envy and disapproval can sometimes be detected. Recent referees have included the late Sir John Mortimer, Ned Sherrin, Sir Clement Freud, Sir James Goldsmith and Michael Winner. One of the best personifications of the term, the first TV celebrity cooking star Fanny Cradock's husband Johnnie, no stranger to the bottle, used to write a column under the nom de plume (which is not a solecism by the way, just an unnecessary calque, or literal translation, of 'pen-name') of Bon Viveur. Bon viveur is still encountered in 'journalese', inevitably employed slightly ironically nowadays in the knowledge that it isn't really French. *Viveur* does exist in French, and on its own (never qualified by bon) means a pleasure-seeker, a – perhaps desperate, sometimes debauched – high-liver, but the correct form of our expression is *bon vivant*.

Other notable examples of pseudo-French include the still current 'restauranteur' (regularly used in connection with TV cooking shows and celebrity chefs; it should be *restaurateur*) and 'double entendre' (actually *à double entente*). *Savoir faire* ('knowing how to behave' or 'how to get by') seems to fill what linguists call a lexical gap in English (a notion that lacks a name), but the French themselves prefer *savoir vivre* ('knowing how to live'), revealing perhaps a significant difference in attitudes. A curious Frenglish phrase that is no longer heard is '(very) à la', often used enviously or with a tinge of disapproval of something fashionable, alien and/or slightly flashy. It is probably a shortening (naturally quite illegitimate and unknown in France) of 'à la mode'. Passé is another piece of faux-French – they would say *dépassé*, *démodé* or *vieux jeu* ('old hat'). On the other hand, the phrase we are proudest of – 'sangfroid' – is, mercifully, not only real French, but is habitually applied to us by the

French themselves. Other useful appropriations are 'fait accompli' and (surely the only elegant, if too flattering, way of describing Russell Brand?) the untranslatable 'louche'. One of my own favourite phrases in any language is 'carte blanche', but don't forget to sound the first 'e'.

Global English increasingly infiltrates other languages, and is sometimes mangled in transit. Trendy French came up with *un mods* for 'a mod' and the self-explanatory *punque*, while *un camping*, *un parking* and *un planning* (schedule) have become standard. German calls a mobile phone a *handy*, while Slovene teenagers express 'excellent' in their language as *ful* ('the best'). Nevertheless, the French have never forgiven us for such outrages as turning the noun 'rendezvous' into a verb – 'we're rendezvousing' – and were bemused by the deliberate garbling that was Franglais, which the English middle classes found so unaccountably hilarious. The imitation of foreign languages for fun, whether by students in common rooms, pub habitués goose-stepping and shouting in 'German' accents, or in the *Fast Show*'s 'scorchio' sketches, is a peculiarly English trait, and though not unknown, is not a staple of folk humour in any of the countries I have visited. Our unwillingness or inability to master foreign languages is legendary (witness World War I's 'plonk' from *vin blanc* and 'san fairy-ann' from *ça ne fait rien*), and to return to Franglais and its near-neighbour Spanglish, it's terrifying to learn that there are Brits abroad – tourists in rural France ('Où est the nearest car méchanique?'), and according to grisly TV reports from the 'Costa del Crime', expatriates in Spain ('Me Inglès, mucho drinko, no arrest, por faveur?!') – who habitually talk like this in real life. This cavalier treatment of other languages is nothing new, but its motives and contexts have changed. From 1066 until the mid-fourteenth century, there was a linguistic apartheid

47

operating in England, whereby all serious business and the conversations of the elite were conducted in French or Latin, while the peasantry communicated in Anglo-Saxon or Celtic dialects. Purely Germanic Old English morphed into hybrid Middle English by absorbing a confusing assortment of words, syntactic features and spellings from those dominant tongues, and this wholesale 'borrowing' (not the best word – the booty is never returned) increased in Shakespeare's time as magpie English authors vastly expanded the lexicon by grabbing useful or colourful terms from Italian, French and Spanish in particular. For the next three hundred years we continued to import vocabulary, notably from the **Empire**, while coining new expressions with the aid of classical languages rather than from Anglo-Saxon roots. It is only since Edwardian times that English has acquired international status and self-confidence, and only really since the 1960s that English-speakers (no longer classically educated and with the USA in the lead) have generated a purely home-grown language of technology and lifestyle based principally on the prepositions and phrasal verbs inherited from our Germanic past.

The contemporary reality is that with our increased mobility and, in some limited ways, our increased cosmopolitanism, we have still not begun to engage with other languages in anything other than a flippant, silly, not-even-gestural way. The dominance of global English is our excuse, and if pragmatism and opportunism (two of our other defining characteristics) are our sole criteria, then it's a bloody good one – if you'll pardon my French.

Bore

In one of his most popular songs, 'The World Is Full of Crashing Bores', fey pop auteur Morrissey singled out 'lock-jawed popstars' and, more curiously, '. . . lamenting police-women . . . educated criminals . . .'. Thirty-four years earlier, in 1968, in another camp tirade against ennui, the Bonzo Dog Doo-Dah Band's 'I'm bored', Viv Stanshall vented his fruity, faux-posh-voiced irritation: '. . . and quite apart from what one hears, I've been like this for years and years'.

Word buff Nigel Rees, in his entertaining collection of curious and everyday phrases, *A Word in Your Shell-like*, wonders why there are no written records of phrases like 'bored stiff/rigid', 'bored to death', 'bored to tears/distraction' before the 1900s. Does this mean, he asks, that 'before the 20th century there was no expectation that you shouldn't be bored? Or were the Victorians so bored that they couldn't even be bothered to find words for it?' In fact the records from the 1780s onward are chock-full of instances of the word bore *tout court*, confirming what we all know to be true: that to bore or to be a bore has for centuries been the worst sin an Englishman (for some time now an Englishwoman too) can commit. It was only in the twentieth century perhaps that the overfamiliarity of the word and the notion created a demand for more elaborate phrases, such as the P. G. Wodehouse favourite of the 1950s, 'bore the pants off (someone)'.

The verb to bore in its literal sense is very ancient, deriving from an Indo-European root meaning 'to pierce'. Figurative uses of the word to mean a boring thing date from 1766, a boring person from 1812; the idea of 'boreism' flourished very briefly around 1833. Puns are sometimes fabricated around the Severn Bore, but this is a different word, coming from Old Norse *bara*, wave or billow.

Sustaining a 1960s contempt for tiresome politicians, witless ads repeated ad nauseam, fatuous and intrusive celebrities and media fads, satirical magazine *Private Eye* has its long-running spoof annual award(s) for 'Bore of the Year'. This impatience with the tedious, the mundane, the predictable was once a mark of patrician English disdain. In the early 1800s, 'bore' as slang was particularly associated with Cambridge University, applied typically to 'six o'clock chapel on a hard frosty morning, sermons at St Mary's, capping a Fellow, dining in Hall, paying a bill or subscribing to the Thirty-nine Articles'. In *Hard Times* (1854), Charles Dickens recounts how '. . . this gentleman had a younger brother of still better appearance than himself, who had tried life as a Cornet of Dragoons, and found it a bore; and had afterwards tried it in the train of an English minister abroad, and found it a bore; and had then strolled to Jerusalem, and got bored there; and had then gone yachting about the world, and got bored everywhere'. It was reported in 1890 that Lord Beaconsfield, just before his death, had been thinking over the best advice he could possibly give, and that it was this: 'Never ask who wrote Junius's Letters [pseudonymous political tracts of the late eighteenth century – their true authorship was endlessly debated], and never ask on which side of Whitehall King Charles I was executed; for if you do, people will think you a bore, and that is the very worst thing they can possibly think of you.' A 'crasher' was a staple of the public school and Sloane Ranger lexicon, abbreviated from the earlier 'crashing bore', but despising earnestness, being bored and complaining about it has become enshrined as an attitude struck by all classes. Modern obsessives excuse themselves by admitting that 'I've become a property bore' or 'I know I'm in danger of becoming a diet bore', while a less self-aware – or self-regarding – version of ennui is conjured up by the contemporary expressions 'bored witless' and its profane twin 'bored shitless'. New synonyms for bore continue to surface – a 'yawn', a 'snore', a 'blah', and its variant, a word that was in vogue on the internet during 2004 and 2005, 'bleh'. North Americans have coined 'bored out of my gourd', 'bored of studies' and 'bored of the rings', while dull, long-winded island-dwellers are said to be able to 'bore for England' . . . but I think I'll stop writing here, as my head is beginning to throb and my eyes are glazing over . . .

Bovver

B ovver, an imitation of a working-class London pronunciation of bother, has made two spectacular appearances
in the English national conversation in the last half-century.
Bother, often in the phrase 'a spot of bother', was part of the
vocabulary of menacing **understatement** and euphemism
favoured by both criminals and the police in the years after
World War II. This style of discourse gave rise to 'a good
seeing-to', meaning a murderous assault, and 'having a word
with' someone, denoting a maiming. Bother (a synonym for
'aggro', which seems to have fallen out of use) thus referred
to extreme aggravation and/or physical violence, and in this
sense was adopted by the skinheads of the later 1960s in
their standard challenge, 'You want bovver?' Once the media
became aware of the skinhead, cast him as the latest in a line
of hooligan folk-devils (teddy-boys and later punks were
others) and fomented a moral panic around him, the public
became acquainted with the phrases 'bovver boy' and
'bovver boots' (first heavy black polished army surplus boots;
later lighter Doc Marten boots worn as part of the skinhead
uniform). Punk group the Nipple Erectors (fronted by Shane
MacGowan, later of the Pogues) included in their 1977

repertoire a song entitled 'Venus in Bovver Boots', which contained the lines, 'She's my venus in bovver boots/And bloody great tall thighs.'

In 2005, bovver, like the US import 'whatever', became a catchphrase symbolising the blasé unconcern for social niceties of youngsters, especially females and particularly, though not exclusively, working-class and so-called chav girls. This time it was part of the phrases 'not bovvered', or the defiant 'Am I bovvered?' ('Does my face look bovvered?' was a slightly later embellishment.) Popularised by comedienne Catherine Tate impersonating the stroppy teenager Lauren, it was nominated Word of the Year for 2006 and featured in Tate's duet with PM Tony Blair (for me his finest moment). As blogger Sarah Phillips recorded in October of that year, 'town centres, branches of McDonalds and playgrounds were suddenly filled with squawks of "bovvered" by excitable youngsters who thought they were being clever'. A media catchphrase imitating the usages of the playground and street had been appropriated, as the jargon has it, by the real frequenters of those milieux. Posher young ladies might prefer to pronounce the word correctly, and the word on its own could function as a sarcastic tag, as in 'So she hates me. Bothered.'

Bother in its standard form is of obscure origin, first noticed by lexicographers in the eighteenth century. Some derive it from Irish Gaelic *bodhar*, which could mean annoyed or deaf, but it has been linked to the now archaic 'pother', denoting fuss or tumult, which had already been in English usage for two hundred years. 'Pother', though, is probably a variant form of 'powder', in the sense of dust thrown up by a commotion, and may be quite unrelated. 'Botheration!' was an exclamation of impatience or vexation used by Victorian and Edwardian ladies and thereafter in parodying their mannerisms. Nowadays it can also be an uneducated or pompous synonym for inconvenience or harassment. 'Bother!', which when an interjection is sometimes a replacement for 'bugger', is still uttered by nicely mannered speakers. The English horror of fuss (see **fusspot**) and fear of engagement and embarrassment often results in meek acceptance of awful responsibilities, expressed by 'Oh . . . it's no bother really', or 'Please don't bother yourself – I'll do it.'

Laura Barton writing in the *Guardian* announced in June 2008 that 'after years in the wilderness the bovver boot is back'. All Saints fashion boutique in Soho was apparently offering a pair of 'faux-distressed lace-up boots for the princely sum of £140'. So far, to go only by my own snapshot survey, the high street seems to be unbovvered.

Brit

Well into the twentieth century, the standard designation was 'Englishman', or, if she had to be mentioned, 'Englishwoman'. The public discussion of the distinction between Britain and England, though long the stuff of pub and dinner-table controversy (Nancy Mitford declared in 1956 that 'British' was middle class and 'non-U', that the upper classes said 'English'), only began in earnest with the devolution debates of the later 1970s. In 1900, a reader wrote to *The Times*, 'Mr Macrae seems to be anxious that we call ourselves Britons, but I would ask him in all seriousness, if he ever heard of any human being who habitually spoke of himself as a Briton. The very name was only invented for modern use in the reign of George III.' That monarch, apparently on the advice of the court favourite, Lord Bute, announced in his first proclamation to his people that he had been 'born and bred a Briton', but the description aroused more resentment than enthusiasm, and when the polemicist John Wilkes called his news-sheet *The North Briton*, he was being savagely ironic as usual. There was in any case a suspicion that Britons weren't English, or at least Anglo-Saxon or Anglo-Norman, anyway: the one universally recognised use of the word has been in the formulation 'ancient Britons', which conjures up woad-smeared tribes speaking unintelligible Celtic languages. As Daniel Defoe put it in his 1703 satire *The True-born Englishman*, 'Nor is it . . . to undervalue the original of the English, for we see no reason to like them the worse, being the relics of Romans, Danes, Saxons, and Normans, than we should have done if they had remained Britons; that is, than if they had been all Welshmen.'

The patriotic/pedantic, hence grudgingly acceptable, adjective 'British' was only occasionally abbreviated by earlier writers, Ezra Pound for instance ('when his Brit majesty lords' in the *Cantos*), and the no-nonsense usage 'Brit' seems to have begun, as adjective and noun, among Australians, from the early 1970s, as a less pejorative alternative to 'Pom'. It was then picked up by North Americans (mercifully supplanting the back-slappingly embarrassing 'Britisher') and subsequently by those being described: the BRIT Awards for pop music began in 1977. This clipped form removes all imperial, traditional overtones and undertones (even the nation designation in the suffix is gone), leaving what is now no more than a brusque-sounding label for a new breed of island-dweller. It is of course a useful piece of journalese shorthand, as in 'Brits abroad' when referring to football hooliganism (including the aged 'Saga louts'), stag nights, tussles over sunbeds, the travails of second-home owners, etc. The *Sun* newspaper has used it around 30,000 times in the last decade, *The Times* around 8,000. Like Briton before it, the new word continued to appear in controversial or ambivalent contexts, as in the expression 'true Brit' that emerged in the 1980s, used by xenophobes and patriots and, with **irony**, also by liberal multiculturalists. The idea of a new, multi-ethnic Britishness was reflected in the title of the controversial award-winning TV drama broadcast in 2008, *Britz* (in this more radical, **yoof**-oriented spelling, it's also the name of a fish-and-chip takeaway in Salisbury).

See also **Anglosphere, Blighty**

Cad

Painful puns have long been an English weakness. From the *Penny Illustrated Paper* of 24 June 1876, in the 'Quips and Cranks' section, comes the following anecdote: 'At the Academy the other day one gentleman pointed out a dandified-looking individual to his friend as a sculptor. "What!" said his friend, "such a cad as that a sculptor? Surely you must be mistaken?" "He may not be the kind of sculptor you mean," said the informant, "but I know that he chiselled a tailor out of a suit of clothes last week."' Eighty-two years later John Betjeman wrote, with a measure of **irony**, 'There's something about a Varsity man that distinguishes him from a cad: / You can tell by his tie and blazer that he's a Varsity undergrad / And you know that he's always ready and up to a bit of a lark, / With a toy balloon and a whistle and some cider after dark.'

Like its disreputable near-relations (forming what linguists call a lexical set), the 'bounder' (originally Oxbridge slang for a vulgar person who, not knowing his place, 'bounds around' offensively), the 'bolter' (an escapee, fugitive or runaway), the 'chancer' (a ruthless, usually small-time opportunist) and the 'counter-jumper' (once an uppity and/or unscrupulous shop assistant, then anyone, especially if in **trade**, who breaches class barriers), the cad was (and still is) exclusively a male epithet – our culture, or at least our language, seems to have no equivalent female category (but compare **slag**). The cad who finessed and seduced his way through the 1940s and 50s is a version of the antique rake, a stock figure in literature and in life, a charming scoundrel. This reprobate is essentially ungentlemanly (see **gentle**), and guilty of unforgivable but not perhaps illegal behaviour: he is often characterised as 'unmitigated'. Of those cads with a public persona, the actor George Sanders (born 1906) was an interesting example – a cosmopolitan lounge-lizard, a languid, supercilious scoundrel, and so suave that he was rumoured not to be English at all – he was indeed born in St Petersburg, but to British parents. Sanders' 1960 autobiography was entitled *Memoirs of a Professional Cad*; his 1972 suicide note, left on a Catalonian hotel bedside, read in part, 'I'm leaving because I'm bored.'

In his heyday, the cad was also incarnated, rather poignantly, in two different guises by the leering, gap-toothed, brilliantined Terry-Thomas (actually Thomas Terry Hoar-Stevens, 1911–90 and really better defined as a 'rotter' – Basil Brush the TV fox puppet is said to be based on him) and by Cardew Robinson (Douglas John Cardew Robinson, 1917–92), the gangling, desperate-looking over-grown schoolboy, who had something of the silly ass about him too. In the fairly recent past, Michael Caine, as Alfie, has been nominated as a working-class cad, and Hugh Grant, in his post-foppish guise, as the more familiar posh version: the epithet has often been bestowed on the late Conservative politician Alan Clark, though in my view, shallow, snobbish, arrogant and childishly lecherous are insufficient qualifications. The former army officer James Hewitt, while cashing in (literally) on his dalliance with the Princess of Wales, embraced the term when it was applied to him.

Cad was first recorded in 1730, abbreviated from the word 'cadet', which in the original French designated a younger son, or the Scottish equivalent, 'caddie'. In English (also sometimes in the archaic form 'caddee'), it referred to a servant or tout or errand boy, then in the 1830s it was applied by university and public-school students to their less privileged contemporaries and acquired the pejorative sense of someone lacking in refinement and respect, such as a 'jumped-up member of the lower classes' with 'ideas above his station'. It soon encompassed ungallant or impertinent behaviour towards women, the basis for an assault recorded in a police report from 1870. 'On the evening of 25th of July, complainant was walking there with a younger brother, when the defendant came up, said he was no gentleman, but a blackguard, a contemptible fellow, and a cad, and that he had insulted his daughters by speaking to them without introduction. This the complainant admitted, but he would not apologise.'

When in 1918 Sir Roger Casement referred to the German officers whose help he had sought in liberating Ireland as 'swine and cads of the first water', he was decrying their lack of good breeding and sensitivity, but by the 1930s the image of the possibly charming, certainly unprincipled womaniser was uppermost among the word's associations. Now, in an age when there are really no universally acknowledged norms of **decent** behaviour, a designation like cad risks redundancy. But the resurgence of class consciousness and the language of class distinction (of 'toffs' and 'proles' and **oiks** and **posh**) that seems to be taking place may rescue it from oblivion. The words cad and caddish may yet survive, and not only in the journalistic repertoire of mockery. They fill what would otherwise be what linguists call a lexical gap: a notion that needs a name. What else can we call a chap (or **bloke**, or guy) who can always be relied upon to let us down, whose superficial charm is positively his only positive attribute, who is two-faced, craven, self-serving and, underneath it all, desperate?

Cellar Door

Asked in 2008 to nominate his favourite word, then mayoral candidate and Tory MP Boris Johnson selected 'carminative', teasing both in its obscurity and in that the word formed from these four sonorous syllables denotes a cure for flatulence. Three quite different, and differently resonant, syllables were chosen by French artist Loris Gréaud as the title of his solo exhibition at London's ICA, part of a large-scale experimental multimedia project dealing in the interplay between rumour and fact, in hidden meanings and in transitions and interruptions. It is no coincidence that the London installation and the project itself go by the name of CELLAR DOOR. The coming together – not for the first time – of these two unremarkable English words is part of a curious sequence of borrowings and allusions, a sort of underground tradition or urban legend that Gréaud is just the latest to tap into.

It was J. R. R. Tolkien in 1955 who first suggested that 'cellar door' was one of the most beautiful, if not *the* most affecting combination of sounds in the English language. He described the phrase on two occasions as being intrinsically inspiring, and since then a series of writers have used

Tolkien's cue to fabricate a quite spurious history of references to cellar door, according to which an American opinion poll, the author H. L. Mencken and various Chinese and Japanese visitors have all, apparently independently, pronounced it the most beautiful sound in English. The cult movie *Donnie Darko* popularised the idea for a pop culture audience, asserting that of all the endless combinations of words in all of history, this was the most beautiful. The film script attributed the claim to 'a famous linguist', but the director Richard Kelly in subsequent interviews name-checked, quite wrongly, Edgar Allan Poe.

We can't be sure of the personal and cultural associations, conscious or unconscious, that led Tolkien to favour this particular collection of phonemes, apart from 'the door of the cellar', there are no sound-alikes in English other than, and of course this might be significant, 'celadon', a colour that is apparently a sort of pale willowy green (and is named, curiously, after the shepherd hero of a seventeenth-century French romance) and 'celandine', the French-sounding name of two different species of flower. It seems to be a prerequisite that cellar door is pronounced in a donnish British RP accent rather than in a provincial burr or North American twang; although for me, and perhaps for Tolkien too, a Welsh lilt might help reinforce its quasi-mythic pretensions.

Celador isn't Welsh but *is* a real word in Spanish: pronounced with initial 'th' in Castilian Spanish, and 'ts' in the Americas, historically it means 'guardian of the bedchamber'; nowadays, more prosaically, it denotes a hospital orderly, a classroom supervisor or sometimes a prison guard. Spanish and Latin American friends tell me that for them, the sound of the word is as humdrum as its modern meaning: it has no special resonance.

Although one explanation of the origins of language, known as the bow-wow theory, holds that all words started out as imitations of sounds found in nature, it's clear that by now, apart from the obviously onomatopoeic like 'splash' and 'plash' and 'smash', sound and sense have become quite disconnected. The word voted the most beautiful in a British Council survey in 2004 was 'mother', for most of us redolent of tenderness, but downbeat and abrupt in terms of its component sounds. Conversely and perversely, James Joyce had earlier proposed 'cuspidor', a nice noise but a nasty receptacle.

The notion, though, that the sounds of a word might evoke certain feelings in the hearer, quite independently of its literal meaning, is a common-sense one, and linguists know the phenomenon variously as phonaesthetics, psychoacoustics or sound symbolism. But these emotional or aesthetic effects are not consistent and vary quite unpredictably across cultures and even among speakers who share a common language. 'Mist', which seems pleasant on the ear, means 'crap' in other northern European languages. The comic actor Stephen Fry likes the word 'moist', but a teenager told me the other day that it's now the most horribly offensive thing you can say in London street slang.

Playing of course on its literal sense, but helped by its new status as a linguistic talisman, 'cellar door' has been used as the name of a host of wine merchants, wine bars and wine magazines, and of a slasher movie too. A café in Guernsey, a London cabaret venue, a jazz band, an indie band, a metal band, a literary magazine have all adopted the title; spelled as in Spanish, it's the name of a well-known TV production company; a new printing typeface, Kellermeister, turns out to be inspired by it, and dozens of internet blogs contrive to work the phrase in somewhere in their mashups.

Why is it that there seems to be this need for a mantra, a

magic set of sounds that can be constantly reinvoked? Is it those phonemes: that front vowel, sibilant and lateral, along with the allusion to something always hidden just beyond our field of vision, that combine to give cellar door its unique charm? Whatever the case, and however impressive Gréaud's work actually is, I'm afraid that I'm quite immune to the two words in question: for me, 'seller' only evokes the housing crisis at the time of writing, and door rhymes with 'sore' and 'poor' – and most tellingly of all, with **bore**.

Chat

For many of us, one of life's small pleasures is 'a nice cup of tea and a chat', an interlude allowing cosy, unthreatening intimacy in domestic surroundings or in a quiet corner of the teashop. *Home Chat* was the name of a women's magazine published in the 1940s, and English journalists in particular still affect a 'chatty' – a cheerfully unstuffy – style in red-tops and the quality press, in magazines and on the air. Are they ensuring that mass communication, however 'technologised', remains within the easy reach of all of us; are they bringing the exalted down closer to the humdrum, or clinging to the trivial and banal rather than aspiring to the transcendental? And then, of course, there is the online chat room: do its users really *chat*? Or do they rather **bore**, hector, ramble, rant, pontificate?

The noun chat was first attested in 1530, already in the sense of an informal conversation. In dialect it once meant 'insolence', and continued to carry overtones of familiarity and levity: a pamphlet written in 1674, a spoof petition by women against the male refuge of the coffee house, recounts how the men 'after an hours impertinent Chat begin to consider a bottle of Claret would do excellent well before

66

dinner; whereupon to the Bush they all march together, till every one of them is as Drunk as a Drum'. Playing on the theme of impudence, W. H. Auden wrote in his 'Letter to Lord Byron', 'So if ostensibly I write to you / To chat about your poetry or mine, / There's many other reasons: though it's true / That I have, at the age of twenty-nine / Just read *Don Juan* and found it fine.'

As a verb, to chat occurs in Shakespeare and Milton: it originated as a shortening of 'chatter', also 'chitter', which were imitations of the sounds of birds or small animals. 'Chit-chat', meaning small talk, is first attested in 1605 as a noun, and from 1821 in verb form (the latest *Rough Guide to England* notes that the English are 'addicted to celebrity chit-chat'), while the affectionate 'chatterbox' dates from 1704. By the 1970s, the formulaic complaint of 'ceaseless chatter' – irritating, trivial 'noise' – had been transferred from the classroom or dormitory to the media.

The dismissive 'chattering classes' was coined by right-wing commentator Frank Johnson in the early 1980s to designate metropolitan liberal-leftist opinion-formers – and 'chatterati', by analogy with 'literati', 'glitterati' and 'digerati', was used by a few journalists in the early noughties. Is our word chat easily translatable? Most languages have a verb that means something like 'to light(hearted)ly converse'. In French, *causer* comes close; better, but too long-winded is *faire un brin de causette*, 'have a bit of a chat'. In Spanish, *charlar* or *trapalear* are offered as equivalents (the latter also has the senses of 'jabber' or 'fib'). This multitasking word is also an essential part of the English repertoire of courtship and seduction: to 'chat up', probably first heard in the late 1950s, could originally mean to flatter, bamboozle or flirt, but has narrowed to the third sense, and a 'chat-up line' can now refer only to an attempted pick-up. Today's university students have altered 'chatting up' to '(le) chat', often pronounced like the French word for 'cat' (and use a synonym, 'chirpsing', that is also inspired by the sounds of birds). In modern multi-ethnic youth slang and hip-hop parlance, chat is a fashionable synonym for to speak or talk, as in 'u chat out ur ass' (London teenager, 2006), or to say, as in 'Jus because we use slang doesn't make us dumbasses . . . so stop chattin fluff' (contributor to an online discussion at www.wass-up.com, November 2003).

Chippy

On 24 July 1999, the *Sun* carried the headline 'When Harry Met Curry . . .' above the story of an Asian fish and chip shop owner who was, in their words, 'facing a battering' from the world-famous chain Harry Ramsden's after calling his business Harry Ramadan's. Harresh Ramadan, 30, had converted his struggling Indian takeaway restaurant to a chip shop two weeks earlier and was now delightedly selling forty portions a day, but inevitably attracted the attention of the existing twenty-seven-outlet 'themed restaurant' chain. Once an inevitable part of the local landscape, wherever you chose to live, the humbler 'chippy' is holding its own, though its owners are just as likely to be Asian or Chinese or Kurdish (which seems to have no detrimental effect on the food, though in the south-east at least, the portions seem to have shrunk). Fish 'n' chips is still touted by tourist boards as the national dish, having displaced the more symbolic than widely eaten roast beef sometime in the 1970s, and despite the late Robin Cook MP's claim that chicken tikka masala had supplanted it. The truth of this was borne out to some extent by a survey of all those English citizens living in streets called Acacia Avenue

69

(see **suburbia**). For this cross-section at least, according to the poll findings, fish and chips remained their favourite food. No longer, disappointingly, tasting of the newsprint in which it used to be wrapped, but still possibly accompanied by mushy peas ('chips 'n' peas' is rhyming slang for knees, usually as in the phrase 'on one's knees': ''E was down on 'is chips, beggin' for mercy'), some 300 million portions are still consumed annually in the UK. In November 2006, the *Sun* was punning again, and this time the headline was 'You couldn't hake it up': 'The boss of a chippy is being probed by town hall officials because his shop smells . . . of fish and chips. Environmental health staff wrote to Steve Morton to say they were investigating an "odour from the extract fan ventilation system".' Fish and chip shops had become established across England by the end of the nineteenth century, though it is unclear where the very first one was located. Charles Dickens has a reference to a 'fried fish warehouse' in *Oliver Twist*, published in 1839, and a fish and chip shop was established by Joseph Malin in Cleveland Street in the East End of London in 1860. Fish and chips became the staple fast food of the less well-off in the 1930s and escaped rationing during the forties and fifties. While no one could dispute the nutritional benefits of fish, the potato chip has had a mixed press: in the sixties, the phrase 'chips with everything', title of a 1962 play by Arnold Wesker (first referring to an institutional diet), came to symbolise a vulgar, limited proletarian lifestyle in much the same way as the loaded phrase 'junk food' does today.

'Chippy' or 'chippie' is also the nickname given to carpenters, from their habitual chipping and the wood chips that surround them, and is listed in dictionaries as *Br* and *NZ*, though I'm sure it is familiar to some Australians and South Africans. It has been heard in England since

Edwardian times and is used by the Irish, too. In the US the same word denotes a promiscuous woman or prostitute, but there it's a shortened form of 'chipping sparrow', a native bird. 'Chippiness', an expression popular during the twentieth century, especially in public-school and armed-forces colloquialism, may not come from having 'a chip on one's shoulder', as is usually supposed, but from the notion of dryness – starchy, brittle, inflexible – chippy defined as 'as dry as a (wood-) chip' was attested in 1866, with some dictionaries claiming that it was Canadian (presumably ascribing it to lumberjacks). It has also been hazarded that the usage may be based on the verb 'to chip in', in the Victorian sense of 'interfere', but again there is no evidence for this. Whatever its provenance, the term encapsulates yet another hard-to-define characteristic of many English males and some females, a sort of surly, resentful, hypersensitive nature that inevitably chafes and irritates. I remember Sloane Rangers using it in the 1980s of one another ('He's small, that's his problem, and small people are often chippy') and of supposed social inferiors ('chippy little **oik**'), but it has also proved useful as a regionalist slur, implying a collective inferiority complex and directed typically at the Welsh, Scots and northerners by southern English-speakers.

The crisis in the UK property market beginning in 2008 brought with it some new chip-related slang terms: when estate agents talk of 'chipping', they mean 'gazundering', that is, driving down a seller's asking price by underhand means and/or at the very last moment before a deal is concluded. In the same jargon a 'fish-and-chipper' is a predatory buyer who fishes around for a bargain, then extorts the best price from a helpless vendor – a tactic known as 'chip and pin'.

See also **crumpet, cuppa**

Chuddies

The most visible – or rather, audible – example of something trumpeted as a new dialect and dubbed Hinglish
(Hindi or Indian English), the jocular phrases 'Kiss my chuddies!' or 'Eat my chuddies!', where chuddies denotes
underpants, have been celebrated by journalists and lexicographers. As Anushka Asthana announced in the *Observer* in
2004, under the headline 'Welcome to the Queen's Hinglish',
'Asian "yoof-speak" is spicing up English, with Hindi words
such as "gora" and slang such as "innit" soon to enter the dictionary and experts predicting an explosive impact of the
language used by second-generation immigrants.' Limited
hybrid forms of English have grown up wherever it 'inter-
faces' with speakers of other languages: Franglais (often,
though, a deliberate spoof – see **bon viveur**) is still the best
known, but 'Spanglish', spoken on the Costa Brava in particular, and 'Chinglish', heard in China and among students in
the UK, are other examples. 'And let's not overlook the
claims of Honklish and Singlish too, lah! All those dynamic
Chuppies (Chinese-speaking upwardly mobile people) can't
be wrong!' (The reference is to Hong Kong and Singapore
varieties, from a posting on the BBC website in 2002.)

72

'Ponglish', essentially a smattering of English words mingled with Polish, is fashionable for both Polish workers in the UK and returnees in some circles in Poland. So-called Hinglish is nothing new, as south Asians, familiar with if not completely fluent in English for historical reasons, and often operating with several 'native' dialects, have been 'code-switching' – the linguists' term for mixing languages – for centuries. As Kiran Chauhan from Leicester wrote in the same online discussion, 'We have always used a mix of English, Gujarati and Swahili in our everyday language: it is so embedded that we do not realise it . . . It's great listening to people in Kenya and those here as well as those from India. We just mix more as we expand use of the internet as well.'

Hinglish is a blanket term for a vocabulary that actually incorporates Panjabi, Urdu and Bengali (see **nang**) elements. As a recent linguistic phenomenon it is closely associated with the multi-ethnic youth dialect, observed by some researchers, which is transforming the accent and intonation of youth in London and elsewhere. The vast majority of youth slang, however, still originates in Afro-Caribbean speech, as speakers of those varieties enjoy maximum street credibility – in inverse proportion to their mainstream social standing. As young Asians become 'cooler' in the eyes of peers, so their slang is likely to have greater impact, a trend highlighted by Gautam Malkani's 2007 novel *Londonstani*. The TV comedy series *Goodness Gracious Me* and *The Kumars at No 42* have simultaneously brought Asian speech patterns to a cross-section audience.

Borrowing from Hindi, etc. into English has been taking place since first contact with the subcontinent: examples are thug, veranda, bungalow, bangle and shampoo, and, of course, the recycled term of approval beloved of mockney

Jamie Oliver, and used by teenagers since the late 1990s, 'pukka'. *Chuddi* itself is Hindi slang and probably comes from *churidar*, traditional tight-fitting trousers.

As well as chuddies, which persists, sometimes in the admonition 'Don't get your chuddies in a twist', and can also now mean buttocks, current youth slang has the unrelated noun 'chuddy', which in the UK denotes chewing gum (as do 'chuttie' and 'chuffie'), and in the US a close friend (blending chum and buddy). As an adjective, the same word means unattractive, ugly or badly designed. 'The chuddy', on the other hand, is a term of appreciation meaning superb, first class.

It may be significant that Asians in England derive humour from underwear, thus buying in to a long native tradition of innocent domestic bawdy whereby underpants have been found both 'rude' and comical. This can be tracked through a succession of terms: from the euphemistic 'unmentionables' and 'smalls', via 'knickers' (a cry of defiance in the 1960s and early 70s) and 'pants', a vogue term of disapproval in the later 1990s (in a breathtaking case of what linguists might refer to as a poor choice of register, in December 2000 the UK Home Office officially apologised to a refugee who was told his asylum application was rejected because Home Secretary Jack Straw thought it was 'a pile of pants'. The Refugee Council said it was 'horrified' by the 'offensive, callous and flippant letter'), to current **yoof** slang synonyms, 'shreddies', 'clouts', 'trolleys', 'underchunders', 'undercrackers', 'underkecks', 'scrapaloids' and 'scripaloids'.

See also **estuary**

Chum

Of all the colloquial English words for 'friend', from the longstanding 'mate', 'pal' and 'mucker' (originally someone who 'mucks in'), to the most recent equivalents in street slang, 'blad', 'bre', 'bezzie', one is especially resonant, albeit sounding a little old-fashioned nowadays. Anthropologists and linguists such as the Polish-Australian Anna Wierzbicka who have analysed the keywords that convey the essence of a particular culture generally take the category of 'friend' as one of the most significant. Comparing and contrasting the nuances of difference within, for example, the Russian *tovarišč*, *drug*, *prijatel'* and *znakomyj*, or the Spanish *amigo*, *compañero* and *compadre* is supposed to reveal deep-seated attitudes peculiar to a people and a language. 'Mate' as used by Australians, for example, is much more than a simple synonym for 'friend'. It has all sorts of shades of meaning – notions of equality, solidarity, classlessness, machismo – built into it, although these will not normally be apparent to non-native users of the language.

Chum is untinged by ideology; it's a much cosier term, conjuring up a pure uncomplicated friendship, togetherness in shared adversity, absolute trust, and – especially significant in the context of a stratified, snobbish and insular culture – the absence of any distinctions of class or race. There are suggestions of loyalty and faithfulness built into it too. If we want to describe a relationship that is at once deep and easy, 'friend' is too bland, 'companion' too formal, 'comrade' too portentous, 'mate' too plebeian; 'pal' comes very close, but is maybe just a tinge too lightweight. It must be significant, though, that the word has always been marked as masculine: friendship among women lacks its own counterpart. Although chum is a quintessentially English word, it has been used, with much the same overtones and undertones, in the US and Canada, notably in children's adventure stories, to describe faithful pets, and for advertising tobacco. In Australia it was used from the late nineteenth century to refer to immigrants from the Old Country, distinguishing between settled 'old chums' and recently arrived 'new chums'.

In September 1892, *Chums*, 'the new penny paper for boys', was launched, and by 1935 the franchise had been generously extended in the form of *The Daily Record Chum Club Annual for Boys and Girls*. But it was above all in wartime that the word really came into its own, given that only then, *in extremis*, did all males became momentarily equal. The word was used by my grandfather in his letters from the trenches, and the 'Old Contemptibles', like him veterans of World War I, were known to each other as 'the Chums'. During World War II, as part of a series of warnings to the public that 'loose lips sink ships', an ominous propaganda poster was circulated, strangely simplistic in design, showing a blood-smeared hand disappearing into the sea, a sailor's hat floating on the ripples next to it, with the admonition 'Keep mum chum'. From the 1940s to the late 70s, 'chummy' (first attested in 1864, though it had previously denoted a sweep's assistant, coming from 'chimney') was favoured by the police as a form of address, full of avuncular menace and condescension, to suspects. It was also the trademark nickname for a diminutive, cheeky-looking Austin motor car manufactured in 1929. The injunction 'don't get too chummy' warns against inappropriate intimacy.

There is an identical word that means 'fish bait', still heard in the North American phrase 'chum-bucket', but this comes from an obscure Scottish dialect term. Our chum probably started out as 'cham', a late seventeenth-century shortening of the phrase 'chamber-fellow', the equivalent of room-mate today, hence from the outset the notion of shared circumstances was present (coincidentally, 'comrade' derives from Spanish *camarada*, which also meant 'chamber-mate'). It was an example of Oxbridge slang, which often employed 'clipping' (the linguist's word for abbreviation, as in 'bus' or 'mob'). In 1793, *The Times* reported on the enforced intimacy among prisoners of the French Revolution: 'There, and under the same roof are to be found *Aristocrate* with a *Patriot*; a Jacobin chum with a *Feuillant*; a *Petit-maitre* and a *Sans Culotte*.' By now a popular usage, among men at least, in the nineteenth century chum spawned a number of derivatives, including 'chummery' (for close companionship), 'chummage' (close collaboration) and the verbs 'to chum', meaning to accompany someone, and 'chummy (up)' (to share digs and/or cooperate with), but these had all become obsolescent by late Edwardian times.

To some degree a leftover from more innocent times, chum is nowadays often employed facetiously, as in 'my old chum Lord Archer' (*News of the World*), or 'Prince Harry's noisy chums' (*Evening Standard*), except where nostalgia is evoked: 'World War Two chums Gilbert Fogg and Tom Parker were reunited after nearly 60 years – when they found they were next-door neighbours' (*Sun*). Modern popular culture has as usual managed to debase a once noble word: 'pedigree chum', punning of course on the brand name of a popular dog food, has been since the early 1980s slang for an upper-class boyfriend or escort (successor to the 'deb's delight' of the fifties and sixties), while 'bum-chum', successor to the archaic 'chuff-chum' (where 'chuff' is an old dialect term for backside), can mean either a (male) homosexual partner or an annoying close companion.

Clever

'It's not big and it's not clever', long a staple of family talk, has in the last few years become a catchphrase, a jokey chastisement of bad behaviour or an ironic put-down, in facetious newspaper pieces, in a Lily Allen song lyric, in online judgements on innovative 'solutions'. I've noticed that clever is a word that foreigners who have learned English, even the most fluent of them, almost never use, although the English themselves often do. It's not a fancy, educated term, but a slight, unassuming word (slipping easily off the tongue like 'clean' and 'clear'). It seems typically English in that it conveys mild appreciation, sometimes slightly lukewarm or muted praise. But the more you examine its connotations and contexts, the more interesting it is. Perhaps, like many of the words listed here, it contains within itself nuances of meaning and allusions that do not equate with, do not translate so easily from, another's mother tongue. The nearest equivalent in French is probably *astucieux* – not at all a plain, day-to-day word – or *intelligent*, which is too straightforward.

How do we define it? 'Ingenious' is probably the closest semi-synonym, otherwise 'quick', 'bright', 'adept', 'skilful', 'talented', 'adroit'? None of them quite does it justice. It's a mum word, a girlie word, almost a nursery word, used especially with or about children in preference to grander, longer terms. 'Clever girl!' I say to my baby daughter when she seems to be picking up the tricks of negotiating the grown-up world particularly quickly. It was one of my mother's key terms of approval when assessing the qualities of cousins, nieces and nephews, schoolfriends. In fact the clever child, usually a girl, was a stock figure in European fables and fairy tales, the child's performances and sometimes comeuppances reflecting the mix of awe, admiration and suspicion that a prodigy inspires. On my bookshelves is a pair of books from the 1840s entitled *Clever Boys of Our Time and How They Became Famous Men*, and its companion *Clever Girls* . . . which bears the caption '. . . whose lives furnish an incentive and encouragement to effort and endurance, and whose example stimulates to industry and perseverance'.

'A clever remark' is smart in a superficial way, or is wounding. 'A clever solution' certainly sounds appreciative – but is there still a tinge of doubt or jealousy? 'Just because you're clever . . .' clearly smacks of envy and/or disapproval, the old English distrust of the intellectual. Hence 'clever-clever', and 'clever Dick' (first recorded in the late nineteenth century) with its variants, the dated 'cleverkins', 'clever-boots' and 'clever-drawers', the more recent 'clever-clogs', 'clever Dan', and 'clever-trousers' (the wonderful *Urban Dictionary* entry on this last runs: 'A person who cannot let anything go by. They always have to answer back in a condesending [*sic*] way. These are usually people who are higher in the academic world than their peers and they use their knowledge in a mean way.' The accompanying illustrative quote reads, 'He had to say that just to be a clever-trousers. Who cares if pigs don't really sweat that much?').

Clever

The origins of clever are interesting too. The *OED*, usually the ultimate arbiter in etymology, precedes its treatment with a big question mark before hazarding that the word is related to the archaic Middle English 'clivers', meaning claws. By this reasoning, clever comes from a dialect sense of 'nimble of claw', 'quick to seize'. The American *Merriam Websters* disagrees: 'Etymology: Middle English cliver, perhaps of Scandinavian origin; akin to Danish dialect *kløver*, alert, skillful. Date: circa 1595.' But note that 'perhaps'. And, oddly, there is no trace at all of the word in the records between the thirteenth and sixteenth centuries. But perhaps this is all just special pleading: maybe I'm only fixated on the word because of a pub conversation that took place thirty years ago. A new acquaintance – one of the regulars – looked me up and down and opined, 'I'm not sure if girls will go for you: you haven't got a car, your looks only just make it, and you're too clever by half.'

Common

In March 2003 it was reported that 'bubbly' trainee teacher Jane Magill had changed her name by deed poll to Lambrini – 'after her favourite wine'. She was inspired to do this by the character Chardonnay in the TV series *Footballers' Wives*. Lambrini, 24, said: 'I'm addicted to the show. But I thought Chardonnay was a bit common. So I chose Lambrini – as I'm always drinking it.' Lambrini, of Eccles, Greater Manchester, broke the news to fiancé Eli Ellwood, 28, after the name change. 'He was stunned.' Unlike Chardonnay, a variety of grape used to make wine, Lambrini, manufactured in Liverpool, is actually a light perry or flavoured pear cider. If common can mean coarse or vulgar, dead common means completely lacking in refinement, functioning as a catty dismissal, or, very occasionally, as a proud boast. In 2005, once-upon-a-time punk controversialist Julie Burchill crowed that she had just made a vast profit by selling her house to a property developer. 'I've got a very Chav attitude to money. I sold it for one-and-a-half million. Huge profit! That's dead common, that is. Real Chav behaviour!'

Since it was adopted into English, via French *commun*, ultimately from Latin *communis*, which meant 'together with one (another)' or 'bound together', the word common has always been associated with rank and prestige, the nobility being contrasted with 'the common' and 'the commons'. As well as shared by all 'in common', it denoted ordinary, undistinguished; hence already in Middle English 'belonging to the commonality' could be pejorative. This is one of only two entries that this book and Raymond Williams' *Keywords* have in common, the other being **society**. In trying to determine exactly when the depreciative overtook the neutral usage, Williams points out that parliamentary troops in the seventeenth-century Civil War refused to be known as 'common soldiers' and insisted on 'private soldiers' as a designation. In 1788, *The Times* lambasted those who celebrated Guy Fawkes night on 5 November: 'It is amazing to think the number of common people who are thus deluded by an ignorant outcast of society . . .' Quotations from 1866 show that the senses 'of inferior quality or value' and 'vulgar' had established themselves by that time, but still at the turn of the century the word could be ambiguous. In 1901, the *Penny Illustrated Paper* lamented the disappearance of ruffles on ladies' winter hats, their fashion expert pointing out, 'I knew they would not last, as they were imitated in cheap material, and had got very common.' Employing a standard formulation in the same paper in August 1910, a Mr Syme complained that 'Thrice already in twenty years, on the complaint of a common prostitute, the House of Commons has ordered an inquiry into the conduct of the metropolitan police.'

For me and for most baby-boomers, common evokes the fifties and sixties in particular, and the keep-up-with-the-Joneses, curtain-twitching competitiveness and petty snobberies of the post-war years. But the epithet endured, and in February 1977, the local press reported that Mrs Victoria

Marshall, 24, of Redditch, had refused to eat Christmas dinner in the works canteen, saying that the shop workers 'ate like pigs', were 'common as muck' and that she would not use the same cutlery as them. That expression was analysed in internet postings in 2004, R. Moore of Lancashire noting that muck denotes manure in the north and observing that 'the saying can rebound on the speaker, who is often female, for it raises the suggestion that jealousy and prudeness [*sic*], rather than genuine contempt, is the cause of the verbal attack'. The same phrase was used as the title of a 'bittersweet' TV comedy-drama about northern bin-men, broadcast in 1994 and 1995, in a song by Ian Dury and the Blockheads (chorus: 'Luvva duck, we're as common as muck') and for the bestselling autobiography of scabrous comedian Roy 'Chubby' Brown (real name Royston Vasey) in 2007. In all these cases the word is employed knowingly and/or ironically, and in an age when what once was deemed vulgar (tattoos, talking loudly about money, wearing sun-glasses indoors) has become commonplace, that seems to be its fate.

Common, fundamental in 'common law' and 'common land', is also of course a component of the noun plural 'common sense' and adjective 'commonsense' (see **sensible**), first attested in English in the sixteenth century, but not originating here. The concept goes back to Greek and Roman ideas of a fundamental human sense underlying the five other senses, but in English usage it came to signify a robust collective pragmatism that by the eighteenth century was, at least by implication, opposable to 'foreign' ways of thinking and behaving. Increasingly through the twentieth century, and still today, English empiricism contrasts, we think, with 'continental' reliance on theoretical abstraction and rationality. In the same way the phrase 'common decency' (see **decent**) appeals to a consensus, a set of shared values that are not enshrined in any written code and are often thought to be instinctive and universal, but which are in fact both imaginary and enormously potent ... and English.

See also **posh**

Cottage

The house I live in, in deepest London **suburbia**, used to have, until I removed it, 'The Cottage' on a wooden plaque displayed prominently on the front gate, with the humble street number much less visible at the end of the path to the front door. The house is not grand, but the designation was hardly appropriate, as the building is identical to all its neighbours, was built in the late 1920s and is neither rural nor noticeably large or small. It was, however, designed with rustic pretensions – wooden shutters outside, wooden latches inside, confirming Pont's cartoons published in *Punch* at the time of building showing couples crouching under a low ceiling or shivering before a mock-baronial fireplace, gently laughing at the English 'weakness for oak beams' and 'passion for the antique'. The ubiquitous interwar semi (and the stockbroker belt's larger 'Jacobethan' or 'Tudorbethan' detached version) was a sort of parody of a tile-hung cottage of the seventeenth century or thereabouts; new developments in England no longer incorporate all the archaic decorative references, but still, usually illiterately and offhandedly, play on a vaguely antique tradition of pitched roofs and porches. In a recent survey of figures kept by the

Land Registry by Mouseprice.com, The Cottage ranked as Britain's most popular house name overall, with The Coach House topping the £350,000 to £800,000 bracket, and The Old Rectory leading the over-£800,000 category. The top five nationwide were as follows: The Cottage; Rose Cottage; The Bungalow; The Coach House; The Barn. Ivy Cottage was at number seven. Giving your house a name, by the way, providing it is not too obscure or far-fetched (or retro-kitsch as Abide-a-wee, Dunrovin, etc.) is recommended by many estate agents as a cheap means of adding value.

A well-known quirk of English usage is highlighted by two articles from *The Times*. On 11 August 1808, their correspondent reported on '. . . a grand public day at the Princess Elizabeth's cottage, at Old Windsor. Upwards of 100 of the neighbouring Nobility and Gentry sat down to an excellent dinner.' In May 1825, at the Royal Academy exhibition, 'Mr T. F. Hunt has *Two views of a cottage to be built in Herefordshire.* The design is exceedingly tasteful; but to call such a building as is here represented "a cottage" has as much reason in it as if we were to speak of Westminster-hall as a closet.' The quintessential Jane Austen and later Enid Blyton also in their works made references to cottages, in which large families together with servants, chattels and visitors could seemingly be squeezed, while Americans adopted the term in the later nineteenth century to designate sumptuous homes such as 'summer residences typically at watering places' (*OED*). In Edwardian England, detached urban or suburban houses were routinely known, at least by builders and estate agents, as 'villas', and the distinction with the out-of-town 'cottage' was maintained: nonetheless the name, along with its cluster of associations, crept across city boundaries.

The archaic 'cot', 'cote' and the contemporary cottage

ultimately derive via Latin and Old French from a prehistoric west European root, something like *kuta*, meaning 'dwelling'. In practice it has designated small, humble homes, as in Chaucer's 'a poure widwe ... was whilom dwellyng in a narwe cotage', while Bacon made a social distinction between the yeomanry and the middle people (free farmers), 'of a condition between gentlemen and cottagers' (landless agricultural labourers). Most European languages have some sort of equivalence, several different names denoting a small, humble rural dwelling, (among them *chata* in Czech, *chaumiere* in French, *Hütte* in German, *cassetta* in Italian), but not just *one* emblematic word as we have, a single carrier of a weight of associations and resonances. Perhaps significantly, the French and the Dutch have taken to occasionally using the English word. Still employed in its homeland as shorthand for rural Englishness, and still embodying the strong identification by an urbanised people with an idealised countryside, the nostalgia for a lost rural idyll, the country cottage is more pragmatically a source of rental income. At the time of writing, of the fifty-nine million references thrown up by an internet search, the great majority are in advertisements for 'holiday cottages'.

'Cottaging' has been gay slang since the 1930s for soliciting (male) sex in public toilets, sarcastically renaming the tiled and rustic-looking lavatories, typically with pitched, tiled roofs, in municipal parks and public spaces. Fulham Football Club players, notwithstanding this, are known as 'The Cottagers' after Craven Cottage, their home ground since 1896.

Crap

From the *Guardian* in 2007 comes a reflection by sports commentator Harry Pearson on the absolute necessity of freedom of speech at football matches: 'at Brunton Park, stewards moved in when a middle-aged women with the solid, matronly build of a prize Jersey and the bellow to match got to her feet and yelled that Carlisle's attempts to defend a corner were "bloody crap". British business slang still talks of 'having a Ratner moment' or 'doing a Ratners' and poor-quality merchandise may be dismissed as 'a load of old Ratners', all referring to the 1991 speech to the Institute of Directors by chairman Gerald Ratner in which he described some of his own jewellery and silverware product lines as 'crap'. The company quickly lost £500m, and its CEO shortly thereafter.

Crap came to national prominence again in 2003 with the advent of the Crap Town section on *The Idler* magazine's website, to which the public were invited to send nominations for the fifty worst places to live, the most miserable of the UK's many awful conurbations. The results (one recent posting, from Yatton near Bristol reads, 'In Yatton, the elderly are like dirty, damaged vultures') were published in two successive hard-copy volumes edited by Sam Jordison and Dan Kieran. The nominations – Hull came top (or bottom) in 2003 and Luton the following year – predictably enraged local worthies, and provoked (mainly excruciatingly embarrassing and doomed) attempts at PR damage limitation. Significantly the nominated towns took in prosperous cities like Bath, Edinburgh and Winchester as well as post-industrial poverty traps.

Thus, although the word is common in all 'native' English-speaking areas, a case could be made for crap, as in 'crap food', 'tourist crap', having a particularly English relevance, given the tradition of poor workmanship, dispiriting, desolate public spaces and abject **naff**ness still prevalent across the country.

Useful as a stronger synonym for rubbish and a relatively mild synonym for excrement, crap may also denote oppressive, petty or otherwise offensive behaviour, typically in formulations such as 's/he doesn't take any crap from anyone' or 'I'm not going to put up with this/his/her crap any more'. Somehow crap (which has been printable and publicly utterable since the later 1960s) seems to evoke an even more pitiable, contemptible condition, even shoddier material, even more irritating nonsense than its stronger synonym 'sh**'.

The word, contrary to folk etymology, has nothing to do with Thomas Crapper (1837–1910), celebrated as the English inventor of the flush toilet (his surname is a variant form of 'Cropper'), and everything to do with Middle English 'crappe', a distant relative of 'crop' and 'crabbed', which meant scrapings, scale, fat residue, ale dregs or chaff. Our colloquialism is also unrelated to the formal, old-fashioned terms 'crapulous' and 'crapulent', which mean suffering from or given to excess and/or debauchery, and come via Latin from the Greek for a drunken headache. (They, rather than crap, may therefore be the origin of 'crappers', twentieth-century armed-forces slang for helplessly drunk.) In the early 1800s, crap was also underworld slang for the gallows, but this probably derives from the Dutch *krap*, meaning to cramp, a euphemism for hang.

Crap was widely heard in robust US military and corporate speech in the 1950s and 1960s and may have been re-adopted from these sources by speakers in the UK, where it had been languishing in folksy or provincial semi-obscurity during the period of Victorian and post-Victorian rectitude. 'Crappy' and 'crappo' are the modern adjectival forms, and to 'crap on' is a stronger version of 'bang on' in the sense of harp on incessantly or rant. The 'crapper' as a vulgarism for toilet appears to derive from crap in the sense of defecate, first recorded in the seventeenth century, rather than the name of its supposed inventor. In so-called cockney rhyming slang, crap, noun and adjective, is rendered by 'pony', from 'pony and trap', while in the slang of younger speakers since the 1980s, it has been embellished in multiple ways, including the North American 'crapola', referring typically to stupid beliefs or useless or inferior products, 'craptastic', 'cra-pitude' and the exasperated exclamation 'crap-cakes!'.

See also **pooh**

Crumpet

O f a party in the late 1970s, a gatecrashing friend slaver-
ingly reported, 'There's wall-to-wall crumpet in there.'
In imitation of the same demotic tone, James Fenton, in a
poem from 1983, gave God the lines, 'Oh he said: "If you lay
off the crumpet / I'll see you alright in the end. / Just hang on
until the last trumpet, / Have faith in me, chum – I'm your
friend."'

They are still there, at the bakers and on the all-night
supermarket shelves, so someone apart from me must be
enjoying their acrid-doughy taste and spongey texture, but
since the demise of the open hearth and the toasting fork,
and the arrival of nouvelle cuisine, they have hardly been
heard of at all. In *Shirley* (1849), Charlotte Brontë wrote of
'Little Mr Sweeting, seated between Mrs Sykes and Miss
Mary, both of whom were very kind to him, and having a
dish of tarts before him, and marmalade and crumpet upon
his plate, looked and felt more content than any monarch.'
As well he might, but not in those days with any thought of
double entendre, as tart and crumpet had yet to acquire their
more modern senses. Tart, just a few years later, was being
used to mean sweetheart, transmuting into 'trollop' by the

end of the century; '(my dear old) crumpet' surfaced as an innocent term of (male to male) endearment in the vocabulary of Bertie Wooster and the members of the Drones Club.

The noun crumpet was first recorded in 1694, perhaps from earlier 'crompid (crimped or curled) cake', the image of a curled or bubbled crust occurring in *The Kelpie Riders*, an 1897 ballad by Bliss Carman: 'By the side of each to cheer his ghost, / A flagon of foam with a crumpet of frost.' It was slang for the head from the late nineteenth century to the 1940s. For an attractive female or females collectively the usage may be ancient, but its first written attestation is from 1936, evoking not so much the sweetness or the challenging acidity of the tart as the comforting combination of soft, hot – and presumably buttered ('buttered bun' was Victorian slang for a prostitute). To push analogies further, the female object of English male desire is everyday, bland, inexpensive, supremely unpretentious. (Less bland but a good deal greasier, 'a bit of crackling' was, from the 1890s to the 1970s, another way of apotheosising an attractive lady.) Unaffected by the class associations that taint 'teacake' and 'scone', crumpet may as easily conjure up Barbara Windsor in her *Carry On* days as, in the formulation 'the 'thinking man's crumpet' first applied by humorist Frank Muir to Joan Bakewell, the middle-class objects of middle-class lust Felicity Kendall and Helen Mirren. The usage is still favoured by tabloid journalists, as in the *Daily Mirror*'s appreciation of an eminent TV historian: 'if history's grand dame Dr David Starkey is Elton John, all flamboyant eccentricity, then Simon Schama is Mick Jagger. With his trademark leather jacket and Harry Potter specs, he is fast turning into the thinking woman's crumpet – the man who puts the phwoar in the Fourteen Years War.'

In the fifties and sixties, 'crumpet-man' denoted a

seducer or notably lascivious male. Since the early 1980s, the sort of people who use the word crumpet in this way (bluff, hapless, unglamorous males, and a few laddish females?) have increasingly favoured the synonym 'totty' (sometimes qualified by 'rampant', the term was probably originally a diminutive form of Dorothy, denoting in the nineteenth century a loose woman), which itself is starting to sound rather dated.

There are sound similarities with crumpet in those saucy synonyms for sexual frolicking 'rumpy-pumpy' and 'rumpo', but these are unrelated, being elaborated forms of rump in the sense of buttocks. They are related, though, in sounding comical: reinforcing the idea that humour is the lens through which we view the Hunnish practices that have long been euphemised as 'slap 'n' tickle'.

See also **toast**

Cuppa

In January 2006, under the possibly slightly tasteless head-line 'Elsie finds eterni-tea', the *Daily Mirror* reported that 'Tea-loving gran Elsie Winterton – who supped 18 cuppas a day – has been laid to rest in her favourite Royal Doulton teapot.' In June 2008, the *Sun* reported that a grieving son had gone one further: 'Cuppa fan John Lowndes had his dad's ashes mixed with clay and turned into a TEAPOT. John, 54, used to enjoy a brew with Ian, 75, and got a potter to make the tribute in Broad Haven, Pembrokeshire.' George Orwell wrote of England in 1940 that 'All the culture that is most truly native centres round things which even when they are communal are not official – the pub, the foot-ball match, the back garden, the fireside and the "nice cup of tea".' In a newspaper advertisement of 1963, the case was put a little more portentously: 'Tea connotes a breaking down of tensions in a neurotic world and amity on a multi-lateral front,' continuing rather bathetically, 'people of sensibility who know what a good cuppa should be . . . firmly insist that the name on the label should be Lipton's.' The importance of this national symbol of comfort was lam-pooned in the WWII soldiers' song:

Kiss me good-night, Sergeant-Major,
Tuck me in my little wooden bed.
We all love you, Sergeant-Major,
When we hear you bawling, 'Show a leg!'
Don't forget to wake me in the morning,
And bring me round a nice hot cup of tea
Kiss me good-night, Sergeant-Major,
Sergeant-Major, be a mother to me.

The homely English remedy for all physical and spiritual afflictions was extended even to the enemy: German airmen captured during the Battle of Britain were routinely given a hot cuppa before being marched away. Whether contained in chipped mug or bone-china cup and saucer, whether strong enough to stand a spoon up in or ever so slightly perfumed, whether served in the late afternoon with biccies or cucumber sandwiches or gulped down with the evening meal, the cuppa appears again and again as a potent symbol of cosiness and togetherness, as when Boy George, in his glamorous pre-convict incarnation, claimed he preferred a cuppa to sex. 'Fancy a cuppa?' is an invitation to take time out from the punishing British work schedule, and 'the search for the perfect cuppa' a focus for (endless but harmless) controversy. Lamenting the disappearance of the **decent** cuppa is a social ritual second only to the serving and drinking itself, indulged in by all manner of ordinary folk and by former PM Tony Blair on US radio in 2007: his publicity-grabbing tongue-in-cheek complaint was obediently turned by the media into a . . . well, a storm in a teacup of the sort we relish.

Tea-drinking is said to have been introduced by Catherine of Braganza to the court of Charles II, but what began as a luxury item (and curative) for the few had by the mid-nineteenth century become the most popular British working-class drink. The idiomatic 'not my cup of tea' seems to be an Edwardian coinage, and at about the same time 'you're a nice cup o' tea!' was a colloquial equivalent of 'you're a fine one!'. In 1970, the UK consumed a quarter of the entire world production of tea, and in 2005, a Mintel survey estimated that 62 billion cups were being consumed annually.

During the post–World War II transition from Old England to New Britain, the cuppa has served simultaneously as a symbol of down-to-earth sociability ('a nice cup of tea and a sit-down') and of an obstinate and insular lack of refinement. In comparing catering services on French and British railways, *The Times* in 1954 contrasted the *poulet rabelaisien* on the menu in Touraine with 'queuing for a cuppa at Crewkerne'. Perhaps a mark of how things have changed in New Britain, one can't help thinking that PG Tips got it wrong when, to celebrate the company's seventy-fifth anniversary in 2005, they toured an exhibition featuring a £7,500 tea bag filled with diamonds (3,000 times more expensive than a whole box of its tea-bearing cousins).

The alteration of 'cup o" to 'cuppa' may be from the pidgin English used in south and east Asia, (there are only rare instances of an alternative spelling, 'cupper') but it has also been ascribed to P. G. Wodehouse. It was also of course the standard cockney pronunciation and appears in music-hall songs of the 1920s. It was often twinned with 'char' (first written thus in 1919, from the Chinese word for tea, *ch'a*, via Hindi), which also gave us a folk heroine, the charlady or charwoman, surviving as the tea lady with the sympathetic ear, a bearer of gossip and good sense along with the refreshment, lone symbol of a more intimate age resolutely wheeling her trolley through the corporate jungle. Cuppa cannot properly be used of the globalised alternative, coffee, and such a cloth-cap word sits uneasily with fruit teas, herbal infusions and novelties such as granules, powders, pellets and pills, so perhaps its days as a cultural icon are numbered. The (English) writers of 2008's *Rough Guide to England*, however, could still contend that the English motto should be 'make tea, not war', and in 2009 came news corroborating the properties of Coronation Street's panacea ('Put the kettle on, I'm parched!'): three cuppas a day reduces the risk of breast cancer in younger women by up to 37 per cent.

See also **chat**

Dear

One of the most essential words in our language is under threat, or at least shows sign of mutating in curious ways. 'Dear . . .' as a term of address in correspondence has all but disappeared from emails, and never figured in text messages at all. Though it has to be used in the few personal (as opposed to circular) letters sent, the accompanying rules of etiquette (if 'Dear Sir/Madam', then 'Yours faithfully' must follow) appear to be breaking down. As a term of endearment, whether private or in public, these days 'dear' sounds positively dated, or associated with the old at heart. In 1946, George Orwell described his ideal, imaginary, pub to the readers of the London *Evening Standard*. For him an essential component was barmaids who addressed their customers as 'dear' rather than 'ducky'. Fifty-nine years on, the elderly Mr Percy Arrowsmith re-emphasised the word's key role, writing to the *Daily Express* to confide that 'the secret of our successful 80-year marriage is two little words . . . "yes dear"' (though a Mr William Gill of Carlisle wrote in the following day: 'I always thought it was "**Sorry**, I'm wrong"'). 'My dear' *tout court* sounds impossibly pompous unless uttered in a rustic accent, in which case it sounds comically

quaint. 'Dear little . . .' or 'little dear', come to that, have come to sound patronising or fey; 'dearest', like the once common 'darling', alarmingly cloying or dangerously, even threateningly, intimate in the cool, affectless discourse of New Britain (unless they are used in written funerary tributes, that is). Rallying cries – 'all that we hold (most) dear', 'a nation dear to my heart' – belong to the alienating language of bombast and jingoism.

So it is no longer cool to write it and no longer cool to say it, but of course dear is not only an asexual expression of affection, it is at the same time (curiously, if you think about it) a humbler and a more genteel way of saying 'expensive', thus tapping into our national obsession with money as well as our limited ability to emote. In earlier times the word was a natural choice, as in 'Salt is this season triple as dear as usual, and we do not think herrings can be shipped under 15s' (a report from 1801), or 'You want jewellery that will last a lifetime, and cheap jewellery is dear at any price' (a 1911 advertisement). Here again I feel that dear is losing ground: 'expensive' sounds more ponderous, more portentous, Latinate and specific – and more urgent, hence more appropriate to our current circumstances; 'costly' has connotations of 'demanding sacrifice' but also of 'precious, splendid, lavish', nuances that the d-word lacks. 'It will cost you dear' smacks of antique melodrama.

Both dear's principal senses, of loved and cherished and of high-priced, were present from the beginning, contained within the ancient Germanic ancestor of our word, something like *deurjaz*. Old Norse had *dyrr*, while the Old English version was *deore*. The noun 'dearth', incidentally, is related, originally meaning a time when scarcity made goods particularly dear.

Perhaps I'm wrong, and dear will simply persist in all its

usages and all its senses, ubiquitous and virtually unnoticed. Perhaps as we grow older we will start, like many of our grandparents, to address all youngsters as 'dear' or even 'deary'. Perhaps we will even re-embrace the language of feeling that led our ancestors to bandy the word about with abandon. It's a safer bet that it will stay with us in the form of real and ritualised laments, hand-wringing and head-shaking: as in mournful comedian Tony Hancock's rueful, exasperated 'Oh dear, oh dear, oh dear', or, if things turn out better than we expect, the chirpier 'dear(y) me'.

Decent

In any scan of transcripts of radio vox pops, press reports and readers' letters, even online discussion groups, one word stands out as what a sociologist or cultural analyst might call our 'self-ascription': the quality we assign to ourselves and to those we identify with or emulate. This word is 'decent'. In *The Way of All Flesh* (completed in the 1880s), Samuel Butler wrote, 'He wanted his children to be brought up in the pure fresh air . . . insisted that they should pass their earlier years among the poor rather than the rich . . . they were still so young that it did not much matter where they were, so long as they were with kindly decent people, and in a healthy neighbourhood.' The distinction made between decent people and their opposite – there is no catch-all term for them, the feckless, lazy, troublesome, slovenly 'others'; the ne'er-do-wells, hobbledehoys and slatterns – is one that resonates through public and domestic discourse since the Victorian era. Although there are no records of the private conversations that took place, the voices of ordinary people can be heard in the Mass Observation diaries that some agreed to keep after World War II and in the depositions made to planning inquiries during the post-war phase of social engineering. Decent is a keyword of indignation and discrimination: again and again we hear that 'the decent families' are made to suffer, while the few on the estate who are not decent are allowed to flourish, long-standing sentiments echoing plaintively in a new world of twoccing, hotting, restraining orders and ASBOs. At the same time, 'decent law-abiding (citizen)' is a formulation deployed by each successive government when issuing pledges or appealing to a consensus.

From French *décent*, Latin *decentum* (from the verb *decere*, to be suitable), the word was first recorded in English in 1539 with the meaning 'appropriate'. It later came also to mean 'proper' and 'respectable', then 'tolerable' or 'passable', then by the early 1700s 'handsome' too. The modern, rather fuzzy though universally understood senses of 'morally acceptable' – actually acceptable to prudes – and 'middlingly good' had established themselves by the end of the nineteenth century: 'French seaside bathing is far more enjoyable for families than the system of separating the sexes adopted in England. Wearing decent tunics and knickerbockers, why should not both sexes bathe together at British watering places?' (from a reader's letter from 1895). 'Common decency', a phrase beloved by counsels for the prosecution and the prim and prurient in general, reinforces this assumption of collective rectitude, but there can be a more benevolent flavour to a conviction that transcends class and circumstance, as in Dr Johnson's 'a decent provision for the poor is the true test of civilisation' and in D. H. Lawrence's poem 'The Latent Desire':

'The latent desire in all decent men today
Is for some more natural, more decent social
    arrangement

Wherein a man can live his life without being a slave to
  "earning
his living" and "getting on".
But of course, this means smashing the present system
  of grab and
devil take the hindmost.'

And again, in the *News of the World*'s March 2000 report,
under the headline 'Shame old story as rivals neglect our
pensioners': 'Our pensioners deserve a decent standard of
living in their old age – but instead they've been forced to
get by on a pittance thanks to recent Labour and Tory gov-
ernments.'

In the language of the normally diffident, thoroughly
English male of folk memory, '**jolly** decent of you!' came
very close to gushing (posh schoolgirls favoured 'jolly D!',
first attested in 1949), and 'a thoroughly decent chap' was
the very highest praise. Looking back at the subterfuges
required by 1950s divorce laws and accompanying clichés,
Simon Armitage, in his 1989 poem 'Not the Bermuda
Triangle', gently mocked,

Of course there is a third party, but
our chap being a decent sort
will do the decent thing: that is
bluff it in a Brighton hotel
with two paid snoops outside the door
and a woman of experience in the adjoining room.

It is hard to imagine anyone anywhere doing the decent
thing today – if that required marrying a jilted spouse, shooting oneself, or merely resigning after being caught in
financial flagrante. The word has dwindled into a lukewarm

endorsement ('they serve a halfway decent pint'), a muted or grudging approval ('after a decent interval'). If we ourselves are decent, we are not outstanding, not paragons – certainly not **flash**y – just quietly, conformingly, dully worthy . . . and, perhaps, by implication only, just the teeniest bit self-satisfied?

See also **fair, gentle, nice, sensible**

Diversity

I've been grappling recently with a rapidly evolving and loaded vocabulary: the sort used in management, human resources and recruitment, as well as public sector discourse, all revolving around the notion of 'diversity'. This key concept for organisations was borrowed from biology and ecology, later linking up with 'equal employment opportunity' (EEO) on the one side and 'globalisation' on the other. Diversity has been commercialised and commodified: there are agencies whose sole function is to analyse, disseminate and market the concept; diversity awareness sessions are a feature of most corporate training programmes; 'Head of Diversity' or 'CDO' – 'Chief Diversity Officer' – have become established as job titles. It's interesting how one emblematic piece of jargon triggers the use of others: conversations and texts about diversity tend to be particularly jargon-rich, as witness HSBC: 'diversity is a source of opportunity . . . competitive edge can be gained from the variety present in our workforce and customer base, and specific attention to market variation'. The Spencer Stuart Roundtable Diversity Practice proclaims: 'diversity is a 21st century business priority — a driver for revenue . . . in order to leverage diversity, companies must diversify the top tier of management'. Even the US Chief of Naval Operations assures that 'we will empower diversity of thoughts, ideas and competencies'. The core term itself is mutating: workers in Western societies are now, we are told, 'living in multicultures in conditions of hyperdiversity'.

Like all fashionable notions, however pervasive, this one has a limited shelf life, and there are signs that its sell-by date is approaching. As long ago as the early 1990s, US human resource manuals were discussing where diversity training had gone wrong and why the term 'difference' was to be preferred. According to Christopher Metzler, Cornell University professor: 'diversity has become a pejorative and must be replaced by the word 'inclusion', which [business executives] believe drives a different philosophy'. Politicians, too, have finally realised that diversity can emphasise separateness and are substituting their alternative buzzword, 'cohesion'. If I'm being facetious, my own favourite replacement, though I doubt it will catch on, is the academics' hugely pretentious 'objective value pluralism'. A much more likely candidate, and the cross-sector term *du jour*, is 'convergence'. In the meantime, diversity's predecessor, 'multiculturalism', has in some circles become the gently mocking, sometimes derisive 'multi-culti'. Motoring journalist James May writes, 'I'm quite a fan of multi-culti Blighty, although I suspect that, like most people, when I say my local community is a vibrant melting pot of the inhabitants of the global village, what I really mean is that there are lots of interesting things to eat and one or two unusual shops that stay open late.' The trajectory of multicultural(ism) as a buzzword has obvious parallels with that of diversity. As with 'minority' and 'community' ('care in the community', 'local community') before it, those it was designed to boost or patronise turned against it, prompting some specialists to replace it with the rather ambiguous variant 'multiculturism'. Growing awareness of the charged nature of such terms and their part in identity politics has meant that in UK official-speak, 'migrant' substitutes for 'immigrant' (losing the real distinction between the two); we are recommended to replace 'asylum seeker' with 'asylum applicant', 'the Muslim community' with 'Muslim communities'.

Diversity – from Latin *diversus*, 'turned in different directions' – did not start out as, nor is it today, an exclusively English keyword, but it does stand for something crucial in considering twenty-first-century Englishness. It is both a recognition of a complex 'new' reality (the reality isn't new, only the collective recognition), and a concept that calls into question many people's idea of an English identity. For me, the missing word in all this, and a worthy candidate for revival, is 'cosmopolitan', a word that has positive connotations and, unlike more recent coinages – 'global soul', 'global nomad', etc. – an ancient and noble pedigree (it's from the Greek *kosmos*, 'world', and *polites*, citizen). *Independent* commentator Amol Rajan, like many of those writing on estrangement and cultural relativism, has made the distinction that cosmopolitanism is 'diversity as lived experience', whereas diversity and multiculturalism are 'state-sponsored ideologies'.

Doily

Familiar things, pillars of a way of life, can slip away while our attention is focused elsewhere: what was taken for granted vanishes, probably for ever. On 11 March 2005, the *Guardian* was in nostalgic mood. Noting the passing of coal fires and male gallantry, the article went on to consider the disappearance of the very English ritual of afternoon tea. 'Gone, too, is all the paraphernalia: milk jugs, tea cosies, doilies ... the latter a gesture of lower-class aspiration to gentility: now people take a break with a mug, a teabag and milk from the carton.'

Doily was first attested in 1678, taken from the surname of a London draper. There are references in 1711 to the 'doily-napkin' – an ornamental napkin used at dessert, which evolved into a lace or imitation lace mat placed under a plate or cup, and in 1714 to doily as 'woollen stuff for summer wear' (Dryden mentions 'doily petticoats'). The epitome of genteel kitsch, of English prissiness – along with the anti-macassar (since 1852 preventing the Brylcreemed bonce from leaving a patina on the stuffed armchair – Macassar was an earlier brand of hair oil), the doily and its equally unac-ceptable-to-snobs alternatives, exists to stop guests leaving a ring on the (also irredeemably non-U) coffee-table. If you look more closely, there are finer distinctions: is the doily not one rung higher on the ladder of gentility than the ornamental place mat, with its reproduction of hunting scenes, or an Eastmancolor view of the English Riviera at Torquay, itself a slight improvement on the coaster, favoured by excessive drinkers and ketchup-users? The doily is placed strategically among the furniture of the English psyche, with all its linguistic bear-traps. Should the table in question be referred to as 'coffee' or 'occasional'? Next to the – not 'sofa' (vulgar, thought erroneously to be American), 'couch' or 'chaise longue' (exclusive province of Jews and would-be theatricals) – but 'settee' (first recorded in 1716, a faintly ridiculous pseudo-French take on the sturdier 'settle'). The 'pouffe' – whether to buy it, how to say it, where to display it? Certainly not in the 'lounge': the 'living room' if you must, but the 'sitting room' is infinitely preferable.

Like the chintz that IKEA urged us to chuck out, beloved by Hyacinth Buckets everywhere, an all-too-easy target for sneering, the word doily even sounds embarrassing, with its echoes of 'dolly', 'toilet' and 'soil'. John Betjeman's satirical 'How to Get On in Society', first published in a *Time and Tide* magazine competition in the early 1950s, ended with the lines, 'Milk and then just as it comes dear? / I'm afraid the preserve's full of stones; / Beg pardon, I'm soiling the doilies / With afternoon teacakes and scones.' In a more boorish vein, the *Sun* blustered in 2005 that women should never be allowed into a man's shed: 'God forbid we lose our sanctuaries, our hideaways – our sheds – to womenfolk. The notion of the fairer sex breaking down the creosote doors to pollute these havens with scented candles and doilies doesn't bear thinking about.' Yet not all doilies can be so easily belittled; in June 1996, twelve silk doilies decorated with original illustrations by Beatrix Potter fetched a total of £59,800 at auction at Christie's, South Kensington. The set represented the front cover and first eleven illustrations for *The Tale of Benjamin Bunny* from 1904.

See also **cuppa, quaint**

Donkey

Donkey rides on the sand were once a familiar seaside attraction: donkey derbies are still a staple of summer fêtes and holiday camps, though in 2008 Health and Safety officials almost scuppered one early summer event by insisting that the children who had ridden the donkeys for the last thirty-nine years must be replaced by stuffed or inflated toy animals. The Donkey Sanctuary in Sidmouth, Devon, founded in 1969, receives around £20m in annual donations, compared, as critics have pointed out, with approximately £17m for refuges for 'battered wives'. The Charities Aid Foundation's most recent annual report shows that the English currently donate more to animal causes than we do to the disabled, the homeless or the elderly.

The hoary controversy symbolised by the two rescue societies, the long-established RSPCA (the most exalted 'royal' endorsement for the animals) and the more recently founded NSPCC (only 'national' for our children) is still regularly reported in the North American press, accompanied by ritual expressions of disbelief at English **eccentric**ity or obtuseness. The cherishing of the donkey (ungainly and lovably obtuse itself) epitomises the well-known English love of animals, small and large, domesticated and wild. The affection we have for animals is deeply ambiguous – we pet them, rescue them, eat them and hunt them. This especially English mix may partly be explained as an aristocratic tradition – respect for the hunter and chaser, inarticulate love for the faithful (dumb and grateful) companion – and partly as the legacy of Victorian and Edwardian sentimentalising and anthropomorphising. It's often suggested, too, that an inability to communicate openly and bond easily with fellow humans is being compensated by overfamiliarity with and overindulgence of animals, but wouldn't it be more charitable to cite a native pantheism or a quasi-Buddhist respect for all sentient life?

We are in any case no longer alone in our affinities – even in Rome, the feral cats are being rescued, and eye-wateringly large bequests to pets are not solely the province of the English, but do feature regularly in media human interest (if that's the right term) stories, such as that of Tinker the cat, who was left a three-bedroom house in north London and a £100,000 trust fund in 2002. Not all of us are so soft-hearted, however: in 2008, the online gossip column Popbitch reported that boogie pianist and TV music host Jools Holland had been enthusing about his new pastime of hare-coursing.

Donkey, incidentally, is an eighteenth-century word for the ass, and its etymology is mysterious. It may be a combining of 'dun' (the colour) with the second syllable of 'monkey' (itself of obscure origin), and was certainly introduced as a conscious substitute for 'ass', whose proximity to 'arse' had begun to disturb the overfastidious. 'Lions led by donkeys' is a phrase popularly associated with the British foot soldiers fighting in World War I, as contrasted with their obtuse and incompetent senior officers, but Nigel Rees in his compendium of phrases *A Word in Your Shell-like* proves that the metaphor is much older.

Dosh

P oet Laureate Carol Ann Duffy mused on the flavour of
hard cash in a poem of 1998: 'Turnover. Profit. Readies.
Cash. Loot. Dough. Income. Stash. / Dosh. Bread. Finance.
Brass. I give my tongue over / to money; the taste of warm
rust in a chipped mug / of tap-water.' In 2002, Barclays Bank
announced, after carrying out a 'nationwide survey', that in
England money 'is most popularly known as "dosh" – a combination of "dollar" and "cash" [*sic*] – with "dough" favourite
in Scotland and "readies" in Wales. But in London it is
"wonga", in the South "moolah", in the North East "bread",
in Yorkshire and the North West "brass".' The same report
confirmed that in the Midlands 'wad' was the preferred
form, while in East Anglia and the West Country 'lolly' prevailed. Among more than two hundred slang synonyms
collected, 'rhino' (inspired by Londoners' first sight of a
priceless specimen in the seventeenth century) and 'spon-
dulicks' (an anglicising of the Greek word *spondylikos*, a
seashell once used as currency in the South Seas, sometimes
shortened to 'spon') were popular alternatives. Barclays' etymology for dosh is often proposed, but is very probably
mistaken, although nobody is certain where and when the

114

word in this form was first used. Its most likely ancestor is 'dash' – a gift or bribe – a word imported in the sixteenth century from the Fanti language of west Africa. It has also been suggested that it is related to 'doss', in the sense of the price of a bed for the night.

Dosh is a favourite with journalists attempting a matey style: 'We've got shedloads of dosh to fork out for stories about people on the show [*Big Brother*]', promised the *Sun* in 2003. 'If you know ANY of the housemates, then call our Big Brother anorak Gary Thompson and his team.' In 2007, Anne Karpf in the *Guardian* asserted, 'You can learn an awful lot by observing how a couple handles its dosh', going on to reveal that seven million Brits have a 'Cashflo', which witty acronym stands for 'a Current Account Secretly Hidden From Loved Ones'. That cumbersome designation didn't catch on, but dosh continues to flourish, sometimes in phrases such as the middle-class 'oodles of dosh' or the proletarian 'doshed-up'.

In the 1950s, dosh was associated with working-class speech and by the 60s sounded dated, but along with the other terms for money quoted here (together with the venerable 'pelf', 'ackers', 'gelt' and 'bunce' and the more recent 'wedge'), most of them having languished in obscurity for decades, it was revived by the yuppie culture of the late 1980s. A side effect of the Thatcherite liberation of entrepreneurship – or greed – was a relaxing of the absolute proscription against talking about money. Since Victorian times, one's income or wealth, or lack thereof, like politics and sex had been a taboo subject in respectable conversation, in most cases even in the intimacy of the family. From the boom and bust eighties on, 'Cashflos' notwithstanding, money talked, and it seemed that everyone over the age of twenty was – is – talking about it.

'He got bare bollers, man, innit!' The cry goes up and fellow pupils turn jealously on their suddenly wealthy friend. For many young people money, though an occasional necessity, may be tantalisingly unattainable, something exotic; one of the most ambivalent of adult obsessions and nowadays a subject of conversation. Nicknames for money fashionable among younger teenagers in Britain since 2000 include 'bollers', probably a playful changing of 'dollars' ('bare' is slang for 'lots of') and 'boyz'. Slightly older students refer to pound coins as 'beer tokens' and cash dispensers as 'drink-links'. A borrowing, according to users, from older siblings in the OTC (Officer Training Corps), is 'shrapnel' for small change, which is also known by teenagers as 'snash'. Terms in use among black British street gangs for denominations are, surprisingly, not very exotic at all: the latest is 'peas' (almost certainly from the abbreviation for new penny rather than the vegetable), 'papes' is paper money in general, a 'brown' is a ten-pound note, a 'blue' is a fiver.

More interesting are the derivations of some words that younger speakers claim for their own generation, but which are really much older. 'Wonga' or 'womba' are well-established Britishisms and used by all age groups, but few are aware that they derive from an old Roma word for 'coal', a hoard of which was a sign of wealth. When interviewed, teenagers often take for granted that such words are recent and have been coined by their contemporaries 'somewhere else in the country'; either that, or they guess at an exotic origin 'in Africa, maybe, or in an old, lost language'. One of the commonest slang terms for money among teenage schoolchildren in the south of England is another example of a misunderstood exoticism. When users are asked to write it down, it appears as 'luka' or 'lookah', which does have an African or south Asian appearance, but is really of course one half of that hoary and often facetious cliché 'filthy lucre', presumably overhead one day in an adult conversation and transmitted across the network of peer groups and playgrounds. ('Lucre' in fact was adopted by English in the fourteenth century from the Latin *lucrum*, meaning 'gain'.)

In the US, younger speakers might refer to plenty of cash as 'bokoo' (French *beaucoup*) or 'duckets', many guessing that the second word may be something to do with ducks. It is actually another venerable term, 'ducats' being the gold or silver currency used in Renaissance Italy and the Low Countries and mentioned in Shakespeare. Other more predictable synonyms borrowed by English youth from North America are 'billies' (for banknotes or bills), 'fundage', and from Canada, 'rocks' (if you are well off, you are 'rocked up'). But it's dosh that is the most universally understood and the most widely used of all the colloquial alternatives. Just as with luka, quite a few youngsters think that their generation must have invented it: in rhyming slang, by the way, it's 'rogan josh', after the popular curry dish.

Eccentric

In October 2001, under the headline 'Cream of crackers', the *Sun* reported that 'A madcap inventor has been named Britain's biggest eccentric – pipping a man who thinks he is a baked bean and a woman who talks to garden gnomes. Lyndon Yorke, 50, who pedals a tricycle-powered catamaran on the Thames, beat some potty opposition to scoop the title.' Other nationalities might think it slightly eccentric to hold a poll of eccentrics, might even count the word eccentric itself as having negative rather than positive overtones (French *excentrique* has sometimes been labelled 'pejorative' in dictionaries).

The American philosopher George Santayana once described England as a 'paradise of individuality, eccentricity, heresy, anomalies, hobbies and humours'. Commonly considered, by the English themselves, too, as a defining characteristic, 'eccentricity' entered the language around 1550 as a geometrical term – it comes, via Latin, from Greek *ek-kentros*, 'out of the centre'. A century later it had acquired the sense of deviant or whimsical behaviour. Eccentric as an adjective describing capriciousness and oddity dates from 1630; as a noun, denoting a nonconformist or crank, it was first recorded as late as 1831. The records show that when applied to males, these words often had a positive 'spin'. In the Regency period, for instance, 'eccentric man of fashion' was a common commendation, and for Victorians the word evoked a 'character' whose quirkiness was to be relished: '. . . his eccentric habits, his charm of look and character, his conversation, his shrill discordant voice' (Matthew Arnold, admiring Shelley); '. . . adventurers who ultimately turn out to be heroes, eccentric characters of all kinds' (Disraeli, in *Lothair*). Women deviating from supposed norms were not seen in the same light: 'I dare say you think me eccentric, or super-sensitive, or something absurd,' a Thomas Hardy heroine apologises. *Plus ça change* . . . Artist Tracey Emin remarked in 2003 that 'If you're vivacious and a bit wild, they call you mad. That's the thing about being a woman and successful. If you were a bloke you'd just be eccentric.'

In April 1999, the UK press carried comments from a German psychologist who had carried out an international survey of oddball behaviour. He concluded that living out one's fantasies keeps the psyche in trim and healthier, with the result that the eccentric English were, he asserted, leading happier lives than their continental counterparts, particularly the Germans, whose deviant tendencies were stifled in infancy. The flamboyant Dr Roy Strong concurred and listed some of his eccentric acquaintances: Lady Diana Cooper, who habitually drove so dangerously as to endanger the lives of hoi polloi; aged dandy and *soi-disant* fashion designer Bunny Roger; recluse Philip Yorke (apparently 'a male Miss Havisham'); the erotic-mural-painting, 'wifelet'-amassing Marquess of Bath, among others. He did also include Lady Lucinda Lambton, whom I can vouch is authentically and charmingly potty, and not at all dysfunctional and tedious.

The freedom to be eccentric can be ascribed straightforwardly to the freedom from outside interference, at a national and an individual level, afforded by living an insular life, although it has also been claimed that what in 1690 Sir William Temple called 'the unequalness of our climate' produces oddities of behaviour – that the Englishman [*sic*] is 'governed by the weather in his soul'. 'We come to have more originals . . . we have more humour' (Temple again) 'because every man follows his own, and takes a pleasure, perhaps a pride, in shewing it.' Robert Burton's *Anatomy of Melancholy*, published in 1621, had amassed authentic examples of strange behaviour, and Aubrey's *Brief Lives* of 1696 memorialised English 'personalities' and their peculiarities. In the following century, and especially at the time of the French Revolution, it became accepted that English rejection of absolutism and tyranny went hand in hand with the right to flout convention and to tolerate those who did so. Eccentricity is a wilder and wackier word than mere 'idiosyncrasy', or the 'individualism' that Americans cherish as a cultural keyword. In England the eccentric has been nurtured in literature and drama and celebrated by the press, not least by professional obituarists. During the twentieth century it came to be associated especially with the privileged castes, helped by Edith Sitwell's *The English Eccentrics* (1933) and successive titles celebrating the odd behaviour of the aristocracy and gentry – those of course with the time and money to indulge themselves and the blithe insouciance necessary to carry it off, what Sitwell called 'that peculiar and satisfactory knowledge of infallibility that is the hallmark and the birthright of the British nation'.

Professor Sir Ernest Barker in *The Character of England* (1947) pointed out the paradox 'that the country of "good form" and plodding habit should also be counted a country of rebellion against conventions and canons'. Nobel prize-winning novelist Octavio Paz made the interesting distinction in a 1990 speech that 'Spain is no less eccentric than England but its eccentricity is of a different kind. The eccentricity of the English is insular and is characterized by isolation: an eccentricity that excludes. Hispanic eccentricity is peninsular and consists of the coexistence of different civilisations and different pasts: an inclusive eccentricity.' Anthropologist Kate Fox, in her 2004 survey *Watching the English*, questions the common view, stressing rather '. . . our sheer ordinariness. With some notable exceptions, even our alleged eccentricities are mostly "collective" and conformist. We do everything in moderation, except moderation which we take to ludicrous extremes.'

To a jaundiced twenty-first-century fogey there's something conservative and selfish rather than revolutionary or inspiring about indulging in spectacular personal obsessions. In any case, English eccentricity can be, and perhaps has been, done to death, institutionalised and devalued by self-promoting 'characters' (horse-racing commentator John McCririck comes to mind, along with anyone who indulges in public cross-dressing, wears a bowler hat or stands for parliament under the banner of the Monster Raving Loony Party), and self-conscious, hence irritating, exhibitionist pastimes such as cheese-rolling, **gurning**, bog-snorkelling, **wellie**-wanging and the like. Rather all of these, though, than those pursed-lipped, baffled foreigners – all of them – with their homogenised, conformist, strait-laced ways.

See also **quaint, queer, whimsy**

Empire

In imperial days, we called Britain
The island where greatness was written.
As many have grumbled,
The Empire has crumbled—
It's here in the damp we're left sittin'.

(Anon)

Between 1785 and 1985, *The Times* printed the phrase 'the British Empire' 39,024 times, not including its use in advertisements, which was common from 1900 to the Second World War. Some modern historians refer retrospectively to a 'First British Empire', based on the colonisation of North America and India from 1583 to 1783, a 'Second', minus North America, but with Africa and Australasia as new focuses, from 1783 to 1815, and a subsequent 'Imperial Century' from 1815 to 1914, during which Great Britain was the pre-eminent global power, though with English, not Welsh, Scottish or Irish, values and attitudes prevailing. In common parlance, it was only from the early 1800s that we began to talk about the 'British Empire', by analogy with the 'Persian Empire' and the 'Roman Empire' of antiquity. (For a time, in the mid-nineteenth century, 'English Empire' was used in the press). By the later Victorian era this could be familiarised as simply 'the Empire'. 'Empire', without 'the', suggesting at the same time the abstract notion, the accompanying assumptions and values and the geohistorical reality, is a *de*-familiarisation, a usage that when first employed recalled the Latin *imperium* (Latin nouns of course are not normally accompanied by definite articles), which itself had been borrowed into English to mean absolute power and domain. 'Empire' on its own became established in academic and journalistic accounts from the late 1970s, about the time that post-colonial nostalgia was reflected in a publishing fad for titles like *Plain Tales from the Raj*. Phrases like 'the burden of empire', 'the end of empire' elevated the word to an iconic status that the familiarity of 'the Empire' denied it, even when it was capitalised.

Scanning the records shows that during the twentieth century, ordinary people, in letters, diaries and those conversations that were recorded, rarely referred to the Empire at all; outside of official, therefore patriotic, discourse and the jingoism of the print media, it seems to have been taken for granted or regarded as something remote, visible only in the names of entertainment venues. In 1883, the Cambridge historian Sir John Robert Seeley had famously observed, 'There is something very characteristic in the indifference which we show towards this mighty phenomenon of the diffusion of our race and the expansion of our state. We seem, as it were, to have conquered and peopled half the world in a fit of absence of mind.' Despite the enormous contribution made by citizens of what was to become the Commonwealth, after 1914 for many the homeland had narrowed down to **Blighty**. By 1958, the year in which Empire Day was renamed Commonwealth Day, a certain ruefulness had set in. John Betjeman could write in 'In Westminster Abbey',

> Keep our Empire undismembered
> Guide our forces by Thy Hand
> Gallant Blacks from far Jamaica
> Honduras and Togoland;
> Protect them Lord in all their fights,
> And, even more, protect the whites.

Since that burst of nostalgia thirty years ago, memories of the Empire have receded, among the 'native' English, whose attention is focused on France, the Costas, Florida or New Zealand, and among those who migrated, who, as Ziauddin Sardar has noted, have stopped calling their restaurants 'The Light of India' or 'The Nawab of Bengal', names evocative of the colonial era, and substituted 'Korahi' and 'Balti' which refer to their own regional origins. Just recently, though, there are hints that the 'white Anglo-Saxon' sense of dominion over foreign parts may be reviving, in terms not of an empire in any traditional sense, but of an informal yet hugely influential network of interests, a so-called **Anglosphere**.

Estuary

The late Malcolm Bradbury, novelist and critic, writing in September 1994, asked rhetorically, 'Is there today a standard English? Estuary English, sometimes called Milton Keynes English, seems to be bidding for the position.' He was referring of course only to the English of England, not the multiple dialects and accents of the wider **Anglosphere**. He went on to characterise this apparent novelty: 'It seems to have been learnt in the back of London taxis, or from alternative comedians . . . it's southern, urban, glottal, easygoing, offhand, vernacular . . . apparently classless, or at any rate a language for talking easily across classes.' Interviewed in 2001, Shirley Jones, a twenty-two-year-old student from Stockport, affirmed, 'Estuary English is nice to the ear . . . it's 50/50 cockney and young southern professional . . . I prefer it to the northern accent but I resent it because of the stigma of not speaking it.'

For virtually the whole of the twentieth century, and some would say still today, the English (and not the Scottish, Welsh and Irish) have been defined above all other markers (dress doesn't count, the school they attended may remain a secret) by their accents. And not by simple regional variance as in other European cultures, but by nuances associated with social class. It was Alan Ross of Birmingham University who in 1954 coined the terms 'U' and 'non-U' (later popularised by the writer Nancy Mitford) to differentiate the behaviour of the upper classes and the masses. Ross believed, though, that by the mid-fifties the upper class was truly distinguished 'solely by its language': its vocabulary and its intonation. It occurred to me that by this measure, looking at the rough statistics for public school and Oxbridge attendance in the 1950s and 1960s, at least 94 per cent of the population were speaking with the 'wrong' accents. Alone at the top of the linguistic hierarchy was what linguists rather unhelpfully termed 'RP', for 'received pronunciation', the non-regional high-status accent acquired from family or from one's place of education and actively promoted by the BBC in particular. Some way below in terms of perceived respectability were the more neutral forms of south-eastern English and Morningside Scots (the lilting educated Edinburgh accent). Clustered at the bottom of the imaginary pyramid were all the regional accents of the UK, with surveys showing that some – Norfolk, Birmingham, Glasgow, Tyneside, for example – were perceived more negatively than others by the general population.

The royal family were not in fact typical exponents of RP, speaking neither 'advanced RP', which itself had at least two sub-varieties, 'Oxford' and 'lah-di-dah' (i.e. theatrical, camp), nor county-set 'cut glass', but a sort of strangulated, clipped, possibly naval or military variety, with oddities such as the famous 'hice' for 'house'. One very noticeable sign of the transition from older prestige speech patterns towards a newer, more generalised and classless accent was the difference between the way Prince Charles and his younger consort, the late Princess Diana, spoke, and recent letters to newspapers complaining of her sons' poor diction confirm that the process continues.

According to Dr Penelope Gardner-Chloros of Birkbeck College, 'a more meritocratic ideology has emerged since the 1960s, which has led to lower-middle-class accents becoming commonplace in contexts previously reserved for the privileged classes – notably broadcasting. These lower-middle-class accents coincide, to a large degree, with the homogenised regional accents of Estuary English, and reinforce its appeal.' The idea of a replacement 'standard' accent actually emerged in 1984 and was promoted by David Rosewarne of the University of Surrey (who chose the term since the accent he had identified straddled the Thames), later by Paul Kerswill and by the Linguistics and Phonetics department at UCL under Professor John Wells, whose website can still be consulted on the subject.

Estuary is only the most recent attempt to describe an accent, or rather a spectrum of similar accents, that have been heard across the Greater London area and in Essex, Kent, Middlesex, Surrey and Sussex for a century or so. It has been linked to the exodus of true cockneys from the East End since World War II, but my own grandmother, a teacher who lived in Woolwich in south-east London, could distinguish precisely the regional nuances in a pre-war London-wide 'lower-class' accent. Something like what is now called Estuary was characterised by my father back in the early 1970s variously as the 'home counties whine', the 'southern drawl' and the 'polytechnic accent'; sometimes simply as 'adenoidal English', as exemplified by David Frost when presenting TV satire programmes in the early 1960s. Before that 'breakthrough', broadcasting had permitted only RP (or the RADA English of trained actors) or the so-called mid-Atlantic accent of game-show hosts. Certainly the broadcast media reversed its prejudices during the 1980s and 90s, actively welcoming regional and 'ethnic' accents as well as the deliberately classless 'DJ-speak' which had been evolving on commercial radio since its beginnings. While as late as the mid-1980s actors in TV dramas tended to have 'actor-y' diction, it is now very hard to find examples of RP on the airwaves (I was told myself by one radio producer that my unassuming teacher's accent was 'too posh' to allow me to present a series on popular culture).

Strictly speaking, estuary should not be confused with 'mockney' (mock-cockney), although it often is. The latter is an exaggerated or feigned working-class London accent, typically employing glottal stops and 'f' in place of 'th', as used by violinist Nigel Kennedy, celebrity chef Jamie Oliver and, in earlier times and with a camp inflection, by sixties icons Mick Jagger and David Bailey. 'Mummerset', the attempt, often by naturally posh-talking actors, at a non-specific West Country burr (made famous by the radio soap *The Archers* and parodied on the comedy radio shows *Beyond our Ken* and *Round the Horne* by the characters Arthur Fallowfield and Rambling Sid Rumpo), is very rarely encountered these days. It may also be significant that regional accents like Brum, Geordie and Scouse have not been re-labelled in recent years. This is not to say that they have not evolved or been modified by contact with other styles of speaking. Linguists have demonstrated what they call 'levelling' of dialects and accents, whereby regional forms lose their most pronounced features and incorporate elements from other sources. One phenomenon I have noticed, but which has not been commented upon in any depth, is a tendency by younger speakers in most parts of the country towards an imitation of childish or 'lazy' pronunciations of individual sounds – again, 'f' or 'v' for 'th', 'w' for 'r' and glottal stops wherever possible – and towards more rhythmic, drawled intonations probably unconsciously influenced by Australian and American speech patterns. This is related to something that may in time be as significant if not more so than Estuary: the rise of a so-called multi-ethnic youth dialect, a form of spoken English radiating from London and to a lesser extent Birmingham and Bristol that is heavily influenced by Afro-Caribbean (including hip-hop and rap) and South Asian rhythms and black and Asian street slang vocabulary. Some linguists suggest that, given the lack of any centralising linguistic authority and the dropping away of social constraints on how we speak, in twenty years or so we may all be speaking a version of the cool, ethnically indeterminate street-cred English satirised by the comic character of the late 1990s, Ali G.

See also **innit, yoof**

Fab

On the *Observer*'s summer 'cool list' for 2008 (a parade of new talent in fashion, art and design: each relentlessly creative, and, painfully for me, all very young indeed), number 11 was a youthful novelist. According to the write-up, 'Poppy Adams, 34, started off as a scientific-documentary maker. Her debut novel, *The Behaviour of Moths*, with its unreliable 70-year-old narrator, is disturbingly fab.' 'No need to phone me, but a text would be fab,' a female executive threw at me over her shoulder just the other day, as she hurried off in mid-conversation. So the other, the three-letter, f-word is still with us.

Jaunty, perky and resilient, though frivolous, fab is noteworthy for other reasons: it was one of a handful of iconic terms from the 1960s to stay the course, it has been successfully recycled several times (perhaps more accurate to say it has partly submerged and resurfaced several times), and, to a linguist the most interesting, it forms part of the 'Polari' or 'Parlyaree' lexicon, the secret code, mixing in elements from Italian, Spanish and Romany, developed by itinerant show-folk, street traders and the gay underground from the nineteenth century. (Polari, from Italian *parlare*, to speak or talk, combined native English syntax with exotic vocabulary items like 'nanty', no(ne); 'omi', man; 'bona', good; and 'eek', face: at the end of the twentieth century, there were still a handful of fluent users of its varieties, and London club-goers have recently revived some terms.) The fad, prevalent in more learned circles, for 'clipping' – linguists' term for abbreviating – took hold in the seventeenth century, and surviving 'mob', 'bus' and the archaic 'cit' (from citizen) are examples, but fabulous seemingly wasn't abbreviated until the early twentieth century, in the English theatrical milieu. It was also recorded in showbiz and fashion circles in the USA in the fifties.

The Beatles were billed as 'the Fabulous Beatles' on local posters and handbills from their return from Hamburg to Liverpool, and it may be for this reason that they were described by fans as and celebrated by the media as the Fab Four. On Merseyside, 'Fab!' became a faddish interjection, indicating enthusiastic – wide-eyed – approval or admiration, and along with the short-lived local synonym 'gear' (originally 'the gear' as in 'the business' or 'the perfect outfit') became forever associated with the Mersey boom and English pop culture of the sixties. Gerry Anderson's ungainly *Thunderbirds* puppet Lady Penelope rode in a pink drop-top limo with the numberplate FAB1, and more prosaically perhaps, but memorably for some, the word was adopted by the pioneering commercial radio station Radio Luxembourg, renamed first as Fabulous 208, then Fab 208, and later parodied by Harry Enfield and Paul Whitehouse's DJ's 'Smashie' and 'Nicey' as Radio FAB-FM.

In 1977, someone wrote in to Janet Street Porter, presenter of ITV's *London Weekend Show*, 'I thought your one [item] on the National Front yesterday was absolutely fab, with lots of things to think about afterwards.' In June 1985, however, a mini-guide to etiquette appeared in *The Times*, warning, 'Whatever you do, avoid tired slang. Nothing is more ill-mannered than to describe your hostess's blanquette de veau as "super" or "fab" or "brill" . . . and no matter how much you are a child of the 60s do avoid such phrases from that period as "good vibrations" and "far out".' Those last two have yet to make a comeback, and there is no guarantee that they won't, but they are in any case quasi-spiritual Americanisms from the psychedelic era, not home-grown English English keywords (the first three are respectively from the fifties, the seminal, 'swinging' early sixties and the late 1970s). In 1991, style journalists belatedly announced the return of fab, along with the late sixties US import, 'groovy', picking up from their ironic use by teenagers mocking their parents. 'Groovy' submerged again quickly, but fab has held on through the noughties, first with a showbizzy, camp-meets-fashionista taint, but now, like 'cool', adopted by the unglamorous mainstream, too.

The full form of the word has epitomised the gushing hyperbole characteristic of the fashion industry and its media, its use revitalised by the TV comedy series *Absolutely Fabulous*, abbreviated by enthusiasts to *AbFab*. *Fabuloso* is Spanish or Portuguese, but is also used across the junior **Anglosphere** in hip-hop slang, texting and teenage 'bloglish', often misspelt as 'fabulouso', even sometimes 'fabboloso' (the correct Italian is *favoloso*). Sometime around the end of the 1950s, possibly from US gay speech, 'fantabulous' appeared, a blend or portmanteau word combining fantastic and fabulous in one. By 2000, this in turn had been elaborated to 'fantubulotastic' (re-adding syllables from fantastic) and 'fantabulistic' (borrowing part of ballistic), as well as joke nonce (probably one-off) coinages 'fantabulicious' and 'fantabulisticesque'.

All of these derive ultimately from Latin *fabulosus*, 'celebrated in fable' (*fabula*, from *fari*, to speak, meant narrative or story). English imported fabulous in the sixteenth century, first with the meaning of 'fond of, or prone to composing fables', then of 'mythical or fictional'. By the 1600s it could mean 'incredible' or 'astonishing'. When lexicographers worry at the differences between words, they sometimes see more than is really there; pedantry and nit-picking are after all part of the job. Nevertheless, I'm exercised by whether fab and fabulous mean the same, or are there subtle differences in denotation or connotations? Fabulous still has overtones of low-level wonder, a mild form of what marketing types call the 'boggle factor', implying something beyond expectations, whereas to me, fab, besides being unarguably shorter and brisker (scanning corpora throws up multiple instances of 'simply fab', 'a fab job', 'looking fab'), has hints of 'just right', 'fitting' or 'suitable' over and above the shared core meaning of 'excellent'. In 2004, two sisters sent the official UK Spam fan club (for the pink processed meat product, not the junk emails) the following encomium: 'Spam is fab, Spam is cool, Spam's enough to make you drool: Good on toast, good on bread, Brill on earrings that hang from your head.'

See also **nang**, **wicked**

Fag

Like many other writers, John Betjeman used the snatched cigarette to evoke the proletarian, the forlorn or careworn, in this case a Land Girl in his 1958 poem 'Invasion Exercise on the Poultry Farm': 'Marty rolls a Craven A around her ruby lips / And runs her yellow fingers down her corduroyed hips, / Shuts her mouth and screws her eyes and puffs her fag alight.'

The Times noted in 1916 that 'Two years' experience [of war] has taught us that the average soldier would sooner go without any other luxury than "a fag"', although three years later the same paper recounted how 'at Willesden Police court the identity of a witness, a working boy of 16, turned on the question whether he was smoking a cigarette. Asked by the magistrate if he was doing so, he replied scornfully, "What, me smoking a fag? I was smoking a cigar."' In 2005, the *Sun* revealed that 'smokers spend nearly a month a year on fag breaks at work'. They were apparently taking on average four ten-minute smoking breaks a day, costing employers 158 working hours a year, equivalent to '7,426 hours during the average puffer's working lifetime'. The traditional 'popping out for a quick fag' may now take the form of 'smirting' – the combined smoking and flirting that occurs when employees are forced out of their newly smoke-free workplaces to huddle together in doorways or stairwells. 'Fag', though, is a venerable word, and in its various forms expresses a cluster of English imperatives. The association of the word with unhealthy pursuits, with hints of a distinctly English desperation, is not restricted to smoking: the fag as a public-school junior performing menial – often demeaning – chores for an older boy dates back to the first years of the nineteenth century (although an encyclopedia published in 1911 claimed that the practice, if not the terminology, was established at Eton and Winchester three centuries earlier). In *Tom Brown's Schooldays* (1857), Thomas Hughes's public-school hero reacts to fagging with 'disgust and indignation': 'what right have the fifth-form boys to fag us as they do?', but in the gung-ho *Big Budget Book for Boys*, published in 1934, 'young Nixon had a sort of blind faith, amounting almost to hero-worship, in Badger Burton. If Burton chose to break rules his fag would join in the affair quite loyally.' That same year J. B. Priestley wrote in praise of what he called the 'Little Englander', the modest, self-effacing version as against 'Big Englanders . . . red-faced, staring, loud-voiced fellows, wanting to go and boss everybody about all over the world, and being surprised and pained and saying, "Bad show!" if some blighters refused to fag for them.' In 1946, *The Times* reported an attempt at regulating fagging: 'None but monitors should have fags. Duties should tend towards what is communal rather than lathering a monitor's chin. There should be no fagging in the morning or after "prep". No boy should be a fag when over 15½, or for more than, say, five terms.'

From the eighteenth century fagging could mean toiling and a fag a tedious or wearying task; 'fagged' or 'fagged out', exhausted. The 'fag end', denoting the last and worst part, actually pre-dates by two centuries the cigarette stub, which was first recorded in 1888. The origin of all these related terms is actually obscure; in the late fifteenth century, fag could mean a knot in fabric, a loose end of cloth or rope, or a sheep tick, but no one is sure where the word came from: as a verb it has been linked to 'flag', in the sense of droop or lag, which in turn looks as if it is related to 'flaccid', but the connections are all unproven. The Americanism fag as a pejorative for a male homosexual was also heard in the UK in the late 1960s and early 1970s but is now very rare here: it is short for 'faggot', once an insult directed at old women, thought to refer to faggots as fuel for burning witches, and first attested in its modern homophobic sense in 1914.

For a hundred years a pint and a fag have gone – literally – hand in hand as the staple comfort of the common man, and it is hugely symbolic that at the end of the noughties the one, if indulged in at all, contains lager, not **ale**, and the other has been banned. At the opening of Britain's first school of darts excellence in 2006, the director, John Gibbs, said, 'The days are gone when darts players had a fag in their mouth, a pint of beer in their hand and a big belly.' Fags and booze continue to be hammered in each successive budget, while cartons of fags, generally smuggled, operate as currency in sink-estate no-go areas. Even the word itself is under siege by the slightly more sophisticated 'cigs' and the robustly north-eastern 'tabs'. 'Fag packet' apparently used to be Cockney rhyming slang for jacket, but never really caught on. I would write at more length about the resonances and symbolisms of this little word, but, like the pub landlord giving in and selling up, like the **bovver**ed generation shrugging off responsibility, like the cowboy plumber I begged to come back and finish the job, I simply can't be fagged.

See also **cuppa, toast**

Fair

In August 1957, under the headline 'Resistance Movement Spreads', the London *Times* reported on one of the first attempts by the French to stem the post-war pollution of their language by English borrowings. A committee was set up to purify the native vocabulary, and 'the first act of the organization was to send a list of current anglicisms to prominent writers, lawyers, doctors, teachers, diplomatists, &c', inviting their comments. The list was: 'best-seller', 'black-out', 'brain-trust' [*sic*], 'bungalow', 'business-man', 'clearing', 'cover-girl', 'dumping', 'fair play' and 'gangster'.' Despite the fulminating and diktats of the Académie Française, the French still haven't developed a satisfactory translation for possibly the most important of these expressions: they still refer, when forced to confront the notion, to *le fairplay*.

'Fair', meaning 'beautiful' or 'favourable' (as in 'a fair wind' or 'set fair', or the now unsayable 'fair sex'), derives from the ancient Germanic *fagraz*. The sense of 'equitable and just' dates from Middle English; it began to denote light-coloured (hair or skin) in the mid-sixteenth century. The sometimes ambiguous use of fair to mean considerable, adequate or middling arose only in the mid-nineteenth century. Fair as festivity is from an entirely different source: it comes via Old French *feire* (modern *foire*) from the late Latin *feria*, a holiday. The ancestor of 'play' was Old English *plegan*, with exactly the same meaning as today. We don't know exactly when the two words were joined, but in Shakespeare's *King John* (1597), the Bastard, having previously scorned 'fair-play orders' and 'compromise', then appeals to 'the fair play of the world'. 'Fair and square' was first written down by Sir Francis Bacon in 1604.

The CIFP, the International Committee for Fair Play, has since 1964 promoted that principle in sport and education and awards annual prizes to outstanding exponents. It explains its inspiration as follows: 'The cradle of modern sports is England. In the 1700's a kind of human ideal had developed, which the social elite wanted to achieve as an emblem of being a gentleman. The demand of these norms was shown in the English public schools and education. And the ideal of conscious fair play had appeared here.' It was in fact a little later, in the 1800s, that the English began to codify the sports they had invented or adapted from elsewhere. The phrase 'fair play', together with 'play fair', 'to see fair' – to enforce fairness – and 'a fair field and no favour', appears again and again in the texts – fictional and factual – of the Victorian age, fairness being seen both as chivalrous and gentlemanly and as evidence of robust common sense. At the same time it was a central tenet, if not the basis, of a nascent political consciousness among the lower orders: many of the humbler petitioners in favour of the Tichborne claimant (centre of a long-running court case that polarised class attitudes in the 1860s) signed themselves 'Fair Play'.

'Fair play' and 'play fair' are of course a mainstay of the mindset associated with cricket, and the plaintive old-fashioned 'just not cricket' is synonymous with 'jolly unfair'.

Fair play in sport, if not always universal fairness, was implanted in parts of the **Empire** along with the games themselves, but attempts to interest other cultures in fair play have foundered. Theodor Herzl, the father of Zionism, in sketching out the utopia he planned to establish, provided that 'all boys born in the Jewish state would learn to play cricket'. In a similar spirit, Pierre de Coubertin (1863–1937), founder of the modern Olympic Games, wanted to instil the spirit of fair play in his countrymen by introducing cricket into France.

Fairness is said to be one of the constituent core values, emanating from England, but held in common by all the **Anglosphere**. Australia has its own variations on the theme, in the phrases 'fair goes' and 'fair suck on the pineapple'. Of course the subversive potential of fair play lies in its dual implications: not only obeying the rules – whether written or unwritten – but giving equal treatment to all, hence 'fair dealing' (the combination 'fair deal' is actually four hundred years old) and the global buzzword 'fairtrade'. In the day-to-day we still resort to sports metaphors to enshrine the principles of fairness; ensuring a level playing-field means not moving the goalposts, but sometimes it's hard to get our overseas partners to play ball. Come on: fair's fair.

Flash

B oss of Manchester United football club, Scotsman Sir Alex Ferguson said in 2003: 'Londoners are different, you know. I think it's something in the water down there, so Sheringham can be a bit flash . . . Incey was flash, but once he settled he was all right . . . Beckham's a Londoner, he's a bit flash at times.' In February 1969, another Scot, the singer Lulu, declared, 'I shall never be sophisticated', but described her then fiancé as 'a bit of flash' because he had a house in Belgravia and a Rolls-Royce while she drove around London in a Mini with green-tinted windows. In June 1851, reporting on the Great Exhibition, *The Times* sarcastically advised British furniture-makers in search of inspiration to visit the French display: 'They will no doubt find there conspicuous evidences of bad taste, flashy decoration and such like.' At the Cambridge Union in 1886, it is hard to tell if the same paper's correspondent was impressed or not: 'their speeches are all flashiness and fluency'.

The word flash was first recorded in sixteenth-century English, where it described the rushing of water, later being applied to light. It probably originated as an imitation of the sound of (s)plashing. By 1605 it had acquired the (then

140

respectable, not slang) meaning of showiness or ostentation. 'Flashy' – showy but shallow – was first recorded in this sense in the later seventeenth century. In the early nineteenth century, a flash was a show-off or fop and a 'flash-house' a thieves' den or brothel, while in the slang of market traders, the word is still used to mean a display or stall.

Mildly pejorative, flash and flashy have continued to reflect the English disapproval of anything too gaudy, too conspicuous, anyone too fond of cutting a dash. They were very commonly used throughout the 1950s and early 60s to dismiss Americans and the visible signs of perceived Americanisation, and were also applied to home-grown chancers and spivs, nicknamed 'Flash Harry', the most famous embodiment, or at least bearer of the name, being the character played by George Cole in the St Trinian films. This folk devil was defined in a poem by G. S. Fraser as 'The man for the three card trick, / The thimble-rigger, the con-man, / With a loverly golden prick', but the nickname is currently reserved almost exclusively for Premiership footballers. Since the 1970s, 'flash git' (in an envious, carping voice), or 'flash motor' (in a grudgingly admiring tone) have been typical formulations; by slight extension the word can mean 'too **clever** by half' when the cleverness takes the form of a performance, and 'impudent and provocative' in prison slang. Interestingly, when the adjective flashy is used nowadays, in an age when visibility is at a premium, it seems to have lost the connotations of cheap and superficial, together with its pejorative edge, its undertone of real resentment. A typical formulation would be 'flashy webpage'. which simply means arresting, eye-catching, 'in-yer-face' – all potentially positive attributes. We are also subjected periodically to celebratory wake-up calls of the sort issued by *Tatler* editor Geordie Greig in the *Observer* in 2004: 'Welcome to the flashocracy . . . now conspicuous consumption is cool . . . stealth wealth is so yesterday.' Billionaire Philip Green's fiftieth birthday party, on which he allegedly spent £5m, was described as 'flash, fast, fun, feckless and fantastically frivolous'.

Foggy

On 21 March 2008, UK newspapers bade farewell to Brian Wilde, aka 'Foggy' Dewhurst of the perennial *Last of the Summer Wine* comedy series, who had died aged eighty. The name of his character was presumably inspired by a bawdy ballad, of which many versions have been recorded since the early 1800s: in the song, a young rake seduces a maiden by protecting her from the inclement weather outside (though some have tried to interpret the phrase as a code for disease or some specific deviance): 'So I hauled her into bed and covered up her head, Just to keep her from the foggy foggy dew.'

In the early 1970s, the 'royals' nicknamed the commoner Captain Mark Phillips, then about to marry Princess Anne, 'Foggy' because he was (allegedly) 'thick and wet'. The word of course is based on 'fog', which is of Norse origin; its exact original meaning is unclear, but it came to refer to damp grass, moss and marshland before, in the sixteenth century, being used to describe thick mist. At the same time its figurative use established itself, as in Chapman's lines from 1595: 'To mee (deere Soueraigne) thou art Patronesse, / And I, with that thy graces haue infused, / Will make fat and foggy braines confesse.' The 'fogged' or foggy brain became an established formulation, from Cobb's 'frequent Fudling does their Spirits drain, / And Bacchus stupefy their foggy Brain' of 1712 down to Barry MacSweeney's 'Grog demon biceps leave me moan groggy, foggy-bonced' of 1997. In the nineteenth century 'fogged' and 'foggy' were slang for tipsy.

In June 1953, Noel Coward took London fog to the Nevada desert for the opening night of his four-week sell-out cabaret run at the Desert Inn. Along with favourites like 'Mad Dogs and Englishmen' and 'Don't Put Your Daughter on the Stage Mrs Worthington', an elaborate number entitled 'So This is London' featured silhouettes of Big Ben and the Thames bridges against a backdrop of artificial fog. At that time the fogginess of London was taken for granted; the 'peasoupers' were thought to be a natural phenomenon and functioned as an internationally recognised symbol of Englishness, along with the rolled umbrella and the bowler hat, double-decker buses and red pillarboxes. The last of the great London fogs occurred in early December 1962 and is still remembered by natives: 'The thick smog, tinged yellow and green, made it impossible to see the kerb from the driver's side of the car, and therefore my passenger had to lean out of the nearside door to keep me on track. Street lights could only be seen as a faint glimmer, and progress was made at a very low speed'; and by visitors like the US meteorologist John A. Day: 'Bus service had been discontinued, so I was faced with a mile-long hike to my house. I wrapped my muffler around my mouth and nose, as was the habit of the locals to strain out the dirty air, and set out to cross the Thames Bridge.' The Clean Air Act, forbidding the burning of soft coal, had just been passed, and from 1963 the fogs – actually 'smogs' (originally an Americanism) – simply disappeared, leaving Londoners immeasurably healthier. Conversations about the weather (or in the locals' language the 'chamois leather'/'hell for leather'/'birds of a feather'/'pigeon feather'/'well I never') could no longer rely on the 'captain's log' and some feared that they had lost a major tourist attraction. Strangely, though, foreigners refused to accept that the fog had gone: London Fog is the 'number one brand of outerwear' in the USA, the London recreated on foreign film sets swirls with thick vapours, a German website reassures potential travellers that they needn't fear the fogs, and my Slovene father-in-law warns me every time I return to the UK to drive carefully in the murky conditions. The old newspaper headline, 'Fog in Channel, continent cut off', is often cited as a comic example of English insularity – in every sense – and self-importance. In common with other word-sleuths, I've been unable to track down the original, but it seems that 'Continent isolated' did appear in more than one press report after stormy weather in the mid-1930s.

Other than admitting from time to time that we 'haven't the foggiest' (a shortening of the early twentieth-century 'foggiest notion'), we hardly ever use the word any more, blissfully ignorant that there is an official definition (visibility of less than 1,000 metres for aviation, 200 metres for driving) and four different types (radiation fog, advection fog, hill fog and coastal fog). In playground language, 'foggy' does survive as a defensive cry in tag games, used by someone who does not want to be 'it', but I'm more interested in an acronym said to be in use among young adults: 'FOG' stands for 'fanciable older guy'. A word I shy away from, on the other hand, is 'fogey', which may have started life (it was first recorded in 1780) as a Scots pronunciation of 'foggy' in the old sense of 'moss-covered'.

See also **wet**, **windy**

Frump

It's difficult for a male to write disparagingly of females in general – or females in particular, come to that – but this didn't stop Digby Anderson in his 2004 pamphlet *All Oiks Now*. Of a fifty-something chav encountered at an airport departure lounge he wrote, 'The fat lady in the tight clothes with the tattoo and [nose] ring is off to Spain or Greece for a holiday . . . Not only does she look repulsive and stupidly inappropriate for her age but she makes, in some small way, English women of her age in general look repulsive and silly.' What Anderson recoiled at is a new in-yer-face version of ugliness, widespread in England but transcending Englishness, based on ageless, classless, globalised trends in eating, dressing and adorning one's body, and on an utter lack of self-effacement or deference. The central theme of his polemic, or lament, was the disappearance of the values of 'Middle England', but one wonders – among many other doubts raised by his vitriol – whether the typical English matron he approves of would present a more aesthetically pleasing prospect, and if so, by whose judgement? Anyone, of any gender, who has travelled widely will be aware that ordinary

Englishwomen (not WAGs, supermodels or It girls) are not known for their in-born glamour or dress sense. Many of them might be described, in slightly dated language, as 'frumps'.

Queen Elizabeth herself, arriving in India from Pakistan for a state visit in October 1997, was greeted by the accusation on the *Times of India*'s front page that she was 'frumpish and banal'. In 2005, a heated chat-room debate on the merits or demerits of Hermes scarves digressed into a discussion of the frump factor: 'I think the Queen is frumpy in a delightful English countrywoman way' opined 'Lippy'. 'How Kate Middleton went from frump to fabulous' gushed the *Daily Mail* in 2006, singling out Prince William's English rose girlfriend's 'frumpy jumper', jeans and Ugg boots to contrast with her more recent svelte, groomed look (helped apparently by image consultant Leesa Whisker). In the *Observer* in 2008, Ruth Sunderland lamented that 'While Parisiennes are stylish, their counterparts over here are still dominated by their inner frump ... some Englishwomen adopt the dishevelled look as a badge of pride, as if it demonstrates their minds are on higher things.' A reader agrees, commenting that 'our female professionals in their dull, dowdy outfits although brilliant in their chosen fields visibly crumble when faced with their continental counterparts. They have worked hard to eliminate overt displays of femininity in order to be taken seriously only to be showed up by someone who has the respect of her colleagues and superiors without having to de-sex herself.' There were, however, signs that the frumpish worm was turning: in 2009, scourge of English womanhood and champions of Original Magic Knickers, that unlikely bossy-boots duo Trinny and Susannah, were dropped from the TV schedules, while singing sensation Susan Boyle, universally acknowledged (pre-makeover, at least) as 'hairy' and 'frumpy', won the nation's hearts.

In colloquial seventeenth-century English, frump denoted grumpiness, from an earlier verb of unknown provenance – though it might be an imitation of a snort of derision – which had the sense of nag, jeer or taunt. It was first recorded in the sense of an unstylish woman in 1817. Although the noun and its adjectives ('frumpish' is an alternative) are well known in North America too, there is a lurking suspicion that frumpiness is itself a condition of English femininity, or at least a certain, important sub-variety of it (though in fairness, in 1911 the *Penny Illustrated*'s correspondent wrote, 'I hate to have to write it, for I have always been a devoted admirer of the fair sex, but I must tell the truth about the German ladies, even though the heavens fall. And the truth is that, always allowing for the inevitable exceptions, the ladies of the Fatherland are frumpish – distinctly frumpish').

Perhaps it was a condition of lingering puritanism that many Englishwomen should be prim, staid, dowdy (like those three words, frumpy has a distinctly respectable ring, unlike shabby or scruffy), and an accident of climate and genetics that many have been considered, to use the innocuous-sounding but loaded adjective that my mother favoured, 'plain'. Our language contains a number of variations on the same theme: first there were the 'bluestocking' (a grudgingly admiring nickname first bestowed in the eighteenth century on redoubtable female intellectuals) and the 'battleaxe' (a usage dating from the late nineteenth century) – much later the 'drabbie', a slang term current in the 1980s and applied, often by journalists, to literary, academic or professional women who deliberately eschewed glamour. The modern slang terms (much loved by City traders) 'Nora' and 'Doris' (see **Kevin**) say much the same thing about a lady, but in my experience are only used by unreconstructed males, not by women about themselves. Frump has no male equivalent – 'bluestocking' might equate roughly with 'fogey', or at least a fogey of a highbrow sort – though until fairly recently, most Englishmen were aggressively impervious to fashion, grooming or indeed any notion of allure.

There is a sub-sense not only of appearance but manner –'sour-looking' is how one dictionary hazards it – integral to the word frump, while sound symbolism conjures up the clumsiness, awkwardness, the lack of shapeliness, the ill temper conveyed by the similar-sounding 'stumble', 'fumble', 'lump', 'frown'. (There were once other words employing this phonology, such as the archaic 'froppish', which meant fretful or peevish, 'frowzy', i.e. shabby, and 'frowsty', stale or stifling.) Sometimes, however, when labelling someone as a frump, an affectionate nuance is present, expressing impatience with someone otherwise held dear, rather as in 'mumsy'.

With the same meaning – shabby, unstylish – though probably in ignorance of its pedigree in standard or educated speech, frumpy was a cool term in US youngsters' 'dawg-talk' (mainly white peer-group slang) around 2000, probably from its survival in black US usage, where it was noted in 1947. Currently the online *Urban Dictionary* lists a slew of slang terms based on frump, including 'frump-a-lump', 'frump-monster', 'frump-dumpty'. Deliberately chosen scruffy attire is described as 'frumpfortable'. Interestingly, the older sense of frump, that of 'grumpiness', has either survived or coincidentally been revived in today's slang in the forms 'frumptious' and 'frumpity'. Frumpy can now also denote physically out of shape: an unsightly paunch on a female is known as a 'frumph' or 'frumpass', though in these cases it's possible that the base word is a deliberate mangling or a mishearing of 'front'.

Fusspot

Fussing is both what, if you are English, you really mustn't do, and what many of the English have been very prone to do. 'Fussy' described the manners of the lower middle classes, with their agitations over niceness and niceties, as well as the decor favoured in their households from Victorian times through to the 1970s and sometimes their clothing and accessories. In the old-fashioned discourse of moderation and understatement, 'fuss' could refer to a storm in a domestic teacup, but equally to an international incident. The word was first recorded around 1700 with the senses, nicely defined by the *OED*, of 'bustle or commotion', 'ostentatious or officious activity', or 'a state of (more or less ludicrous) consternation or anxiety'. Its origin is unknown, though it may be an imitation of the noises of agitation – sounds of bustling, or hissing with frustration. To 'make a fuss of' in an affectionate way and to 'fuss over' someone are more recent elaborations.

For my own mother, 'whatever you do, don't make a fuss' and 'I don't want any fuss' (said for the last time about arrangements for her own funeral) were phrases used almost daily. Though delivered in softly reproving tones, fusspot, a term dating from the 1920s, was one of her most damning dismissals: a put-down conveying the impatience of the puritan with the flutterings of the hot and bothered and with precious continental habits of expostulating and emoting; a gently firm reminder of the need to remain unperturbed at all costs.

Looking at instances of its use, fusspot was often applied to elderly males such as the irascible old colonel or the Oxbridge don. In the early 1980s, conservative commentators sometimes referred to 'the fusspot state' when criticising economic intervention by government; when this notion widened to encompass intervention in matters of morals and manners too, '**nanny** state' was preferred. Alan Bennett has celebrated the fusspot in his monologues, and Patricia Routledge, among others, has incarnated her. Babies and children can be fusspots too: in the form of a pointy-faced schoolgirl, the cartoon character Fuss Pot, in the words of Toonhound website 'the most stuck-up, arrogant, irritating little minx ever to grace a comic page', appeared successively in *Knockout*, *Whizzer and Chips* and *Buster* comics between 1971 and 1990. And in a further poignant footnote to pop-cultural history, the *Manchester Evening News* reported in 2006 that 'a cardigan worn by Coronation Street busybody Norris Cole could raise only £21 in an internet sale . . . fusspot Norris was often seen wearing the sleeveless, woolly top as he worked in the Kabin newsagents with Rita Sullivan . . . after 19 bids on eBay, the cardie was sold to an unknown bidder'. The fusspot hasn't disappeared from English society, though it may have mutated from grump and **frump** to a more modern incarnation: the *Sun* has thus described the miserabilist singer Morrissey (bringing his own bedding to a luxury hotel), and Victoria 'Posh Spice' Beckham (agonising over lactose intolerance). 'Fussy-boots' and the venerable Americanism 'fussbudget' are other forms of the phrase, though harsher terminology —'obsessive-compulsive', 'nit-pickingly paranoid' – might be substituted these days. More often fusspot is now employed defensively, especially by journalists wishing to cavil: 'Call me a fusspot if you like, but . . .' Lower-middle-class pernicketyness is out of fashion anyway, and in matters of decorum most of us are probably not fussy or not fussed. In younger milieux, blasé (the pose, not the word) is cool and nobody wants to be a 'fuss-bucket' (the most recent variant, popular among North American moms and teenagers across the **Anglosphere**): better not to be **bovver**ed.

Gentle

The Distressed Gentlefolk Aid Association, a charity founded in 1897 to help 'gentlemen and their families' who had fallen on hard times, recently changed its name to Elizabeth Finn Care, after its founder, simultaneously recording a 150 per cent rise in requests for financial support from architects, doctors, lawyers and other professionals. Along with 'kind', and **decent**, gentle has been one of the key adjectives of Englishness, according to Middle England itself, significantly also used of the English climate, for wind ('a gentle breeze') and rain and topography ('gently rolling hills'). Now defined as 'benign, amiable and tender', with an implication of deliberate, voluntary kindliness, for Chaucer 'gentiless' denoted something more high-flown: good breeding, courtesy, elegance. 'Gentil', in the sense of 'well-born', came to us from French in the thirteenth century, itself deriving from Latin *gentilis*, 'belonging to a clan', from *gens*, 'family'. 'Gentleman' was coined at the same time in imitation of the French *gentilz hom* to refer to a member of the nobility or landowning classes, slightly later to someone who behaved in the chivalrous, honourable, courtly way identified with the elite. The combinations 'gentleman farmer' and 'country gentleman' appeared in the eighteenth century, implying someone who cultivates the land more for pleasure than for profit, while 'gentleman's gentleman' for valet was used by the eighteenth-century playwright Sheridan. 'The gentry' is from Old French *genterise*, the state of being high-born, and came to define the members of the landowning classes who were entitled to a coat of arms but not an aristocratic title. Daniel Defoe wrote in 1736 of the rich tradesman metamorphosing into a gentleman, and from that time the word could be used of anyone leading a moneyed, leisured existence; it also came to be a courtesy term for all males, sometimes in facetious formulations like 'the little gentleman in black velvet' (for a mole), 'gentleman of the fist'(a pugilist) and 'gentleman of the road' for a vagrant.

Trying to define the iconic gentleman is tedious and has been attempted so many times before, though Anglophile literary giant Jorge Luis Borges pointed out an interesting contrast. Sir Thomas Browne described a gentleman as someone unassuming and unobtrusive who tries to avoid being a nuisance, while Borges' fellow Argentinian author José Luis Lanuza said that a gentleman, in the Hispanic view, deliberately imposes his presence, is a nuisance and is constantly on the watch lest somebody slight him. Examples of the phrase 'gentlemanly conduct' are now confined to sport, and like 'gentlemanly behaviour' as employed by women they are almost always used in the context of a complaint. As for the abbreviations of the g-word, 'popping to the gents', which I still find myself mumbling, now sounds a little old-fashioned. Since the advent of Essex boys, nouveau-spivs and hedgies – and indeed bankers in general – the old notion of the upstanding 'City gent' seems doomed, but let's hope people still have occasion to call someone a '(**nice**) old gent' or convey approval and genuine affection by 'he's a proper/real gent'.

Curiously perhaps, English adopted the French *gentil* all over again in the sixteenth century, this time rendering it both as 'genteel' and, by approximating the French pronunciation, 'jentee', meaning elegant or rakish, which turned into our 'jaunty'. 'Genteel' is a semantically complex descriptive, one which is no longer common now that there are no recognisable codes of decorum or taste. Originally meaning 'noble' or 'stylish in a patrician way', it now encompasses the notions of 'well-behaved', 'refined to some extent, yet not cultivated', 'restrained rather than assertive', and for me there are also hints of 'effete' or 'prissily (over-)polite'.

It was not until the seventeenth century that gentle's modern role as an antonym for rough and harsh came to predominate. Except among the elderly ('oh for a kinder, gentler society') or semi-indisposed ('a gentle stroll'), timidity and moderation are out of fashion, and like 'kind', gentle is not heard very often these days, except in advertisements for skin creams and in the ominous-sounding phrases 'a gentle reminder' and 'gentle persuasion'. The remonstrances 'gently', 'gently now' or 'gently does it' are still useful, and possibly 'be gentle with me' is still murmured in intimate surroundings.

Ginger

It was once observed of US President Ronald Reagan that he had gone prematurely orange. For most genuine redheads the process is from bright ginger through a series of indeterminate russets and auburns to a sort of dirty white, as I, a carrot-top myself back in the day, can attest. Reporting on the national Grammar Schools Soccer Tournament of 1965, *The Times* concluded, 'It was, perhaps, fitting that the youngest of the company division, the Sussex centre forward, should steal the limelight. Only 16 years of age and with the fighting spirit that goes with ginger hair, he scored both the goals which gave Sussex a 2–0 lead at the interval.' In 1994, however, according to the *Sunday Times*, Chris Evans, then presenter of Channel 4's *Big Breakfast* show, admitted that before fame struck, his carrot-coloured hair had made him a target of bullies and a failure with women, 'something that thousands of other men with similar shades of orange can easily sympathise with'. In the years between these two reports, popular attitudes towards the redheads among us moved from varying degrees of appreciation to cruel and systematic mockery, seemingly on a national scale. The 'ginger' (the adjective now a pejorative countable noun) is not only the butt of school playground jibes but a joke-figure for university students, bar-room quipsters and professional would-be humorists. In 2000, the energy company npower ran advertisements depicting a family of redheads with the slogan, 'Some things in life you can't choose', and at the time of writing, the gossip website Popbitch is, with the help of its readers, gleefully 'outing' ginger celebrities from the black-and-white era.

Researchers into bullying at the Institute of Psychiatry at King's College London, claim that genetic influences explain 73 per cent of children's risk of becoming a victim and 61 per cent of their risk of growing into a bully: as well as genes for character traits such as aggression or timidity, children inherit physical characteristics such as being prone to obesity or having ginger hair that make them more likely to be bullied. This is bad news for around 10 per cent of Brits and 13 per cent of Scots, who have mutations of the melanocortin 1 receptor gene, resulting typically in milky-white skin, copious freckles and hair colours ranging from 'strawberry-blonde' via bright orange to auburn. Only 2 per cent of the global population falls into this category and the numbers are declining as those who have the gene tend no longer to mate with partners who carry it. People with this type of complexion are exceptional in other ways: they tend to be more sensitive to pain, are more vulnerable to skin cancer and are often unphotogenic. Of course redheads have always been noticed and labelled, but it's doubtful whether any other European language has as many nicknames as does English: 'ginger-hackled' and 'ginger-pated' were first recorded in the later eighteenth century, 'ginger' alone in the nineteenth, while 'ginge' and 'ginger-nut' (from the biscuits of the same name) probably date from the 1950s. 'Coppernob' and 'carroty', 'carrots' or 'carrot-top' were heard in Edwardian times and are probably older; 'sandy' in this sense dates from the nineteenth century. 'Belisha beacon' was presumably coined in the 1960s, when it denoted a road crossing sign topped with a yellow-orange light. By the 1990s, the elaborated forms 'ginger minger' (where 'minger' is slang for a repellent person) and 'ginger whinger' (applied to Chris Evans among others) had been joined by 'Agent Orange' (a defoliant chemical weapon notorious in the 1970s), 'Jaffa Cake' (an orange-centred chocolate cake) and 'Duracell' (a gold-banded battery). As the name of the spice, the word ginger has a long and complex history, borrowed into Old English from Latin *gingiber*, but ultimately deriving from Sanskrit *srngaveram*, 'horn-body', which referred to the shape of the root. To 'ginger up' in the sense of enliven comes from the practice of inserting ginger into the rectum of a horse in order to rouse it, but 'gingerly', meaning very cautiously, seems to comes from the quite unrelated Old French *gensor*, 'pretty' or 'dainty'.

I can testify from experience that forty years ago, ginger-haired children were admired and freckles seen as a sign of a healthy constitution, though redheads were generally assumed to have fiery tempers; 'ginger' might indeed function as a friendly insult in the playground, but there was as far as I know no endemic 'gingerism' or 'hairism', no victimisation of the red-haired 'other'. Superstitious fears of the red-headed surely do not figure in post-industrial societies, so some experts have suggested that today's discrimination is racist, directed at members of the 'Celtic fringe' such as immigrants from Ireland, but there seems to be no supporting evidence, either documentary or anecdotal. It is true, though, that this seems to be a specifically English phenomenon; in other parts of the UK, and more so overseas, the redhead naturally stands out from the crowd but is not picked upon: in the USA, red-headed females at least are seen as glamorous, while in Australia the nickname for a redhead, 'blue' or 'bluey', like the American 'rusty', is invariably affectionate. In countries where dark hair is prevalent, the blonde or redhead is commonly viewed as rare and desirable, and in neighbouring France the colouring still has romantic Celtic or Pre-Raphaelite associations.

Back in England, meanwhile, according to one 2006 survey, an astonishing 81 per cent of the population think it's OK to 'slag off' people with ginger hair, and when in 2005 Reading footballer Dave Kitson spoke out publicly against racist language, the *Daily Star* reported his remarks under the headline 'Kitson's a right ginger whinger'. Throughout the noughties, tabloid letters pages and online forums featured *cris de coeur* from across the country: 'I have been spat at, as well as physically and verbally abused in the street because of the colour of my hair' (Hannah from High Wycombe); 'We are treated almost like aliens' (Bridget from Milton Keynes). The cause has perhaps not been helped by the (coincidental?) unpopularity of such figures as one-time Labour leader Neil Kinnock, Simply Red's Mick Hucknall, the **cad** James Hewitt, Geri Halliwell ('Ginger Spice' as was) and, at times, Liberal Democrat politician Charles Kennedy and Prince Harry, but for some time now the ginger constituency has been fighting back, notably by way of websites such as redandproud.com, 'the home of the redhead', and the dating agency Redhedd.com. In 2009, the *Daily Mail* reported a German study that claimed that redheads were more sexually active: some *Mail* readers concurred, adding that they were noisier about it too.

But what lies behind the rise in ginger-baiting in the first place? Could it be that in a progressive society where tolerance and **diversity** are enforced and enshrined in legislation, all the other targets for racism, sexism, religious hatred or victimisation are now off-limits, that this is the only colour prejudice we can get away with, that 'gingers' are the one visible minority not fully protected by the law, thus fair game for the 'wicked sense of humour' of the mousy majority? The murmurs of protest are, however, growing louder, as when in 2009, columnist India Knight railed against the casual use of racist language by, among others, Prince Harry. Reader Michael O'Donnell of Leicestershire was one of many to recoil at her characterising of the hapless royal as 'some ginger simpleton'.

Grotty

A very English word, evoking a very English distaste, 'grotty' is rarely heard in other Anglophone regions, though US Valley Girls of the 1970s had their modish equivalent, 'grody (to the max)' and the noun 'grot' denotes a dirty, disreputable person in Australian slang. First becoming widespread in the 1960s, grotty, like **fab** and 'gear', was Liverpool slang associated with the Beatles and the Mersey boom. George Harrison, in the 1964 film *A Hard Day's Night*, famously said of supposedly stylish shirts he was asked to endorse, 'I wouldn't be caught dead in them, they're dead grotty.' Grotty was also, however, part of the vocabulary of London debs, hoorays and educated Bohemians at roughly the same time, and in the early 1980s was used by Sloane Rangers too. Although it originated as an alteration of 'grotesque', that is not what it means. Referring to places ('a grotty bedsit'), facilities ('grotty loos'), clothing or footwear ('grotty trainers'), it often has the specific sense of squalid, seedy and dirty, palpably inferior, sometimes a more generalised sense of nasty, unpleasant. Applied to goods or artefacts, it denotes offensively cheap, shoddy (compare **naff**). 'Feeling grotty' suggests irritation, if not mild revulsion, as well as discomfort.

The first instance of the term in *The Times* dates from 1966, while London estate agent Roy Brooks often used the word in his jocular house ads, which ran in the *Sunday Times* through the 1970s: 'Fully modernised family house in the grotty part of Chelsea'; 'So do you still think N1 is grotty? Surprise yourself . . .' Before becoming the playground for publicly riotous underaged drinkers that it is today, the city of Nottingham supposedly declined in the 1980s and experienced a crisis of self-esteem, during which local residents and visitors referred to it as 'grotty Notty'.

Unfortunately for a handful of citizens, Grotty exists as a surname: it seems to have originated in Ireland, and its etymology is obscure, but it's certainly quite unrelated to our adjective. Derived forms of the English word include the noun back-formation 'grot' denoting filth (in Wales at the time of writing, 'grots' is slang for revolting underpants), the compounds 'grot-bag' for an unwashed, slovenly and/or extremely disreputable person, and 'grot-hole' (just possibly associated in some minds with 'grotto', which is actually the origin of 'grotesque') for a very unpleasant, often cramped as well as dirty location.

Why and how, then, is grotty so quintessentially English a pejorative? It may have become so popular so quickly in the 1960s because it signalled the tentative beginnings of a slow rebellion against the sordid shabbiness of much of post-war England, with its substandard hotels, poor plumbing and heating, its contempt for hygiene and for public aesthetics. Since 2000, grottiness has often been deliberate; artist Tracy Emin's Turner Prize exhibit of her seamy bed unsurprisingly earned the epithet from the *Sunday Telegraph* in 2005; the London *Evening Standard*, reviewing a west London bar, declared: 'So hip, it's almost grotty: waxed leather, polished ebony, Britpack art – The Westbourne is more grit than glamour.' As a footnote, Domestos has begun to market a bathroom cleaner aimed specifically at the most unpleasant recesses, under the name 'Grotbuster'.

Grumble

Only a month after war was declared in 1939, British brewers placed an advertisement in the quality broadsheets exhorting the public to drink beer and frequent pubs as a patriotic duty, adding that 'the precious things we are fighting for [are] Good-feeling. Relaxation. Laughter. Leg-pulling. Yes, and the free Briton's right to grumble.' Fifteen years earlier, the then prime minister, Stanley Baldwin, in a speech to the Society of St George on St George's Day, held forth on the nature of Englishness: '. . . we grumble, and we have always grumbled, but we never worry. Now there is a very great truth in that, because there are foreign nations who worry but do not grumble.' It is surely true that we have never been prone to *angst* – the word itself is foreign; quiet desperation is more our style. But we have never committed to suffering in absolute silence. Sir Ernest Barker, in *The Character of England* (1947), noted that for the English, grumbling and humorous chaffing very often went hand in hand: 'Often the joke is mixed with a grumble . . . alike in the North and South this mixture of grumbling and joking is characteristic . . .' In more militant mode, in December 1971, the first issue of the north-east's alternative magazine, *Muther*

Grumble, started its editorial, 'A lot of people have started grumbling lately – at work, at home, at play. Honest anger lost forever ... or perhaps not quite.' In 2007, Neil MacGregor, director of the British Museum, singled out one part of the museum's collection, the eighteenth-century caricatures, as representative of the national spirit: 'Ephemeral, brilliant and cruel, they sum us up as we saw ourselves at the very moment the museum was founded: the pushy and sententious Scots; the high-minded, garrulous and quarrelsome Welsh; the Irish feckless, but so charming they carry all before them; the English grumbling, perversely content in their gin-sodden xenophobia.'

'How's your wife's lumbago? Ooh, mustn't grumble!' is a slice of cod-cockney dialogue from the mod-turned-psychedelic group the Small Faces' hit 'Lazy Sunday', and Mustn't Grumble was poignantly chosen as the title of the memorial concert for singer Steve Marriott after his death in a house fire in 2001. Professional cockney musicians Chas and Dave chose the same expression as the title of a 1981 album, to go alongside *Don't Give a Monkey's* and *One Fing 'n' Anuvver*. 'Mustn't grumble' is a stock response to an enquiry about one's condition, but is it neutrally noncommital, an avoidance, or sometimes, like it's near-relative 'can't complain', an out-and-out hypocrisy – a dysphemism for 'I'm doing very well indeed' or a euphemism for 'things have never been worse'? It *is* nearly always a hypocrisy in any case, in that grumble is just what the English enjoy doing. They are not alone in this, but as anthropologist Kate Fox observes in *Watching the English*, grumbling is more than a coincidental national tendency, it is a powerful bonding ritual and a way of harmlessly venting frustrations in a climate and a culture in which doing so will probably not make the slightest difference to the status quo.

Xenophobe's Guide to the English is a Russian website offering advice on our national foibles. It warns its readers that the response 'mustn't grumble!' is English hypocrisy writ large, for grumbling is a national pastime, and finding fault, sometimes venomously, encompasses one's own health, bureaucracy, the government, the price of food, the young and the old. 'Nodding sagely and united in discontent, they lay into anything and everything, and finally, refreshed by a good grumbling session, they unite in the moaners' amen – "Typical!"' Unlike some other conversational staples of the last few decades, the refusal to grumble survives, even if it is often used knowingly and ironically, inside virtual quotation marks, as by Mark and Lard in their afternoon show on BBC Radio 1. It's interesting to compare two recent books that took the same phrase as their title. Prolific expatriate Joe Bennett followed in the footsteps, or tyre tracks, of H. V. Morton (author of the 1927 travel classic *In Search of England*) to rediscover the nation he had abandoned for New Zealand. Online reader reviews, though, took him to task, grumbling that the author grumbled far too much (he was accused of 'churlish moaning'), and pointing out the irrelevance of trying and failing to hitch-hike in modern England and the folksy absurdity of a strictly pub-to-pub itinerary. Terry Wogan, hugely genial Irish expatriate and English 'national treasure' (a phrase repeated in many listeners' endorsements), entitled the second volume of his autobiography *Mustn't Grumble*, and this time the reader reviews were almost all flattering to the point of sycophancy ('Terry exhumes [*sic*] the same humour he always has'), one asserting in passing that his hero was 'entitled to whinge'.

The word grumble is related to imitations of mumbled menace or complaint in other northern European languages: *grummeln* in German, *grommelen* in Dutch, *grommeler* in

French. These were themselves descendants of even more ancient words that echoed the sound of thunder. In the form we recognise, grumble was first recorded in English as a verb in 1586; the noun, meaning a 'subdued utterance of complaint' (*OED*), in 1623. Contemporary 'grumble and grunt', incidentally, is well-established rhyming slang for the rudest word in the English language; hence 'grumble mags' are pornographic magazines.

However downbeat grumble sounds, it's surely preferable to its rivals for inclusion here: it sounds a fraction jollier than its synonym 'grouse' (apparently no relation to the game bird), much less craven than 'whinge', the nasty-sounding (it blends 'whine' and 'cringe') habit ascribed by Australians to themselves since the 1930s and to the English since the 1970s, or the northern English dialect 'mither', the venerable noun 'misery-guts' or the childish 'moaning minnie'.

GSOH

'House-proud – and with good reason – career woman (admin, sausages and cheese) seeks aspiring career man GSOH N/S, nice physique i.e. broad shoulders, for friendship, support, understanding . . .' Not really a lonely-heart ad, but a parody from the BBC Radio 4 website for fans of the long-running rural soap *The Archers* . . . keen listeners (but not me) will recognise which of the characters is reaching out via the *Borchester Echo* personal column.

For the English today, being amusing or being amused isn't just an occasional indulgence or a quality to be appreciated, it's a default state. A good sense of humour, or GSOH in the poignant, somewhat dated jargon of magazine lonely-heart ads, now shorthand used primarily in online chat, IM, email, blogs or newsgroup postings, is an absolute requirement, of everyone, at all times (no, not quite true: undertakers and the Home Secretary are probably exempt). This was not always an uncomplicated reality: in 1915, P. G. Wodehouse told the *New York Times* that the Great War then raging would restore England's lost sense of humour by destroying class prejudice, while in 1922, Canadian author Stephen Leacock entitled a chapter of his transatlantic travelogue 'Have the English any Sense of Humour?'. He concluded that they did, but at the time, such was their staid and serious reputation that other English-speaking peoples doubted it.

Within their borders, members of many different cultures commend themselves on their humour, but few are internationally defined by it. For a 'western' audience, possibly only Jewish humour is a staple of Jewish and Yiddish identity with the same significance as it holds for the English. Many nations, though, seem to suffer, by our standards at least, from NSOH (more fashionably known nowadays as a 'sense of humour deficit' or 'bypass'). In 1971, *Time* magazine reported that Britain, in negotiations to join the European Common Market, had offered 'to pay only 3% of the EEC's annual $4 billion budget the first year of membership and 15% after five years. The figures are so low that [French President Georges] Pompidou dismissed them as an example of the British sense of humour.' When Britain did enter in 1973, another French statesman commented ruefully, 'Now we shall all have to learn to have a sense of humour.'

Humour came into English, via French, from Latin, *humor*, which meant fluid or moisture. It later denoted the bodily fluids that in combination supposedly dictated a person's character, and by the sixteenth century could already mean a capricious, wayward and/or facetious spirit. (For many years it was pronounced 'you-mah', the aspirate 'h' being restored in popular but not posh or affected speech in the twentieth century.) Humorous came to mean droll around the end of the seventeenth century; humourless, not surprisingly, was first recorded in early Victorian times. A 'sense of humour', or the capacity to appreciate or generate drollery, was first referred to at the beginning of the seventeenth century but became established as a stock phrase only as late as the 1880s – just when the Americans and the Irish were questioning our capacity to see the joke.

Of course being funny all the time, rather like deliberately cultivating **eccentric**ity or adopting a permanent pose of rebellion, is tiresome in the extreme, and institutionalised humour – as in UK TV commercials, for instance – eventually palls. In native English conversation it's more specifically facetiousness that dominates, and misplaced levity – the national taste for flippancy – that most often shocks all those painfully literal-minded and excessively earnest visitors from the rest of the world.

See also **irony, whimsy**

Gurning

Reviewing *Perils of Paragon*, a BBC2 broadcast in January 1974, *The Times* wrote, 'It was nice to be reminded that comedy acting can be something more than pulling funny faces, gurning through the horse-collar of a 21-inch screen.' The allusion was to a rural practice said to date from the thirteenth century, the pulling of faces at country fairs and carnivals, with competitors' heads framed by a horse-collar, or 'braffin'' in dialect. In September 2000, the *Evening Standard* announced that the World Gurning Championship was due to rear its ugly head again – that year's face-pulling competition would be held at its traditional site at the Crab Fair in Egremont, Cumbria. 'Contestants are doubtless keeping their ears crossed,' the paper ventured, 'that Ozzy Osbourne doesn't return to his old drinking haunt in the village, the Blue Bell, else there will be stiff competition.' There is now a junior category for talented young face-pullers, while some older entrants take the event very seriously indeed. In 2002, forty-six-year-old Alan Hornell had twelve teeth removed in a bid to make his face more flexible for that year's contest. Despite such dedication, this remains essentially an amateur, not a professional performing art, although comedians George Formby and Les Dawson, the former perhaps involuntarily, gurned for a mass audience. Nowadays practitioners can gurn at home and share it with a global audience via a webcam online. Alternatively, at www.rubberfaces.com you can tamper with and distort the features of famous people.

Gurning keys into a demotic love of self-ridicule and celebration of the grotesque that is quintessentially English (though Australians also amuse themselves by making 'duck faces'). My wife, a Slav body fascist, remarked uncharitably on a recent outing to the seaside that most of the English people she saw appeared to be gurning. She feels that this ritualising of the hideous is a veiled acknowledging of a national genetic failing. Our collective enjoyment of exhibitionism, self-abasement and cringeworthy amateurishness is now facilitated by a genre of TV spectacles such as *Britain's Got Talent*, described by one viewer as consisting largely of 'singing, dancing, simpering and gurning'.

The term itself originates, unsurprisingly, in rustic usage: in fourteenth-century Scottish and northern English dialects this variant form of 'grin' could mean 'snarl', 'complain peevishly' or 'grimace'. Grin comes from Old English *grennian*, which meant 'to bare the teeth in anger or pain', from an ancestral Indo-European root meaning 'open-mouthed': the modern sense of 'smile' dates from the fifteenth century. The word has taken on a secondary sense: it now often means, in the slang of clubbers and students for example, '(helplessly) drunk or under the influence of drugs, or recovering therefrom'. This derives from the jaw-grinding effects of amphetamines and ecstasy, as well as the comical gaping of the very inebriated: a practitioner defined it thus: 'Roll your eyes back, chew your bottom lip and have a faraway look.'

Handbag

The Economist reported in August 1983 that 'one of her less reverent backbenchers said of Mrs Thatcher recently that "she can't look at a British institution without hitting it with her handbag"'. This may well have been the first time that this enduring image was invoked: by the end of the year, the same publication was announcing that 'Treasury figures published last week show how good she has proved at handbagging the civil service.' Five years on and the *Guardian* was still giggling: 'Don't we all . . . simply adore the idea of foreign politicians (male) and recalcitrant members of her own party (mostly male) being handbagged?' Margaret Thatcher administered her handbaggings to, among others, her then Health Secretary Kenneth Clarke (memorably visualised in a Gerald Scarfe cartoon), her sports minister, the diminutive Colin Moynihan, German premier Helmut Kohl (and the entire EU when she was insisting on the UK's £2bn rebate) and, according to SNP leader Alex Salmond in 2006, to Scotland itself during her ascendancy. She herself was eventually handbagged in her turn by the poodle that roared, Geoffrey Howe, of course. As a figurative thrashing, a dressing-down, browbeating or prolonged vilification, the word has since become established in the colloquial political lexicon, and it's no longer always gender-specific. Though most people nowadays are unaware, it also echoes the old term 'sandbagging', when that described hitting someone with an improvised cosh, literally a bag filled with sand (a weapon favoured by muggers, deserters, etc. in the forties and fifties); figuratively it meant stunning an opponent with a surprise attack.

In a number of recent online discussions, the new sense of the word has had to be explained to foreigners. In some circles it functions as a *Coronation Street*-style colloquialism: 'As I'm from the UK, the old Maggie Thatcher "handbagging" thing has become a figure of speech. Now, at least where I grew up, the word means any kind of gentle and humorous rebuke from a lady to a man.' In the journalese jargon of sports commentators, and equally among supporters, the expression is a useful way of jocularly describing an on-pitch display of ill-temper, 'a handbag situation' and 'a bit of a handbags' denoting a minor altercation or scuffle; 'handbags at ten paces' or 'handbags at dawn' a stand-off. In whatever incarnation, handbag must never, ever be confused with 'manbag' – which, if a tote or purse, is not just un-English, but un-British, the sole province of the metrosexual (a word dreamed up by a New Yorker), while so-called 'manbag surgery', cosmetic procedures to reduce puffiness around the eyes, is surely equally suspect. In fashion and showbiz parlance, handbag is well established with the meaning of a male escort or, in the raffish speech of small-time gamblers, money. 'Handbag-positive' in medical slang may refer to any panic-stricken, immobile patient, based on the image of a supine middle-aged lady clutching her handbag to her upper body.

Sometimes playfully treating violence as a mere display, a

comic set-piece, in its more aggressive, Thatcherite sense, handbag conjures up a nation of irate grannies, but also prompts thoughts of other terms that describe the pronounced British tendency to (despite our vaunted stiff-upper-lipped reticence) fitful, petulant aggression. 'Chucking a hissy-fit', 'throwing a wobbly', 'having a strop', 'throwing one's toys/teddy out of the pram', all of them modern versions of the foot-stamping, in the *Just William* stories, of Violet Elizabeth Bott's tantrums. Notched up by several degrees, the same tendency may result in the various 'rages' ('trolley rage', 'desk rage', 'phone rage' and especially on budget flights, 'air rage') diagnosed since 'road rage' was voted word of the year in 2000. While citizens of other nations also 'lose it', statistics show that we, in our overcrowded, overwrought island, have the highest incidence of road rage ending in real violence.

See also **grumble**, **nanny**

Hedge

From hawthorn and beech to privet, and on to ley-landii . . . the ubiquitous, defining feature of the English countryside, and an utterly familiar curiosity (in that it simply isn't visible to anything like the same extent elsewhere), the hedge gives our lowland fields and lanes and our suburban gardens their deep shadows, their privet-y privacy (often with the accompanying privet scent of cat). The hedgerow is a habitat, an ecosystem and a child's bestiary, and a boundary among hundreds of boundaries criss-crossing the landscape. It's also a symbol of what, to use the jargon, is an idealised, romanticised notion of a rural idyll: a collective fantasy actually based on a constructed rather than a natural environment. Once upon a time it was a symbol of dispossession, too, in that the successive enclosures of common land by the wealthy, in the thirteenth, eighteenth and nineteenth centuries, drove many poorer country folk (apart from those who hired themselves out as hedgers) to destitution.

For centuries, 'hedge-' could be used as a combining element imputing poor quality or falsity – 'a hedge-marriage' and 'hedge-wine' were examples, and in 1550 a 'hedge-priest' was an illiterate clergyman. In colloquial language, a rural vagrant is still known as a 'hedger' and a supposed bumpkin or rustic down-and-out by youngsters as a 'hedge-monkey'. The word began as Old English *hecg*, related both to 'haga'; haw(thorn), of which enclosures were woven (as early as Roman times) and to old Germanic words for pasture. By the sixteenth century it referred to a field-boundary, either a remnant of ancient wildwood or newly 'layed'; by 1850 to the orderly line of bushes we now know it as. Times have moved on: across southern England the characteristic patchwork quilt (one estimate gives 500,000 miles of surviving hedges) is still visible from the air, though the old hedge banks and their complex ecologies are in many places under threat.

Stretching a point, it could be said that hedging and hedging one's bets (figurative senses that came into use from the seventeenth century) are also typical of a cautious, tentative, thrifty-but-greedy people. In media references at least, hedge now means hedge funds (a concept dating from 1909) and 'hedgy' (which once meant 'abounding in hedges') is the nickname for fund-managers and their ilk, the noughties incarnation of the 1980s yuppie (and the greedy-and-not-thrifty bugbear of 2008's credit crunch).

Innit

O ne of the problems that English poses for foreign learners is that in standard, that is 'correct', speech, it
requires the question tags at the end of sentences to vary
according to the preceding verb, as in 'They do, don't they?';
'We can, can't we?', etc. Some other languages have invariant
tags, like French '*n'est-ce pas?*' or Spanish '*no?*'. However,
south Asian English, as spoken in India, or by Asians living
in the UK, for example, often uses the form 'isn't it?' regardless of the main sentence verb, and in the early 1980s, in the
youth slang of the south-east UK, the same usage appeared.
The unvarying question tag in this case was 'innit?', a
London working-class version of 'isn't it?' used especially in
emphatic or provocative exchanges. (Interestingly, in Dennis
Potter's script for the musical *Pennies from Heaven*, set in
1937, the cockney hero peppers his speech with what Potter
rendered as 'ennit'.) Innit and 'int'it' are also characteristic of
Brummie (Birmingham) speech, and East Coast US has
'ed'n'it', but it was a London intonation, usually turning the
terminal 't' to a glottal stop (i.e. swallowing it) that swept the
country. As well as a sort of ritualised question-ending, the
word can be used at the beginning of a statement, and as a

separated exclamation of agreement, as in 'We should split up and meet back here later.' 'Innit!' Once the term was recognised by outsiders and reported in the press, its users evolved alternative forms like 'ant'it', 'in't it' and 'don't it', but these don't seem to have caught on to the same extent.

By the end of the 1980s, innit had become identified especially with black British and later Asian British speech patterns, so much so that in the mid-1990s my students at King's College London, were referring to their Asian fellows collectively as 'the innit crowd' (by facetious analogy with 'the in crowd'), and when Sacha Baron Cohen's comic character Ali G parodied Asian and white 'wiggas' ('white niggas' or imitators of black styles), he incorporated innit in the title of a 1999 collection of TV shows. Since 2000, innit has been seen as one of the most recognisable features of so-called 'Hinglish' – south Asian English – and of multi-ethnic youth dialect, supposedly a new accent and vocabulary common to younger speakers across a range of ethnicities and mainly urban environments, which may eventually come to influence mainstream English. It is also seen as emblematic of the troublesome underclass known as 'chavs', and in 2005, jokes were circulating playing on the fact: 'What do you call a chav in a box? Innit.' And 'What do you call an Eskimo Chav? Inuinnit.'

Innit as a question tag is now actually written down – it occurs in prison letters sent by Blake Fielder-Civil, singer Amy Winehouse's estranged husband, published by the *Sun* in July 2008. In April 2008, the same newspaper had carried a hilarious but apparently true report of a teenage girl from London who telephoned directory inquiries to book a taxi to Bristol but ended up having a cabinet delivered – because she asked for 'a cab, innit'. The nineteen-year-old first requested the number of a cab firm using the cockney rhyming slang 'Joe Baxi'. When the baffled operator told her she could not find anyone listed by that name, the teen snapped back: 'It ain't a person, it's a cab, innit.' Here the girl is using the term in its original way, but when put in touch with a seller of display cases she insisted, 'Look love, how hard is it? All I want is your cheapest cab, innit.' She was charged £180, paid with a credit card and the next morning the company delivered an office cabinet to her home in south London. (She was eventually refunded, added the *Sun*, who accompanied the story with a photo of a taxi lest readers in their turn misunderstand.)

See also **chuddies, estuary, nang**

Irony

In June 1914, *The Times*, under the title 'Stay-at-home Husbands – Troublesome Superfluity', commented on the ahead-of-its-time phenomenon of men who had taken to working from home instead of commuting to the office: 'This is "against nature" and natural law imposes retribution . . . it is an added irony that the generality of husbands who work at home are thralls to the life contemplative, and consequently alive to the philosophic anomaly of their lot.' The popular and more populist *Penny Illustrated Paper* was also fond of pointing up the quirks of fashionable behaviour to its readers. In 1906, it lamented the disappearance of a feature of the *fin de siècle*: 'The languid girl is dying out as a type. By a curious irony, the times that created her have . . . made her impossible. These are strenuous days, and to men the hours are precious. They cannot afford, if they want to make money, to waste time lavishly, and the languid girl is a terrible "waster" in this respect.'

For many of the English, irony, like humour (see **GSOH**), is not an occasional indulgence or lapse, but a default conversational (and possibly deeper-seated psychological) mode. The French, too, are capable of irony, as are other European neighbours, particularly those, like Czechs and Hungarians, whose history has required of them 'coping mechanisms' involving rueful contemplation, detachment and deceit. Here, the word itself is bandied about, invoked too lightly, for anything slightly paradoxical or only mildly surprising. Since the seventeenth century, irony has been prized as part of a repertoire of refinement: 'Mr Sheridan went through many ingenious arguments, great delicacy of wit, and pointed irony', wrote a critic in 1785, while the same cluster of attributes was applied to Coleridge's lectures in 1811: 'However serious the design of Mr C's lectures, in the execution he shows himself by no means destitute of talents of humour, irony and satire.' But when it is relentless or laboured it irritates; as Carlyle noted, 'an ironic man . . . more especially an ironic young man . . . may be viewed as a pest to society'. Prefacing with 'ironically . . .' allows the speaker to distance themselves and assume a superior, knowing air. Irony can be savoured as 'an exquisite irony', lamented as 'a bitter irony', or marvelled at as 'the supreme irony', or, as in a 2003 report from the *Daily Express*: 'Oh, irony of ironies: ageing lothario Peter Stringfellow, whose nightclub specializes in nude dancing, says he is "shocked" by the way society has become "sex mad".' The use of irony is a dual defensive-and-offensive strategy: provided you say it ironically, you can say almost anything, anywhere, to anyone, however gauche, vulgar or hurtful. It appeals to a people who are far gone in dissimulation, avoidance strategies and veiled cruelties, but equally can be a result of healthy self-awareness and self-mockery. It is also a conceit, a pose, part of what the contemporary critic A. A. Gill has described in his knockabout way as 'that sneery Soho snobbery that says being Brit is enough, and Americans are irony-resistant naïfs who will roll over and simper at any

European sophistication'. Back in 1875, English commentators wondered whether the King of Portugal was wise to commission a translation of Shakespeare into his language, given that the works were shot through with 'baffling, subtle irony', while in the 1930s, letters to English newspapers took Herr Hitler to task for the total absence of irony in his speeches.

Among his rulings on grammar and usage in *The King's English* (1908), the great panjandrum H. G. Fowler observed that 'the word *irony* is one of the worst abused in the language'. He went on to lambast writers who employ supposed ironies 'for ornament not for utility', especially those who patronise their readers by flagging said ironies with italics or quotation marks. Irony is too easily invoked, as when the *Daily Express* (again) asserts: 'For the man who coined the term big brother, it is an irony that George Orwell might possibly have appreciated: that for the last 20 years of his life he was kept under surveillance by the British secret service.' Is this really ironic, or is it, while quite unpardonable, entirely predictable? D. C. Muecke, who in 1969 devoted a whole book – *The Compass of Irony* – to the subject, reminds us, too, that cheap sarcasm ('I didn't expect you to arrive at the correct conclusion') and **understatement** ('I'm partial to the odd oyster' – after consuming several dozen) are not ironical, unless 'the ostensible meaning differs from the intended meaning'. A real potential irony, as *The Times* noted in its 1848 review of Thackeray's *Vanity Fair*, is that the irony that permeates an author's work may be lost on a later age.

Irony was of course one of the mainstays of classical rhetoric, and, in the form of feigned ignorance, was a tactic in formal debate. The word is originally from Greek, via Latin *ironia*, and was first used in English around 1500: it is not related to the word for metal, which comes via Old English *iren* and Old Germanic *isen*, possibly from an even older Celtic *isarnon*. 'An irony of fate' is a direct borrowing from the seventeenth-century French *ironie du sort*.

See also **sarky**

Jobsworth

O ur English rejection of intrusive officialdom on the Austro-Hungarian or Gallic model, our impatience with over-zealousness and small-mindedness, with cavilling and pedantry in general, have given us the words 'pettifogging' (from 'petty fogger', nineteenth-century slang for a customs officer) and 'nit-picking' from the 1960s. For much of the twentieth century we suffered from a 'lexical gap' – there was no catchy, catch-all term with which to label the oppressor, although 'jumped-up' (a Victorian colloquialism) was the adjective invariably employed. The standard rebuff by the surly ex-serviceman, 'I can't let you come in here/park there/turn up that amplifier, sonny, it'd be more than me job's worth, was eventually distilled into a new expression, for a new hate figure (a minor 'folk devil' in the language of ethnologists), a focus for our day-to-day frustrations. The bugbear in question is the jobsworth, a petty official exercising his – sometimes her – authority in a way we don't like: insisting on doing it by the book, turning down a perfectly reasonable request.

The term first appeared in print in the 1970s, disseminated by the pop music papers *Melody Maker* and *New Musical*

Express. It was also the title of a record released in 1973 by singer-songwriter Jeremy Taylor. By the eighties, it had been picked up by the mainstream media (the lightweight TV consumer series *That's Life* ran a 'Jobsworth Award' feature from the autumn of 1982), and by the 1990s was well established in colloquial speech across the country. The music press had picked it up from rock musicians, their hangers-on and groupies, who themselves had probably got it from the roadies – their point of contact with the real world of car parks, tradesmen's entrances and fire regulations, and a conduit for all sorts of slang and jargon.

In those days the word evoked an England hobbled by red tape and bumf, a place that at street level was still dominated by demobbed other ranks, armed with rule-books and buttressed by bureaucracy, resentful at the liberties being attempted by a younger generation. The typical jobsworth then was a doorman or park-keeper, now, in a world of health-and-safety procedures, noise pollution, surveillance and so-called political correctness, it's likely to be a traffic warden or a local authority apparatchik or flunkey. In 1994, *The Times* reported that 'The public struck back against the "jobsworth" culture last year by increasing the number of complaints about civil service rudeness, incompetence and awkwardness.' Eleven years on, Max Wells of Southampton was writing to the *Sunday People*, 'What sort of jobsworth could fine a one-legged man £106 for having his disabled badge accidentally upside down on his car. He's got one leg! What more proof of disability do they need?' Other examples gleefully pounced upon by the press (an average of thirty per year in the *Sun* alone) have included a Battle of Britain veteran aged ninety-four being thrown off a bus because his OAP pass was not valid for another forty minutes, council officials interrupting a Holocaust commemoration because

an official car had one wheel on the pavement, and star musicians Jools Holland and Nigel Kennedy being told to stop
playing an impromptu gig to a crowded hotel bar as it was too
loud (I think I'm with the jobsworth here).

It may be significant that railing against petty obfusca-
tions, encouraged as it is by the media, channels our anger
and distracts us from the bigger issues, like private finance
initiatives, bovine spongiform encephalopathy, banking bail-
outs, health and education, etc., in the face of which we are
utterly powerless. The other side of the coin, though, is illu-
minated by a leaked manual circulated a year ago to local
council bin inspectors across England. It advises them on
how to react to members of the public who abuse them: 'If
you are shouted at, say, "I am not prepared to carry on this
interview whilst you are calling me a w***er and a jobsworth"' (the use of 'whilst' may, I think, be ill advised).
The desperately detailed tract advises inspectors to look out
for the warning signs of bin rage, '. . . changes in breathing
patterns, the throbbing vein in the temple, the opening and
closing of their fists'. It also recommends venting stress by
'screaming and shouting (in a safe place)'.

Meanwhile, my students report that the 'little Hitler' syn-
drome still afflicts the music scene. Their constant oppressors
at clubs, gigs and festivals, they say, are jobsworths otherwise
known as 'arsey bouncers', where arsey means truculent and
bumptious. For more proof of the survival of the genus, con-
sult www.b3ta.com/questions/jobsworths/.

See also **nanny**

Jolly

I n *Mr Jolly Lives Next Door* (1987), a knockabout black
comedy from the Comic Strip ensemble, the eponymous
hero is a contract killer, played by the late Peter Cook, who
hacks up his victims to the sound of Tom Jones hits from the
1960s. Mercifully, the best known Mr Jolly active at the time
of writing is a real-life children's entertainer from Preston.
Modern jolly is from Old French *jolif*, 'festive', of mysterious
provenance but possibly deriving from Old Norse *jól* or *jül*,
the midwinter or Christmas celebration(s), which also gave
us Yule(tide). The everyday equivalent of convivial, jovial,
our word epitomises a spirit of exuberant, uncomplicated
good cheer that the English take pride in, just as the French,
especially in the first half of the twentieth century, valued
their *bonne humeur* and *bonhomie*. (In modern French, *joli* can
only mean pretty.) From its first adoption, in varying
spellings, the English word was used as an appreciative nickname, later becoming a common family name: a John le Goly
was recorded in Wiltshire in 1275, Henricus Joly in Yorkshire
in 1379.

In the seventeenth century, jolly was notably polysemous
(linguists' jargon for having multiple meanings): it could also

mean amorous, lustful, brave, good-looking, healthy (and plump), overbearing and, attested from 1652, slightly intoxicated (two hundred years later, Dickens' cockney character Sam Weller was still referring to 'the gen'l'm'n as beat his wife with the poker, venever he got jolly'). 'Jollity' is now defined as gaiety, lively good spirits, but in the seventeenth century it could additionally refer to sexual pleasure or impudent behaviour.

Sadly, a scan of twenty-first-century examples confirms that this venerable noun is mainly reserved these days for carping, typically in phrases like 'forced jollity', 'attempted jollity', 'unrelieved' or 'relentless jollity' and the plaintive 'adding a touch of jollity (to an otherwise sad occasion)'. 'Jollification', though, straightforwardly describes revelry, festivity, merry-making, while in colloquial conversation a jolly (probably a nineteenth-century shortening of 'jollification' rather than an adjective-turned-noun) denotes a splendid time, in particular a one-off outing at someone else's expense. In the Sloane Rangers' lexicon it was a euphemism for sex, just as 'to get one's jollies' (first attested in the USA in 1962) can refer to undeserved or illicit enjoyment. The phrasal verbs 'jolly up' or 'jolly along', in the sense of keeping someone's spirits up or cajoling them, also seem to have started as Americanisms in the late 1800s, while 'jolly on' is currently a North American synonym for 'party on' or 'rock on'.

There's a folksy, kitsch flavour to hackneyed combinations like 'Jolly Jack Tar' and pubs called the Jolly Sailor (from the end of the seventeenth century, sailors were routinely presumed to be jolly and played up to this, bestowing the nickname on one another; the Jolly Roger pirate flag dates from 1785 and Royal Marines were called Jollies from the 1820s) or the Jolly Brewer. I'm bemused by the Jolly

Farmer, an unfeasible image these days, and when the Scots appropriate our word, as in the Jolly Judge Lounge Bar, in dour Edinburgh, it doesn't quite chime.

'I'm jolly well not going to stand for this,' mutters May, as her sister's schoolfriend Thelma surreptitiously rummages in her family's treasure chest (from *The Popular Book of Girls' Stories*, 1930). Jolly is often an intensifier before an adjective or adverb, since Victorian times a usage emblematic of wide-eyed, innocent, gleeful approval ('jolly fine'), or of earnest admonition ('jolly dangerous'). 'For He's a Jolly Good Fellow' (the tune is ancient but the words seem to have been added around 1830) is said to be the second most popular song in the English language, after 'Happy Birthday to You' and just ahead of 'Auld Lang Syne'. Surprisingly, this collo-quial sense of 'very' or 'exceedingly' is not, like the archaic 'bally', a euphemism for something stronger, but dates back to the early sixteenth century. 'Jolly D' (where the letter stands for **decent**) was a staple of public schoolgirl slang and was a catchphrase of the foolish upper-class character Dudley Davenport in the comedy *Much-Binding-in-the-Marsh* (King George VI's favourite radio programme, it ran for a decade from 1944). At the same time, **cad**dish comedian Terry-Thomas used 'jolly good show' as one of his trademark expressions, as did smoothie Leslie Phillips a little later. From 1950, the radio series *Educating Archie*, starring a ven-triloquist's dummy, 'Archie Andrews', also featured 'Monica', a hearty public schoolgirl played by the actress Beryl Reid who coined the enduring formulation 'jolly hockey sticks', evoking the boisterous sportiness, the breathless enthusi-asms, pashes and crushes of female boarding-school life. Another such combination is 'jolly super', a punning sobri-quet bestowed by unkind colleagues on the journalist Jilly Cooper, chronicler first of the proto-Sloane semi-posh of

London in the early seventies, later of the horsey county set of fictional Rutshire (another pun). While hippies and feminists ushered in New Britain, Cooper wrote teasingly about the upper middle class day-to-day, going on to pioneer the rural 'bonkbuster' (in which Old England and new hedonism combine). In the words of Giles Hattersley, her journalism and novels 'succeed because of her unfaltering sense for what the ... English ... are really obsessed with: class, sex, shopping, anti-intellectualism and dogs'.

For some time now employed mainly by journalists for mockery and condescension, as in 'oh, jolly unfair'; 'and jolly exciting stuff it is', (the adjective was being used ironically as early as the sixteenth century), jolly, like its stablemates 'splendid', 'horrid', 'my word', 'awfully' and 'bother!', may be making a comeback, at first self-consciously or ironically, but actually in earnest. Old England is waiting in the wings and periodically re-emerges in the form of overgrown schoolboys like the broadcaster James May, for instance, while public-school dominance of politics and the media, covert under New Labour in the nineties and noughties, reasserted itself in the make-up of the first government of the tweenies.

Kevin

In 1987, the Sloane Rangers' house magazine, the snooty *Tatler*, wrote of pupils at one minor public school, 'Other schools just can't understand why they look so "Kevin-ish" . . . white socks and footballers' haircuts.' Though it's an anglicising of the Irish name Caoimhín, composed of Old Irish *coem*, 'handsome, kind and gentle', and *gein*, meaning 'birth', nowadays the name Kevin, especially in its shorter form, 'Kev', has very different connotations in England. It is one of the many synonyms for the new feckless underclass, the tracksuit-, gold-chain- and trainer-wearing 'chav', 'townie', 'pikey' or 'scally'. A Kev is, according to one contemporary, 'a twat in a Burberry cap from a housing estate', and his female counterpart is a 'Shaz', from the first name Sharon. This is the English love of minute differentiations of status and class in a new incarnation. Rather than the contentious 'lower-upper-lower middle class' distinctions of yesteryear, we have ironic categorisation by given name. 'Sharon', 'Tracy', 'Mandy', 'Wayne' and 'Darren' can all be used generically to refer to unsophisticated members of what used to be called the 'lower orders', and by, for instance, middle-class financial professionals for the working-class or lower-middle-class 'Essex boys' and 'Essex girls' who work alongside them in the City. 'Trev' or 'Trevor' is also used, by university students among others, to deride an unlikeable fellow student, considered either too fashion-conscious or not fashionable enough. I'm told that in 2008 the name Jono (pronounced 'John-oh'), usually short for Jonathan, began to be used mockingly in the same way.

The tricky question is, is there a demonstrable difference between a Kevin, a Darren and a Trevor? And what exactly is a Jono, unless it is someone who takes after the cheerfully rotund TV and radio presenter Jono Coleman? This stereotyping goes back at least to the 1960s, when a Nigel or a Rupert could be shorthand for a 'chinless wonder', 'hooray' or 'toff'. Tarquin has since been used with much the same intention, and on a weekly basis *Sunday Times* TV critic A. A. Gill dismisses posh and/or precious BBC programme-makers as 'Tristrams'. In ordinary conversation, gormless males used to be known as ''Erberts' (often qualified by 'spotty' or 'scruffy'), with Wally taking on the same role from the later 1970s. In the 1960s, trendies dubbed tedious conformists 'Erics'; beatniks and later hippies castigated 'Norman Normals', which, shortened to 'norms', was still in raffish use in 2000. From the 1970s to the 1990s, 'Brian' was the jokey nickname for any footballer or sports commentator, and those in service jobs sometimes call their customers 'Billies', but this is an example of rhyming slang – 'Billy Bunter' (the rotund Edwardian schoolboy character), standing for 'punter'. In surfer and skater slang, girls and girlfriends may be lumped together as 'Betties', originally inspired by the character played by Michele Dotrice in the 1970s TV comedy series *Some Mothers Do 'Ave 'Em*. Older women, especially if they are thought to be **frump**s and/or harridans, are called '(a right) Doris', or 'Nora' (after Nora Batty, the character in *Last of the*

Summer Wine). The former Conservative MP Ann Widdecombe was cruelly nicknamed 'Doris Karloff' by colleagues, and in cockney banter Doris may also, like ''er indoors', simply denote one's wife or partner.

In English there is an ancient tradition of using given names as nicknames for particular types, or for activities or parts of the body: examples include biddy (short for Bridget, originally suggesting an Irish maidservant), roger, dick and, of course, willie. In other languages, names can be used in fiction, especially comedy, to suggest a social category – in France, 'Jean-Charles' is a toff, 'Roger' a suburban hairdresser. In Norwegian, there is something more similar in that chavs and chavvishness are described as 'Harry', or in local dialects as 'Johan', but only in English is there such a full taxonomy. Kevin, interestingly, is also a generic nickname among US high school and college students, but there it signifies an attractive, (over)confident male. In France, Kevin has, since the 1980s, been a very fashionable baby name, probably inspired by Hollywood leading men Kevin Costner, Kevin Kline and Kevin Bacon.

When in 2005 the Churchill Insurance Group carried out a survey of car-owners and matched them with first names, they discovered that statistics confirmed assumptions. Their database determined that Darrens drive downmarket Ford Escorts and so do Waynes and Traceys. If you are called Gary, Carl or Lee, you are likely to own a Vauxhall Astra. And with owners called Joyce, Doreen and Beryl, Nissan Micra drivers evidently come from the older members of the population. The typical (Ford) Mondeo Man is (somewhat unbelievably) Rodney, Laurence or Julian, Renault Clio owners include men called Matthew, Adam and Alexander, while Gavins were likely to buy a Renault Megane. The unlisted Kevs do own cars, or perhaps twoc them (from the police terminology 'take without owner's consent'; my informants describe them 'skidding around in souped-up 1.1 litre pimped bangers, pumping out techno music at full volume'), but they probably don't insure them.

In the same year, Barclays Bank surveyed their high-earning customers and found that professionals called Susan or David were more likely to earn over £100,000 a year. Elizabeth, Sarah, John or Michael were also likely to command a six-figure salary. A spokesman for Barclays noted that names such as Darren and Wayne were noticeably absent from the list. But 'in some way this could just be a reflection of social backgrounds as much as luck or financial acumen'. Kevin once again was nowhere (as was my own first name, incidentally). A teachers' website subsequently posted a list of pupils' given names that, allegedly, in themselves sound warning bells. The female name that inspired the most dread was Paige; lesser offenders were Chantelle ('spawn of the devil'), Courtney ('trouble'), Danielle ('a nightmare'), Kayleigh ('a pain') and Keira ('live in fear'). Disruptive boys were especially likely to be called Ashley, Chase, Conor, Dylan, Grant, Reece, Shane, Tyler or Wayne (again, it is probably entirely coincidental that in the USA, a statistically disproportionate number of murderers have Wayne as one of their names).

Nameism, it seems, is here to stay. In 2009, tour operator Activities Abroad promoted its adventure holidays with two lists of names: those 'you are likely to encounter' on one of their holidays and those you are not. Apparently Alice, Joseph and Charles were welcome members of the customer base, but Britney, Chantelle and Dazza would feel out of place. Among those roused to protest was Candice (one of the proscribed names), who wrote as follows: 'I own my own business, have a postgraduate degree, an undergraduate degree, four A-Levels, an Advanced Diploma in Life Skills, a Diploma in Performance Coaching, GCSEs, speak French and Italian and drive a Merc. Happy slap that you idiot.'

Kip

I n May 2005, British Airways published an online guide to English slang and popular sayings for overseas tourists. It explained that 'leg it' means to run quickly; 'peckish' means hungry; 'kip' means nap; 'laughing gear' means mouth; 'readies' means available cash; and 'chuffed' means delighted. I was struck by the fact that kip was by far the oldest of these colloquialisms, but in what way is it typically or quintessentially English? It does seem to be one of those small words that somehow have a special resonance. It's a **chum**my sort of word, sounding like a friend's nickname, which of course it is, being one of the short forms of Christopher. It's odd in that it doesn't sound like the action or state it defines. S-l-e-e–p is a long, gentle word; kip is a highly abbreviated, snappy one. So is it for a puritanical, hyperactive society something crucial, yet truncated and provisional ('forty winks'), to be snatched where and when one can; likewise for our contemporary overworked, sleep-poor culture (in the form of a 'power-nap' for instance)?

Is it because it carries suggestions of shared fatigue, brief respite, thus symbolises the camaraderie of the old 'gentlemen of the road', exhausted soldiers in two world wars, and today a whole rootless, huddled community of dossers? Could it possibly have something to do with the lurking apprehension, common to males between fifteen and sixty for as long as any can remember, that any one of us might hit rock-bottom one day? It was once a proletarian usage: when quoting a burglar caught on a roof in Mayfair ('when challenged Evans said "I'm having a kip"'), *The Times* in 1928 had to translate for its readers. Eight years later, describing London's homeless, 'begging eloquently for a night's "kip" or congregated in a charitable night shelter', quotation marks were inserted. In modern usage the word is classless, though more often employed by male speakers. It came into English, presumably part of the lexicon of poorer travellers, from Danish *kippe*, or Low German *kiffe*, for a hovel, later used to denote a mean inn (as a cheap place of lodging, hence a bed for the night) or a brothel. The verb to kip, to bed down, was first recorded in Britain in 1889, while the forms 'kip down' and 'get some kip' appeared in the early twentieth century. From Victorian times until the 1930s 'kip-house', 'kipping-house' or 'kip-shop' were synonyms for the surviving 'doss-house', and during the 1950s 'kip-in' was used by young criminals ('borstal boys') in the sense of 'take it easy' or 'keep mum'. In Irish usage until recently the noun has referred to a squalid room – a 'dump' or 'tip' – but speakers there now also employ it in the English sense of 'sleep', as do Americans. In London rhyming slang it is rendered by 'lucky dip' or 'feather and flip'.

Not surprisingly for such a short, matey word, it often features in the *Sun*, which has over the years reported that 'More than one in five workers admit to having a kip on the job. It costs companies an estimated £20 million a year in lost business' and 'The average worker misses out on nine hours of kip a week – a whole night's sleep – due to job worries and irregular shift patterns' and curiously, 'Britons kip in an average of 818 beds in their lifetimes, said a survey.'

Lurgi

'The sneeze in English is the harbinger of misery, even death. I sometimes think the only pleasure an Englishman has is in passing on his cold germs' (Gerald Durrell, writing in 1956). The grand English tradition of not treating **serious** things seriously extends not unnaturally to sickness and disease. Whether talking about a slight seasonal 'chill' (itself a very useful, very English word now shunned by the medical profession), snottiness caused by an allergic reaction, a viral infection or a full-blown communicable epidemic, one word will serve for all. Normally preceded by 'the dreaded', the term in question, lurgi ('lergi', the colonial-looking 'lurghi', and 'lurgy' are alternative spellings, while playground usage sometimes shortens to 'lerg'), looks exotic, sounds both unpleasant and comic, and for most people is of unknown etymology. In institutional settings such as schools it has come to denote an undiagnosable, perhaps imaginary affliction, nonetheless touted as scarily infectious.

In fact, lurgi, sporting its 'dreaded' prefix, first emerged from the *Goon Show* radio comedy series in 1954 – the episode of 9 November that year was entitled 'The Lurgi

Strikes Britain', giving the smoggy, **wet** and **windy** country a new catch-all expression with which to laugh off successive pre-vaccine flu epidemics and all the other climate and pollution-related ailments that faulty plumbing and absence of central heating exacerbated: 'She's gone down with the lurgi' or 'Don't touch him, you'll get the lurgi!' being familiar cries through the sixties and seventies.

It's not certain whether the *Goon Show* invented the word, or whether it pre-existed in baby talk or in public-school and/or armed-service slang: it is almost certainly a jokey deformation of the word 'allergy', a deliberately 'ignorant' mispronunciation. Perhaps significantly, perhaps coincidentally, 'lerg' is attested, with the same derivation, as an obscure American colloquialism of the late 1940s. 'The dreaded' probably originated in nineteenth-century penny dreadfuls when introducing a supposedly notorious villain, and has become entrenched in facetious banter of a nerdish variety. Lurgi is still heard, usually in family conversations or between colleagues (for the school, 'Damian seem to have gone down with a bug'; for the boss, when throwing a sickie, 'It's a case of acute rhinitis complicated by lactose intolerance'), but sounds a little dated, perhaps inevitably in today's health-obsessed, over-medicated – increasingly self-medicating – society for which specific, named conditions and remedies (even when spurious) are an absolute requirement.

Merry

As a word – perhaps *the* word – chosen by the English to define themselves, merry has a long history, coming as it does from the Old English adjective *myrige*, 'delightful' (even then there was a flavour of hilarity associated with the term: it is closely related to the noun that became 'mirth').

The phrase 'the merry month of May' dates from 1567, and surprisingly, the euphemistic meaning 'slightly tipsy' was first recorded as early as 1575. Robin Hood 'and his merry men' apparently borrows an authentically medieval clichéd designation of a feudal knight's close companions or followers. The 'merry monarch', as applied to King Charles II, restored the image of a cheerful if not riotous court and partly resurrected what was already to some degree a utopian folk myth, the medieval festive life that had been put aside for a Reformation, then a Puritan interregnum. 'A very merry Christmas' was first wished for in the seventeenth century, while merry in the sense of brisk – 'a merry pace', 'lead someone a merry dance' – dates from around a century later.

But of course the best known 'collocation' or 'co-occurrence' must be in the formulation 'merrie Englande', first recorded as long ago as 1436 and still evoking – or mocking – the appealing idea of a past idyll, a time of unending good cheer and fellow feeling, perhaps at a slightly deeper level expressing the notion of a joviality transcending social distinctions, a whole people united by jollity, making merry together, playing merry hell with stuffy convention. Good humour must be a universal, and we can't really, reasonably, claim the quality of being merry for ourselves alone, can we? And yet the word as it's understood and embraced by natives, with all its overtones and undertones (connotations of bluff, hearty, unrestrained, convivial, uncomplicated enthusiasm . . .), is difficult to capture in translation. French has *gai*, *joyeux*, *divertissant*, but these do not have the echo of 'good old times'; Italian has *festoso*, *giocondo*, *lieto*, but none of these is a perfect match. German equivalents might be *froelich* or *lustig* but these are more common and less nuanced, as are Finnish *hauska* and *iloinen*.

Muddle

'Incapacity, muddle, petty jealousies, intrigues, ineffi-ciency, amateurishness, and do-nothing' was how one cynic privately characterised the Royal Navy's bureaucracy in 1911. 'Muddle' had by then already become a keyword of Englishness, still inside the quotation marks indicating a colloquialism in the 1820s but flourishing in the late-Victorian period when it would typically be applied to non-bellicose foreign policy or ill-organised households 'in a perpetual/frightful/deplorable muddle'. Victorians also used muddle as a transitive verb meaning to lose or destroy through indecision or confused tactics, as in Queen's Park Rangers 'muddling a goal' or a farmer 'muddling his inher-itance'.

Citizens of all nations suffer confusion, behave clumsily on occasion, but I think we rather enjoy portraying ourselves as vague, amiable, disorganised naïfs without a clear idea of where we are going – and then **grumbl**ing about the fact. The implication of course is that we are therefore *not* self-seeking go-getters, single-mindedly pursuing narrow goals. On 5 November 1910, the *Penny Illustrated Paper* declared, 'At the present moment we are a nation of muddlers. We muddle through with our navy, with our army, with our education, and with nearly every other department of social life.' According to word-buff Nigel Rees, the US humorist H. L. Mencken said that he first heard 'muddle through' around 1885. Ira Gershwin used it in his song 'Stiff Upper Lip' in 1937 and claimed that it was coined by English MP John Bright circa 1864. In everyday usage from Edwardian times onward, the phrase, with its variant forms 'muddle along' and 'muddle on', all meaning to proceed in a haphazard, makeshift manner, was employed especially in references to the armed forces and the railways (the Midland and Great Northern Railway was jocularly renamed the 'Muddle and Go Nowhere'). After World War II, muddle was rife in a world of rationing, of inefficient nationalised utilities and petty bureaucracy. Diaries and letters from the time reflect ruefully that, in the words of a Wigan housewife, 'we just seem to muddle through somehow'. The refrain bundles together stoicism, resignation to the inevitable, a jaundiced attitude to any notion of progress. Little successes will come in spite of oneself and in spite of the overwhelming array of obstacles. Of course clinging to a model of muddle, a compromise of comforting confusion, like the cult of amateurism and a disdain for taking oneself **serious**ly, was swept away, like everything else, in the 1980s. Resignation, cynicism and ploddingness gave way to earnest, impatient, unapologetic aspiration to affluence, a culture of targeting, benchmarking and auditing. Yet we can still get ourselves in a right royal muddle. Now the muddlers might be public- and service-sector employees improvising in a context of borderline chaos; as a hapless prison guard admitted to an undercover reporter from the *News of the World* in 2005, 'We just muddle our way through the shifts . . . to be honest we don't know what to do.' But, lest we forget, in an overcomplicated New

Britain, just as in clotted, constipated Old England, to muddle, just like its close relative 'dither', can be creative, or at least deliberate – a low-key strategy that avoids extremism, juggles alternatives, reflects before acting.

Muddle possibly derives from Middle Dutch *moddern*, to 'make muddy', and the English word first meant 'wallow in mud' or 'grub in dirt'. 'A bugger's muddle' (fiasco, 'cock-up') shocked my mother when a crusty ex-officer used the expression to characterise government ineptitude back in the early 1970s. 'Muddled' used to be a synonym for drunk, while in current slang, 'muddling' can mean fondling or fornicating. As a definition of 'muddle-headed', an example from the *Leicester Mercury* will serve. In 2006 it informed its readers, 'Oo-er la la – a survey of muddle-headed motorists has found that one in 10 people thinks Ashby-de-la-Zouch is abroad.'

Naff

An untranslatable (into American, let alone other languages) nailing of much that is quintessentially and
enduringly English, of what is not simply in bad taste and/or
inferior, but embarrassingly, painfully so. A word equally at
home among thespians, lesbians, fashionistas, suburban
housewives (if we are still allowed to use that expression)
and university students, in fact almost anyone except the
terminally, full-time pompous. As the late Miles Kington
noted in a 1984 column discussing tasteless postcards, 'Naff
is a word we hear a lot these days but which has seldom to
my satisfaction been defined, hovering as it does between
kitsch and **grotty**.' A staple of 'raffish speech' as it used to
be described by lexicographers, naff circulated in the same
milieux as the Polari/Parlyaree argot of the camp and the
theatrical, formerly of hucksters and pedlars and the like.
Slang collector Eric Partridge claimed to have heard it pronounced 'narf' in the armed services in the 1940s, but it
first appeared in writing in Keith Waterhouse's novel *Billy
Liar* in 1959, then in 1965, in the form 'naph', in the scripts
of the radio comedy series *Round the Horne* and *Beyond our
Ken*. It was given much wider currency by Ronnie Barker's

character 'Fletch' in the 1970s prison-based sitcom Porridge (scripts by Dick Clement and Ian La Frenais). He employed it as a disguised form of the then forbidden f-word, as did Princess Anne at the Badminton horse trials in April 1982, using the euphemism to tell photographers to 'naff off'. The following year marked the apogee of the now fashionable, classless word, with *Times* columnist Philip Howard commenting on the many conflicting etymologies being put forward, a couple of which are still periodically advanced, although they are spurious: it does not come from NAAFI and is not an acronym once used in the sex trade for 'not available for f***ing' or anything similar.

When it first caught on in the 1970s, naff was merely a useful conversational novelty and a handy euphemism, but for me, its heyday in the mid-1980s marks a significant moment – the realisation by the aspirational, impatient New Britain that was then coming into being of just how shamefully shabby Old England had become. Not all of that old awfulness was swept away by the coming of the me generation; in its senses of inferior and shoddy, naff is especially relevant in the land of botch-up, cowboy workmanship and desperate **muddl**ing through.

The word is still in use, especially by journalists who favour space-saving epithets, and in conversation: 'truly'/ 'irredeemably'/ 'hopelessly'/ 'terminally' are typical collocations. An elaborated form of the adjective that North Americans are currently fond of is 'naffola' (using the mock-Spanish '-ola' suffix to add emphasis). Recent examples from internet postings include 'truly naffola moments'/'the naffola Jim Morrison ep[isode) of *Dark Skies*'; 'grown-up bridesmaids are truly naffola'. The meaning is still 'in lamentable taste', sometimes generalised to just 'awful, repellent', as in 'the weather here is naffola'. Once again, a Britishism has crossed over into North American usage, a reversal of earlier trends, largely an online phenomenon, and confined to colloquial youth use.

There is a women's perfume called Eau de Naphe, the word here being a poetic name for orange blossom, but this is nothing but coincidence. Naff's continuing popularity points up the English predilection for simultaneous amusement at, and disapproval of, vulgar tastelessness. Its importance reflects the fact that, for all our affluence and mobility, most of us – **Brit**s, that is, not only the English – are still deficient in a basic everyday aesthetic sense. Whether unconsciously or deliberately we still regularly commit outrageous breaches of the taste barrier in our choice of clothing, accessorising and body decoration, domestic architecture and design.

See also **quaint**

Nang

In January 2006, *Times* reporter Michele Kirsch is riding on a bus en route to Islington Green School alongside a noisy gaggle of teenage girls she calls the 'scary bitches'. 'They scare the other passengers – meek, tired and irritated – and use a secret language punctuated with words such as "sket" and "nang" and "buff" and "bredren", which mean whore, cool, good-looking and mate, in that order.' By August 2006, this teenage code is being 'taught' to visitors to London. Under the headline 'How to Talk Nang Teen', the *Sun* reported on outdoor lessons in five languages: Bengali, Spanish, sign language, cockney and 'rap-style' teen slang, or 'gangsta-lingo', as popularised by TV star Ali G. 'The move comes,' the paper informed its readers, 'after researchers revealed kids have swapped traditional Cockney rhyming slang for a new dialect dubbed "Jafaican" . . . mixing English, Jamaican patois, Indian and West African dialects.'

Probably the highest-profile and most resonant examples of youth slang are the succession of synonyms for 'great' or 'excellent' that have come in and out of fashion since the 1950s. Called 'vogue terms of approbation' by linguists, these range from 'smashing' back in the 1950s through **fab**

and 'gear', those emblematic Scouser terms forever associated with Merseybeat and the Beatles, via 'groovy', 'far out'
and 'too much', the hippies' favourites (which I have to
admit I sometimes blurt out even today, to the derision of
younger listeners). The end of the 1970s brought 'ace' and
'brill', occasionally elaborated by younger speakers into 'ace
to base' and 'brillo pads', as well as **wicked** (sometimes subsequently shortened to 'wick'), the UK's response to North
America's 'bad' and its near-contemporary 'rad'.

Although they are invented in order to replace outdated
forms, and rely for their power on novelty, these expressions,
if they catch on at all, actually stay around for some time,
migrating from the cutting edge of linguistic innovation to
outlying regions as provincial or younger speakers discover
and cherish them. Thus it is that ultra-fashionable words
from the late 1980s and early 1990s like 'mint', 'fit' or 'top'
are all still to be heard somewhere in the UK. In the 1990s,
skaters introduced, and still favour, 'sick' as an all-purpose
positive, to the intended bafflement of the older generation,
and 'brutal' has been used in the same way, first by the mods
of the mid-1960s and again by schoolchildren since around
2000.

Probably the most significant of these badges of approval,
acceptance or admiration in recent years has been a word
that is also important as the first term of south Asian origin to
make a real impact across the entire British youthscape.
Nang, which began to be heard in areas of east London at
the turn of the twentieth century, is thought to be from a
Bengali word for a naked woman, but it is also claimed that
it is a Thai proper name, that of Nang Phan, a former pupil
of Kingsland Secondary School in Hackney. According to an
internet posting by an anonymous 'Nang's best friend', 'It
came about through boys in years above her chiding "ahh,

Nang you're nang" . . . it caught on like wildfire from there.'
Peppering the conversation of multi-ethnic youth in districts
like Hackney and Tower Hamlets, the word was quickly
picked up in other parts of London as the preferred replacement for 'safe', 'dope' or 'rated'. It is often heard in the
forms 'bare nang', where 'bare', from Afro-Caribbean usage,
is slang for 'totally', and more recently 'nangin'', probably by
analogy with other words for 'exciting' like 'bangin'' and
'kickin''.

Knowing and using nang was for some time a badge of
allegiance for youth from London, specifically from the particular multi-ethnic mix in inner east London, but since 2004
its use has spread across the UK with the growing dominance of that variety of **yoof**-speak, even in areas where no
black or Asian speakers are in evidence. The proof of this
importance is that some young commentators in web-based
discussions use the designation 'nang-slang' (like 'bling-
lish' – from 'bling' meaning hip-hop-style ostentation –
before it) to refer to their entire code, or what linguists more
portentously call the 'new multi-ethnic youth vernacular'.
Nang is interesting too, in that unlike some earlier faddish
teenage terms ('fab' and 'brill' in particular), it hasn't crossed
over into mainstream, adult or media usage.

See also **innit, wicked**

Nanny

The nanny is an enduring English icon, metamorphosing from the upper-class nursery to the middle-class mother's help. Her complex role as surrogate carer and often disciplinarian, too – especially if she additionally possessed Mary Poppins-like qualities – left an indelible impression on many males. Even now that the roost is as likely to be regulated by a young au pair, probably Slovakian and possibly even of masculine gender, the antique maxim 'nanny knows best' still calls forth the image of the stiff, stern male quailing before the raised finger. Some of the murkier aspects of English masculinity may thus come into play: privileged childhoods blighted by parental absence or neglect, fantasies involving submission and domination.

'Nan', a familarising alteration of Ann(e), was a nickname given to young maidservants from the eighteenth century, with the alternative form, nanny, coming to denote in slang a whore (a 'nanny house' or 'nanny shop' being a brothel) and in colloquial speech a nursemaid. It was first attested with this sense in 1832 and by the 1930s was in fairly widespread use. 'Nana', which could also be rendered as nanny, was first recorded in the nineteenth century, when it was a

Nanny

child's deformation of 'grandma'. Today, of course '(yer) nan' is the un-posh equivalent of the more generalised 'granny'. 'Nannyish' means overprotective and/or authoritarian, and the verb 'to nanny' to nurse (someone else's) children or to be fussily controlling. Meanwhile in rhyming slang, 'nanny' is short for 'nanny goat' – providing over the years a rhyme with 'anecdote', 'coat', the horseracing 'tote' and journalistic 'quote'. In French, the nanny is known as a *nou-nou*, a baby-talk version of the English 'nurse', but for most of our European neighbours the role is irrelevant as, traditionally, the extended family provides.

The government, when seen as patronising, overprotective and interfering, has been referred to as 'the nanny state' since the formulation was coined by the Conservative politician Iain Macleod in the *Spectator* in February 1965: he was attacking the idea of government intervention to control smoking. A scan of the print media throws up thousands of instances of the phrase, employed more often by reactionaries and conservatives (of the late Dr Rhodes Boyson in 1976; 'He distrusts managers in politics and the influence of "middle class mandarins" in creating "the nanny state"'), but also sometimes by 'progressives' complaining of illiberal social policies. During Margaret Thatcher's administration, 'nanny state' became a sort of anti-mantra, along with 'spoon-feeding' and 'welfare scrounger'. For the tabloids, the phrase is a trigger inserted into scores of populist articles highlighting instances of heavy-handed intrusion into the day-to-day. The *News of the World* instituted a 'Nanny State Award' in 2004, and also ran a column by former Conservative leader William Hague called 'Nannied by Ninnies': 'This week's winners are the busybody council officials in South Shields who have drastically cut back some much-loved horse chestnut trees to try to stop children hurting themselves while

213

gathering conkers.' Protests at 'nannying' and 'nannyism', along with the words themselves, have now gone global, with blogs across the **Anglosphere** featuring sections such as 'Nannied to Death', in which the 'blogerati commentariat' inveigh against what they see as infringements of individual freedoms, such as health-and-safety legislation, enforcement of so-called political correctness, or Lyme Regis council's recent banning of a conger-eel-cuddling contest (obliquely, a sudden flashback reminds me that a 'nannyism' also used to be, in British English, an adage of the sort once uttered by stern domestic carers, such as 'You need not brush all your teeth, Master Antony, merely those you wish to keep').

It seems that no one is willing to speak up for Nanny, but in 2008, playwright Alan Bennett announced that he was donating his life's work to the Bodleian Library in Oxford. Noting that 'the state isn't something that people would normally thank or think well of, hence the phrase "the nanny state"', he recalled that he had been given a free education: 'now if that's being nannied, I'm all for it'. In 2010, *Daily Telegraph* columnist Matthew d'Ancona urged the new coalition government to impose an alternative 'manny state', invoking the male nannies increasingly favoured by fashionable families. 'They are generally employed to help ease children out of total reliance upon their parents, to show compassion and provide help to the young without hesitation, but to urge the children in their care away from dependency and towards responsibility for themselves and others.'

Nice

Two of the keywords of Englishness come together in the phrase 'naughty but nice', conveying as it does charming (another keyword, this) sauciness. Wasn't it applied to the 'lovely Aimee McDonald', airhead presenter of the pre-Monty Python TV comedy *At Last the 1948 Show* in 1967? And don't I remember it as the slogan used to promote cream cakes in two separate campaigns in the 1980s, coined, it is said, by the young Salman Rushdie in his job as copywriter? Certainly Huntley and Palmers' Nice biscuits have been a well-known genteel (see **gentle**) accompaniment to a **cuppa** since 1904, but here the word is really the name of the southern French city, Nice, though no one pronounces it thus. Throughout the 1970s, the cockney (London working-class) phrase 'nice one', expressing admiration typically for a smart move, was popular among all classes, helped enormously by its adoption as a slogan – 'Nice one, Cyril, nice one, mate!' – for TV commercials for Wonderloaf bread, then by supporters of Tottenham Hotspur football club cheering their player Cyril Knowles.

'Here Comes the Nice' was a song by the Small Faces in their psychedelic incarnation, and the phrase was then used

215

in druggy code for a banned substance or the person who provided it. Celebrity former cannabis smuggler Howard Marks has been promoted as 'Mr Nice', the title of his 1996 autobiography and more recent stage show. So pervasive, so fundamental to English intercourse is nice that the TV comedy series *The Fast Show* had two characters based on its use as a catchphrase: the jazz critic, inspired by 1970s rock presenter 'Whispering' Bob Harris, who follows each and every cacophonous performance with an approving 'N-i-i-i-ce', and the plummy, smug Patrick Nice, who relates self-satisfied anecdotes.

Nice, the adjective, has undergone a remarkable transformation in meaning since it was borrowed from the French, who had inherited it from Latin, in which *nescius* (combining a negative prefix and the verb *scire*, 'to know') meant ignorant. Once arrived in England, some time in the later twelfth century, nice, probably pronounced 'nee-say' or 'nays-uh', was used to refer to a foolish or frivolous person. It subsequently went from meaning 'timid' in the thirteenth century to 'fussy' in the fourteenth. In the fifteenth century it had the sense of 'delicate' or 'dainty'; in the sixteenth 'precise' or 'careful', preserved in such terms as 'a nice distinction' and 'nice and early', but it could also denote 'difficult' or 'strange'. In the seventeenth century, it continued to function as both pejorative (as in 'coy' or 'over-refined', even 'wanton') and appreciative ('modest'), depending on context. By the mid-eighteenth century it had come to mean 'agreeable' or 'delightful' and by 1830 had added the denotations 'kind' and 'thoughtful'. In 1914 it could still be used in two differing senses in one article in *The Times*: 'the maiden ladies in *Cranford* are too nice [fastidious] in their ways to eat oranges except in the privacy of the bed chamber'; and further on, 'to the plain man no peach ever grown can come up to a nice [agreeably tasty] juicy orange'. The adverb nicely, as in 'nicely browned on both sides', still retains two of nice's shifting senses, conflating 'precisely' and 'agreeably'; in the 1920s it was used in **society** circles as an adjectival euphemism for inebriated ('She's nicely this evening'), probably starting out as an abbreviation of 'nicely cooked/done/lit up' or similar.

By now widely seen as emblematic for fatuous or muted approval, lukewarm enthusiasm, blanket complacency, the adjective was mocked by Jane Austen in *Northanger Abbey* in 1817: 'This is a very nice day and we are taking a very nice walk, and you are two very nice young ladies. Oh! It is a very nice word indeed! It does for everything.' In 1926, Fowler, the prescriptive, and proscriptive, grammarian par excellence, dismissed the term as '. . . too great a favourite with the ladies, who have charmed out of it all its individuality and converted it into a mere diffuser of vague and mild agreeableness'. Only in 1934 did lexicographers at Merriam-Webster stop labelling the use of the word as 'colloquial' in their dictionaries. It still epitomises an English inability to state things clearly or express emotion openly and straightforwardly, and the *Bloomsbury Good Word Guide* suggests that it is often best to replace it with an appropriate synonym, such as 'a pleasant [not nice] afternoon' or an 'attractive [not nice] garden'. Yet while the n-word is seemingly almost empty of significance, it manages to remain hugely significant, perhaps because it is so useful in so many day-to-day contexts. Among thousands of typical usages are homely, straightforward appreciations like 'I felt nice and cosy', 'that bread smells nice', 'his mother sounded very nice on the phone'. Even with the addition of an intensifying adverb, nice still conveys only a diluted version of enthusiasm: 'he's really an awfully/exceptionally/extremely/incredibly/jolly/really/terribly/very nice chap', and sometimes the effect is double-edged or ambiguous, especially if the preceding adverb is 'perfectly' or 'thoroughly'. It can be employed for **understatement**: 'It has not been a particularly nice experience', and for expressing doubts and reservations: 'I'm sure she's perfectly nice really', 'He's nice enough, I suppose, but I don't think I want to have dinner with him.' 'Nice!' and 'Very nice!' may often function as ironic interjections, while for Bohemians nice has long been a pejorative, signalled in speech by exaggerated intonation: 'very *nice* people . . . but outside their tiny world of consecrated mediocrity, nothing exists whatever' (Colin MacInnes). There are still people who refer to behaviour being 'not quite nice', in other words unseemly, though the phrase smacks of prissiness and invites the mocking pronunciation 'naice'. My friends in the City of London tell me that when heard in the Square Mile, 'nice guy' (as in the US 'nice guys finish last') or 'nice **bloke**' is invariably pitying, as conveyed by 'Nice guy – but he goes home at six/but he's seriously henpecked.'

Ethnolinguists have demonstrated that for the French, being nice (*aimable, sympathique*) is less important than for the English and Australians – being *engagé* (involved, concerned, committed), for example, can count higher in Gallic estimation. For most of us, however, it signals the crucial importance, if you live in one of the most socially stratified, complex and diverse societies on earth, of being able to rub along with one another, of being kind, polite and considerate, or at the very least, inoffensive. Here is retired and temporarily disabled *Guardian* editor Peter Preston waiting outside a London courtroom with a random group of strangers: 'I can't lift my arms properly, so somebody hangs my coat up, then puts it on me at the end of the day. Somebody calls a lift. The court officials apologise for delays as though they mean it, and soon know us all by our first names . . . young men in t-shirts and trainers, mobile-phone junkies, Nigerians, Arabs, West Indians, Cockneys. . .they are still utterly nice in that old, familiar, English way.'

'Apples and rice' was the old east London rhyming slang equivalent, from the days when both were regarded as delicacies or associated with celebrations such as weddings; it was often shortened to simply 'apples' and in this form is still occasionally encountered, though those saying it may be ignorant of the derivation. 'Chicken and rice' is a more recent variant, and the obscure phrase or possible pseudonym 'Obie Trice' has also been mentioned in online discussions. However strenuously the slang devotees and we sophisticates may try to avoid the word in its standard form, it keeps on cropping up. I found myself just this morning attempting to bond with the neighbours, unbelievably, by way of 'Turned out nice again, hasn't it?'

Oi

'Our customer is more design-led than label or trend-led. He probably doesn't like to admit it, though, or he'd look like a knobhead,' says Steve Sanderson, who runs Manchester's Oi Polloi boutique. His shop's name is of course a play on the snooty pejorative 'hoi polloi', in the sense of the lumpen masses (it's Greek for 'the many'), and 'Oi!' the defining, inarticulate cry of the English **yob**.

For some jaundiced commentators (I'm among them), the little interjection 'oi' sums up the brutishly unreconstructed machismo (if that isn't too grand a word) of a certain kind of Englishman, epitomised in three catchphrases in particular: 'Oi, you lookin' at my bird?' (relentlessly mocked in a series of punning cartoons by *Private Eye* magazine), the 'Oi, you, you're barred' of the pub landlord, and 'Oi, fancy a shag?' which anthropologist Kate Fox sees as a key term in the repertoire of English masculinity. In the late nineties, comedian Harry Enfield's boorish characters the Self-Righteous Brothers would end each of their pub tirades at absent celebrities with the admonition 'Oi [name of celebrity]! No!' On the real streets of twenty-first-century England, 'Oi mate!' is not absolutely invariably a challenge;

it can occasionally precede a solicitous 'need any drugs?', for example.

So resonant was the word – if it qualifies as such – that it inspired its own pop music genre, following on from punk at the end of the 1970s. The main exponents of this ultra-abbreviated, high-volume, thrashing-guitar-and-chanting style were the Gonads, the Cockney Rejects, the Oppressed and the 4-Skins. The movement's rallying cry, nicely appropriating a Nazi slogan, was 'Strength thru Oi!' Its whole stance was ambivalent, endorsing punk's glowering 'loser' pose, while dispensing completely with its (albeit disguised) subtleties and sensitivities, and seeming simultaneously to mimic, mock and espouse the mindless aggression of the skinheads of a decade earlier. Perhaps the Oi! bands and their followers were, like many outsiders, ironically adopting the language of their oppressors, the policemen, teachers and irate parents who told them 'Oi, get yer hair cut!', which they did, shaving it to the bone. An ephemeral fad, Oi! the 'music' disappeared, bequeathing oi the word to a new generation of hooligans, brickies and mockney-affecting journalists.

The menacing, provocative Oi! *tout court* should not be confused with the winkingly familiar and/or suggestive 'Oi, oi!', as in the expression, 'oi-oi saveloy'. The saveloy (a red smoked sausage sold in fast-food takeaways), like the iconic chipolata, has become established as a homely phallic symbol. Describing Nice 'n' Spicy, one of six Spice Girls tribute bands touring in 1997, Stephen Armstrong noted appreciatively, 'They smoke like chimneys, swear like troopers, dance a bit better than the originals and scream, "Oi, oi, saveloy!" at passing men.' Just recently Fleur Britten, having joined guests at a house party, disrobes for a dare: 'Soon, though, I'm tittering like a Japanese schoolgirl as I adjust to the Carry On hilarity of it all. Ooh, matron. Oi, oi, saveloy.'

Used thus, the oi-phrase is an example of what linguists used to call 'nursery talk' being appropriated or imitated by adults (the high-flown term for this is 'hypocorism', from the learned Greek for a child's pet name). It helps enforce a cheery democratic mateyness or introduce a cheekily provocative tone into a po-faced gathering. Like the jocular expressions of assent 'okey-dokey artichokey' and 'aye-aye shepherd's pie' it probably originated among primary or junior school pupils, but during the early 1990s was adopted as a catchphrase by grown-ups, particularly those working in advertising, the media and finance in London.

Oik

In 2004, Dr Digby Anderson, retired director of the right-wing think tank the Social Affairs Unit, published a book ('crass and patronising' the *New Statesman* called it) entitled *All Oiks Now: the Unnoticed Surrender of Middle England*. The publicity for the book read, 'Once Middle England was as immovable as a rock. It was a minority but a sizeable one. Now, however, as far as public life is concerned, it has surrendered to the oiks.' Commenting on Anderson's polemic, vicar's wife, novelist, broadcaster and right-wing controversialist Anne Atkins gushed revealingly, 'I want to stand up for the oik . . . I think it's wonderful, for instance, that a lot of the taxi drivers who drive me around when I'm doing media work can afford a house in a village in Spain.'

When, in 1950, Anthony Buckeridge's fictional schoolboy hero Jennings arrived at Linbury Court Preparatory School, he was shown around by Venables, two years his senior: 'You new oiks are dim at picking things up.'

Coupling class prejudice and sexism – there is no female equivalent – combined with condescension, hostility and implied self-satisfaction, this abrupt and enduring little word conjures up a very English nexus of nastiness. It has usually been employed to disparage or dismiss someone perceived as socially inferior and irritating – perhaps simply because they are socially inferior – or to label as uncouth, coarse and/or vulgar. Typically used by public schoolchildren or Oxbridge students to refer to 'townies' or pupils from state schools, sometimes to younger fellow pupils too (often prefaced with 'spotty little'), oik has also been part of an adult repertoire of snobbery and spite.

In their 1968 glossary of Hobson-Jobson colonial-era slang, Yule and Burnell defined 'competition-wallah' as 'any scholarship oik who got into the service without going through Haileybury' (a public school specialising in the unintellectual but biddable). The 'scholarship boys', sometimes 'scholarship oiks', were also a feature of the pre- and post-war years, when a few managed the transition to universities without having the means to pay fees. In the 1960s, there were grumblings about 'grammar-school oik(s)', as members of the elite state-school system threatened the assumed superiority of public schoolboys who were not always their intellectual equals.

The Times highlighted the return of class-conscious language in 2007: 'The *Daily Mirror* uses the words "Tory toff" as a prefix almost every time the Conservative leader's name appears. Imagine if *The Daily Telegraph* used "Labour oik" before every mention of John Prescott. Inverted snobbery is just as offensive as traditional snobbery.' To confuse the picture slightly, Will Buckley in the *Observer* in 2008 pilloried 'the man who would be Chancellor, George Osborne . . . who changed his name from Gideon to George to gain admission into the Bullingdon Club at Oxford University because they were no more likely to vote in a Gideon than they would a woman. Having gone to all that effort did his new friends call him George? Don't be absurd, they called him "oik".' (In fact he was so called because he had been a pupil at St Paul's, the cerebral London day school, rather than the *ne plus ultra*, Eton.) The word caused consternation again when, in June 2010, Labour lord (former defense minister, erstwhile philosopher and chartered accountant) John Gilbert informed his fellow peers that if proposed Coalition Government reforms turned the Upper House into an elected chamber 'you would get the sort of oik – and for Hansard's benefit, oik is spelt OIK – that could not get into the Commons, Europe, the Scottish Parliament or the Welsh Assembly and probably not into a half-decent county council.'

Earlier alternative spellings of the o-word were 'oick' and 'hoick'. No one is sure how and where the term originated – it was first recorded in the late nineteenth century, and some guess that it began as an imitation of the sound of inarticulate speech; others that it is from Greek *oikon*, 'family' or 'household' – or how it might be related to the Australian 'ocker', another resonant cultural keyword signifying a boorish male. 'Ockerism' and 'ockerdom', however, quite unlike oik, can have appreciative overtones of comradeship and unaffectedness. Oik has also been confused with 'hoick', meaning to spit, and 'oink', the sound made by pigs, but any link is unproven. It has also been used ironically or self-effacingly, by working-class males or journalists affecting demotic mateyness, to refer to themselves; as an advertising executive said to me in 1986, 'I'm constantly amazed that a couple of oiks like me and [his business partner, also of humble origins, also with a strong London accent] have managed to make it.' In the yuppie ascendancy of the later 1980s, OIK was an acronym for (a person or a couple) with 'one income and kids', as opposed to the better-off OINK ('one income, no kids') and DINK ('dual or double income, no kids').

It's important to note that, *pace* Digby Anderson, the classic oik is essentially an obnoxious *individual*, as opposed to the 'chav' (vogue label of 2004, originally a traveller's term of address or endearment, from a French nickname for a young fox), who represents an imagined social grouping, a troublesome, truculent, feckless, shameless underclass delighting in petty criminality and conspicuous consumption (of, inter alia, illicit substances, electronic stimuli, pimped technology and 'bling'). The revival of oik and the adoption of chav have assisted in the sneering and jeering at the lower orders that characterised the noughties. Superficially a standing joke, at a deeper level this crude version of us-and-them class distinction points up the paradoxes of a culture for which fame and gain have displaced all other values.

One

Oblique, obtuse, evasive, provocative – or commendably self-effacing? As the theologian and crime-writer Ronald Knox put it, '. . . Suave *Politeness*, tempering bigot *Zeal*/Corrected *I believe* to *One does feel* . . .' One of the things that is sometimes thought to set English English apart from its Scottish, Welsh, Irish and overseas cousins is the high-flown, possibly snooty, occasionally downright affected use of the little impersonal pronoun 'one'. In September 1955, a *Times* correspondent rather reluctantly agreed to provide his readers with a 'man's eye view' of a women's purview: 'Frankly, one had expected to be one of a very few men looking in at the international wool fashion festival yester-day, and accordingly one had nerved oneself for something of an ordeal.' More portentously, in April 1969, the politician, controversialist and man of letters Enoch Powell stated his belief that 'in myths and institutions the individual con-sciousness is absorbed in that of the group: the nation is the body in whose blood stream one is oneself a single corpuscle, the collective mind in whose thoughts, for an instant, one shares oneself'.

If one does decide to use one in this way, the poser has

been to decide which possessive pronoun to follow it with: 'one's', 'his', 'his or her', 'her', 'their' – or even 'your'? The American humorist James Thurber pronounced on the subject in his *Ladies' and Gentlemen's Guide to Modern English Usage*: 'Such a sentence as "One loves one's friends" is considered by some persons to be stilted and over-formalized, and such persons insist that "One loves his friends" is permissible. It is not permissible, however, because "one" is indefinite and "his" is definite and the combination is rhetorically impossible.' Thurber described this solecism as an example of hendiadys, which it isn't, but in any case objections to 'one . . . his' these days are more likely to invoke sexism than faulty rhetoric or grammar. I have taught learners of English that in British English 'one' should be followed in formal or academic discourse only by 'one's', but in less formal contexts with 'their', as this is the only neuter form available. In American English I would recommend they substitute 'his' or 'her', or preferably 'his or her', though it is cumbersome.

One as numeral comes from a presumed prehistoric oinos, via Old Germanic *ainoz* (equivalent to Latin *unus*). Old English had *an*, but used *man* as a generic neuter, and this evolved into Middle English 'me', though there are relatively few examples of this in the records. By Shakespeare's time 'one', usually spelled 'oon', had been adopted as the pronoun of choice (he has 'Why, may one ask?' for example). It is interesting that now, however, we are, as so often, out of step with our nearest neighbours. The French and Germans have their equivalent generic pronouns, *on* and *man* respectively, and these are still used to generalise without any of the overtones of patrician conceit that cling to the English usage: Spanish has *uno*, which is restricted to formal contexts. The modern English tendency, even in academic

discourse, has been to move away from affectations of gen-
derless neutrality and towards personal responsibility, usually
by the substitution of 'we' or 'you', or in the case of opinions,
'I'. It seems to have been the Victorians, clergymen in particular, who gave one a bad name by overusing it in
expressions of pomposity and bombast, its reputation com-
pounded by its identification with hoity-toity-sounding
observations by the royals in the twentieth century. Thus,
generally speaking, one substituted for the first person – like
Margaret Thatcher's invoking of the royal 'we' – sounds
worse than one in place of the third person. 'Oneself' is still
fairly common in written discourse and has proved
extremely useful for journalistic pronouncements, especially
sweeping ones, where there is no preceding subject speci-
fied, as 'it is hard to reconcile oneself to such harsh
measures', 'the traditional British virtue of keeping oneself
to oneself', 'the main intention was to please oneself', etc.
Many 'ordinary people' nonetheless still agonise over the
use of one, typically asking each other (on online message
boards) or 'authorities' (teachers, lexicographers) if it is correct. The standard linguist's response is to invoke not
'correctness' but the two benchmarks of 'intelligibility' – is it
generally understandable? – and 'appropriacy' – does its tone
fit with the setting in which it is being used? Unless the
intention is ironic detachment or self-mockery, it is increasingly hard to satisfy this second criterion.

Permissive

On 19 June 1969, the then Labour Chancellor of the Exchequer Roy Jenkins announced, in a speech in Abingdon, Oxfordshire, that 'the permissive society has been allowed to become a dirty phrase. A better phrase is the civilised society.' His attempt to banish a contentious cliché with an anodyne alternative did not work. On 4 May 1970, Mr Peter Fry, Honourable Conservative Member for Wellingborough, succeeded in getting a parliamentary debate on the permissive society, which he introduced with the following words: 'I beg to move, that this House views with grave concern the continuing decline of moral standards and the increases of violence, hooliganism, drug taking and obscenity and the consequent undermining of family life; and calls upon Her Majesty's Government to enlist the support of parents, religious leaders, school and university teachers, broadcasters and social workers to give help to those members of the rising generation who may be in need of adequate discipline and a better example.'

Permissive society was a formulation first used by US psychologists and later sociologists in the 1950s. It crossed the Atlantic in 1967, first attested in *Punch*, then in January 1968 in the *Listener*. Permissive, which formerly could mean 'done with permission' or 'optional' as well as its current sense of 'not forbidding or preventing/tolerant', came to us in the fifteenth century from the past participle of Latin *permittere*, literally 'to let through or let by', which also gave permissible, 'that can be or ought to be allowed'. In 1975, *Permissive Society* was used as the title both of a Mike Leigh film, dealing with fraught sexual relationships, and an episode of the TV comedy *Rising Damp*, dealing with Scrabble, smuggled fiancées, double dates and thoughts of suicide. It has since been borrowed twice to name music ensembles: once in 1991 by the pseudonymous Mike Fab-Gere for a novelty cover-version band, more recently for an indie band from Manchester. In the interim it established itself as an indispensable label, reached for by conservatives and non-aligned cultural analysts, but almost never by the liberal/left, whenever the post-swinging-sixties 'sexual revolution' or 'new morality' (to cite two other – no, three other – glib catchphrases) were under discussion. Like 'affluent', in J. K. Galbraith's 1958 title *The Affluent Society* ('In the affluent society, no sharp distinction can be made between luxuries and necessaries'), permissive is a watershed word, marking a profound change in attitudes and behaviours, or at least marking the recognition of this change. While 'affluent' and 'affluence', like Harold Macmillan's spivvish Americanism 'you never had it so good', signalled the transit from a society of scarcity, via self-imposed **austerity**, to a society of plenty, so permissive and permissiveness epitomise the shift from a culture of restraint and repression to one of moral relativism and unfettered indulgence. Progressives and liberals do sometimes use the words, but usually in a slightly different context, when for example referring to themselves guiltily as 'permissive parents'.

Whether we ourselves are liberal or illiberal, we are now living in a society in which instant gratification, hedonism and an ethical free-for-all undoubtedly predominate. Words like 'severe', 'strict' and 'stern' are just no longer heard (and nor is the antonym 'repressive', except in connection with alien regimes), there are no acknowledged authority figures – let alone universally acknowledged authority figures – left in England, Philip Pullman, Lynne Truss and – heaven help us – Richard Dawkins probably coming closest. Though loaded, permissive nowadays sounds somewhat too flimsy a word to carry all the connotations with which it has been freighted.

See also **society**

Pluck

Ninety-four-year-old great-grandmother Edith Buck of Brierfield, Lancashire, attacked and drove off a burglar who was trying to break into her home in the middle of the night – and said she'd do it again if she had to. Local councillor Sheena Dunn praised Mrs Buck for her actions, saying, 'Edith is a very plucky lady . . . it is wonderful that people have this sort of courage but it is awful that they need it.' The story is one among dozens, if not hundreds, of 'pensioner confronts burglar'/ 'granny defies muggers' stories to appear in the English press in recent years. It is principally in this context, or in sports reporting, that the old words 'pluck' and 'plucky' live on. Humble Mrs Buck was pre-dated by seventy-five years by posh Mrs Bruce . . . or rather the Hon. Mrs V. A. Bruce, lady motorist, who drove 9,000 miles solo from John O'Groats to Morocco in 1927, a feat celebrated in an advertisement for Ovaltine: 'Roads sheeted with ice, blizzards and fog were encountered but nothing daunted this plucky little woman, whose motto seemed to be "Onwards, ever onwards."'

In fact pluck and plucky in particular have, even more than their close relations 'grit', 'vim', 'nerve', etc., played an essential role in journalistic evocations of heroism since the nineteenth century. At first, in the early 1800s, they were identified with the lower classes and specifically with pugilists and their fans, the usage having derived from the 'pluck' in the sense of the guts pulled from the carcass of an animal, signifying, like 'spleen', 'kidney' and 'heart', the essential spirit. An 1806 court report describes a woman's part in a tavern brawl: 'Mary Hurlston flew at him again with the ferocity of a tigress; kicked him about the belly, and with all the energy of slaughter-house eloquence, threatened to tear out his pluck.' Although the losing crews in the Oxford–Cambridge boat race and the Thames Regatta were annually commended for their pluck, Sir Walter Scott condemned the word as 'blackguardly' in 1827, and it was apparently not used by any but the 'fastest' ladies until after the Crimean War. In *Tom Brown's Schooldays*, published in 1857, the 'big boys' say of the young hero, 'he must be a good plucked one'. Generally referring to the courage or daring of the underdog, not the heroism of the superman, pluck was often used in the later nineteenth century in relation to the armed forces – there are hundreds of examples in the populist *Penny Illustrated Paper*, celebrating the merits of a young soldier or a particular regiment. There is an enduring link between youth and pluck. Lieutenants and below were routinely referred to as 'plucky', whereas higher ranks were more often deemed 'courageous'. Jingoism regularly made use of the same terms ('the pluck of the Anglo-Saxon race'/ 'native pluck') and they have been used of foreigners, but in an interestingly ambivalent way, seeming to mingle admiration with condescension, as when *The Times* wrote in 1897 of the Greek king: 'Britons always admire pluck . . . though the expedition was in the teeth of the opposition of the great Powers of Europe, it was undeniably plucky of stalwart and handsome King George to send a Greek army Corps to the succour of the Cretan Christians.'

After 1900, the words were more widely used, in relation now also to civilians and women. Pluck and plucky echo through advertisements, military logs, diaries and broadcasts, evoking not only acts of bravery but the qualities of readiness and resolution. Children's author Enid Blyton was very fond of 'plucky' and it appears in many of her stories, more often applied to Anne, the feminine girl in the Famous Five when she managed to summon up courage, than to Georgina (aka 'George'), the tomboy. In addition to pensioners, the p-words are nowadays typically bestowed upon children ('the plucky youngster kept smiling'), especially if sick or disabled, animals ('Plucky pooch Beau, who was shot in the head TWICE with a crossbow, is looking forward to a new home after a miracle recovery') and, as always, potential or actual losers in sports contests ('plucky Paula Radcliffe/Bangor'). To 'pluck up one's courage' brings us back to the base verb, which comes via Old English *pluccian* from late Latin *piluccare*, 'to pull out hair'.

See also **The Few**

Pooh

In his jocular *fin de siècle* ballad *The Aesthete*, W. S. Gilbert wrote of his eponymous anti-hero: 'Of course you will pooh-pooh whatever's fresh and new, and declare it crude and mean, / And that Art stopped short in the cultivated court of the Empress Josephine.' Ninety-one years later, 'General Melchett' (played by Stephen Fry) in the TV comedy series *Blackadder Goes Forth* embarks on a peroration:

> General Melchett: Is this true, Blackadder? Did Captain Darling pooh-pooh you?
>
> Captain Blackadder: Well, perhaps a little.
>
> General Melchett: Well, then, damn it all! What more evidence do you need? The pooh-poohing alone is a court-martial offence!
>
> Captain Blackadder: I can assure you, sir, that the pooh-poohing was purely circumstantial.
>
> General Melchett: Well, I hope so, Blackadder. You know, if there's one thing I've learnt from being in the Army, it's never ignore a pooh-pooh. I knew a major who got pooh-poohed, made the mistake of ignoring the pooh-pooh. He pooh-poohed it! Fatal error! 'Cos it turned

out all along that the soldier who pooh-poohed him had been pooh-poohing a lot of other officers who pooh-poohed their pooh-poohs. In the end, we had to disband the regiment. Morale totally destroyed . . . by pooh-pooh!

The double expulsion of air is a very English expression of scorn, showing up our national propensity to dismiss out of hand anything and everything that smacks of excessive seriousness, avant-garde 'continental' notions, strong feelings openly expressed . . . erm, in fact, at one time or another almost everything. Whether this brisk dismissiveness reveals commendable stoicism, demotic irreverence or corrosive, subversive cynicism – or just blind insensitivity – is an interesting subject for consideration – but probably not on the part of pooh-poohers.

As long ago as 1593, the plosive puff appears in the records as a single noise, expressing exasperation and contempt: Shakespeare has it in the form 'puh'. In the reduplicated form, still used as an exclamation, it was first attested in 1697, then as a verb in 1827. 'Pah!', a shorter, possibly more aggressive version of the sound, came to be associated with impatience and disdain as expressed by the proud and privileged from the seventeenth to the nineteenth century, but was not reduplicated (into 'pah pah!') and is now archaic. It is probably the same sound symbolism that has given us 'poobah', a name that has come to be used – in the USA perhaps more than in the UK – as a mocking title for someone self-important and/or high-ranking, who acts in several capacities at once, and/or who has limited authority while taking impressive titles, from Pooh-Bah, the haughty character in Gilbert (again) and Sullivan's *Mikado*.

'Poo' meaning faeces or to defecate was recorded in

family and playground slang in the UK and Australia from around 1960; it became an acceptable term for general use in the mid-1980s, sometimes also in the form 'poo-poo(s)', and by extension can be used adjectivally as in 'completely poo trainers' or 'that film was utterly poo'. The variant 'poop' probably originated in the US, where it was first recorded in this sense in 1948. Both forms are either imitative of the sound of breaking wind and/or defecating itself, or of blowing out the cheeks in reaction to a bad smell.

The 'pooh' in Winnie the Pooh does not originate in an English toilet fixation but does sound like an example of the baby talk we love to imitate, which was probably the origin of the combining form '-poo(s)' used in terms of endearment or teasing ('Suzie-poos'; 'icky-poo'). In fact A. A. Milne's character borrowed the pet name for a swan that the author's son had seen on holiday (while 'Winnie', short for Winnipeg, was a Canadian black bear who lived at London Zoo from 1919).

'You're getting good at this – extra poo tonight' promised a character in Caryl Churchill's 1987 play *Serious Money*. Here the word refers to champagne, first nicknamed 'shampoo' and then abbreviated by Sloane Rangers and Yuppies. Those homophobic insults 'puff' (attested as tramps' argot in the eighteenth century), 'poof', 'poofter' and the 1960s variant once favoured by *Private Eye* magazine, 'poove', are also quite unrelated and probably come, despite the many alternative folk etymologies on offer, from the French *poufiasse*, meaning a prostitute or depraved person of either sex.

Posh

In November 2002, the *Sun* reported that footballer's wife 'Posh Spice' Victoria Beckham had launched a legal bid to stop second division football club Peterborough United from registering its nickname Posh as a trademark. The former Spice Girl claimed the word had become synonymous with her. '*Sun* readers,' the paper affirmed, 'back the club, which has used the name for eighty years.' This little word epitomises both the English obsession with status distinctions and the jokey tone in which such a contentious subject is often addressed.

Fictional characters in the novel *The Diary of a Nobody*, published in 1892, and the musical *Lady Madcap*, playing in London in 1904, sported the name Posh, and in a 1918 *Punch* cartoon a young swell is seen explaining that it is 'slang for swish'. The first use of the word in *The Times* was in a crime report from May 1923, headlined 'The Taxicab Murder'. 'A walking stick was left at the scene of the crime, which the murderer left behind after shooting the driver, which belonged to his friend Eddie Vivian. He said . . . that he went out with Eddie's stick because he wanted to be "posh".' In 1935 in the same paper the use of the word, which still appeared between quotation marks, was excused, as 'inevitably the idiom of the younger generation creeps in'.

The popular derivation, from the initial letters of 'Port Out, Starboard Home' allegedly affixed to the cabin doors of first-class passengers on P&O Orient Line steamships, is certainly false, as demonstrated by, among others, word-buff Michael Quinion in his 2005 book, which took the phrase as its title. Posh seems to have been used in low-life slang for some time before it was first recorded in a dictionary of 1889 with the principal meaning 'money' and the subsidiary sense of 'dandy'. It may be the same word, in the form 'push', meaning 'swanky, showy', that featured in Edwardian upper-class student slang ('quite the most push thing at Cambridge' was P. G. Wodehouse's description of a fancy waistcoat, from 1903). The ultimate origin, then, is obscure: in the Romany language, which was a rich source of pre-twentieth-century argot, *posh* could mean 'half', often referring to half a shilling/crown/sovereign, etc., so may have come to denote money in general, then the trappings of wealth.

In 1966, cuddly TV presenter and 'personality' Michael Aspel was carpeted by the BBC for selling records of elocution lessons featuring his voice and that of Jean Metcalfe, the ads for which implied, the corporation said, that broadcasting required a posh voice. Like class-consciousness itself, and like the assertively upper-class accents it often described, the word posh seemed to fall out of fashion after the end of the 1960s, only to reassert itself at the new millennium. At the end of the noughties, it took on a renewed importance with David Cameron's accession to the leadership of the Tory party and fellow Old Etonian Alexander Boris de Pfeffel Johnson's election as London mayor. As a literal synonym of privileged/wealthy/upmarket it is usefully inoffensive. Very frequently, however, it is used ironically, as in references to 'posh nosh' (typically very expensive sausages), and what online gossip site Popbitch dubs the 'too-posh-to-push brigade' – pampered mothers who opt for Caesareans at private hospitals. Reviewing Joanna Lumley mocking her own accent in a 2005 TV commercial, the *Independent on Sunday* commented, 'In the 1960s, After Eights, Harvey's Sherry and Cockburn's Port were sold to Mrs Buckets everywhere on class – the idea that posh people bought them . . . if you want to do posh now it has to be spoofy and retro.'

In pop culture contexts posh has proved to be handy as an antonym of 'chav', especially in the numerous test-yourself quizzes claiming to assess the underclass/toff factor. From around 2000, 'posho' in UK campus slang has denoted a fellow student perceived as from a wealthy or privileged background (the noisy-and-posh are known as 'yahs' and 'rahs'), while the litigious Victoria Beckham should note that in the same circles, 'Posh 'n' Becks' is rhyming slang for 'sex'.

Pseud

Though the designation has changed over time, the implication remains the same: if the English distrust, fear and in some cases despise the intellectual, they utterly abhor the would-be or phoney intellectual. In an environment where even to be seen to be earnest is (still to some extent) a social solecism, and where (until recently) prevailing attitudes were influenced by upper-class and public-school philistinism, a cerebral demeanour or a continental delight in theoretical debate are definite no-nos. Even the term 'sophisticated' still has an un-English ring to it, and until the *Sunday Times* adopted it in the 1990s as the title of its arts section, the word 'culture' was only ever used about other nationalities.

In *The British Character*, his series of caricatures illustrating English attitudes published in 1938, the cartoonist Pont entitles one drawing 'The Importance of Not Being Intellectual'. It shows a room full of well-dressed people all desperately edging away from a glowering, slightly scruffy male with bushy eyebrows and wispy beard, apparently waiting to hold forth on some **serious** subject. Curiously, on the same page is a little sketch of a grotesquely pointy-headed ('egghead'?) Jewish-looking male wearing thick-lensed spectacles, presumably a second version of the intellectual. In yet a third take on the theme, reproduced on the facing page, a Dr Bronowski-like figure waving a cigarette fixes the reader with an owlish glare and demands, 'Tell me, are you a believer in elemental disproportion or de-energised statics, or do you just stick to the Propkoffer theory?' Under the heading 'Political Apathy', Pont also has a pipe-smoking, clubbable type ignoring a gesticulating, dishevelled activist (wearing a dark shirt, the badge of the thinker, the do-gooder and what an elderly acquaintance labelled the 'brown-bread-and-bicycle-clip brigade').

In the 1950s, public-school slang reflected schoolboyish prejudices, and the words applied to bright, hard-working, possibly unsporty fellows – 'swot', 'brainbox', 'weed' – were pejorative. Anyone who flaunted their own intelligence or stylishness was a swank or a show-off. For educated adults since the 1930s, 'bogus' (originally a nineteenth-century nickname for a counterfeiting machine) had been a key word in a repertoire of contempt, to the extent that intellectuals (itself virtually a foreign term until the end of the 1980s) used it themselves. 'Sham' and 'phoney' were in the same way easy accusations to level in a society whose categories were thought to be rigidly definable. 'Highbrow', with its middle- and low- counterparts, was another controversial designation during the 1950s, applied, often enviously or ironically, to the hapless intellectual.

In colloquial speech, pseudo was the abbreviated form that found favour from the 1930s, either as a noun or adjective: the noun pseud (formerly an abbreviation for pseudonym printed after an author's pen name) appeared in the 1950s and was consolidated by its use from 1961 in the satirical magazine *Private Eye*, whose feature 'Pseuds Corner', in which instances of pretentiousness sent in by readers are reproduced, is still running (now enhanced by a 'Pseuds Corporate' section reprinting samples of business jargon). The original pseud(o)- as combining form is from Greek *pseudes*, 'false', from *pseudein*, 'to lie'. It was imported into English usage in the Middle English period to signify counterfeit, artificial and false, or an imitation.

'Pseudy' is a more modern dismissal, used across the **Anglosphere** to ridicule such irritants as the language of wine snobs, but there are faint signs that the tendency to deride the thinker, though not the poseur, is receding. Current student slang still calls a show-off a 'ledge' (from the ironic 'legend in his/her own lifetime/lunchtime/mind'), and in UK street slang the adjective 'neeky' (from 'nerd' and 'geek') describes some-one who is over-serious and less than stylish. Grown-ups tell the closeted that they 'should get out more', and big-heads are said to be 'up themselves'. But in the globalised virtual world in which many of us now spend work and leisure time, the nerd, the geek and the wimp (all originally imports from US slang) rule supreme. In the media, if not yet in the academy, since the arrival of Australian pioneers Clive James and Germaine Greer, public displays of erudition and intellectual posturing are tolerated, and even when they fall embarrass-ingly flat (everything in the now defunct magazine *Modern Review*, Stephen Fry debating with Christopher Hitchens, Martin Amis denouncing cliché, Will Self), not much is made of it. Pretension and pomposity are seen as necessary tricks of the trade for pundits and politicians, and self-promotion is a requisite rather than a violation of good manners.

'A bit of a/a dreadful/frightful pseud' can still be heard from time to time but sound a little dated (I'm told it sur-vives in Indian English, though): the most recent examples I can find in print have been directed at the Slovene stand-up philosopher Slavoj Žižek, so *plus ça change* . . .

Quaint

Describing the grand opening of the Royal Albert Hall on 30 March 1871, *The Times* correspondent focused on the yeoman guards standing outside: 'Their halberds, their Tudor frills, the scarlet uniform and plentiful gold lace, the quaint black velvet caps with circlets of gay-coloured ribands added a quaint tone of medievalism to the otherwise specially eighteenth century spectacle.' The word 'quaint' epitomises the ambivalence of the English towards the odd, the whimsical (see **whimsy**), the recondite. It is not quite appreciative and not quite pejorative, yet a little of both. It may be simultaneously affectionate and condescending. As a qualifying adjective it is also, like **nice**, a little vague in a typically English way. It describes the charmingly peculiar, the olde-worlde curious, sometimes the poignant, as in Sebastian Barker's 'Lines for my Unborn Son': 'Look, the millions dead, their quaint, old-fashioned dress / (The sunlight glinting on the monk-smoothed stone)' or Ted Hughes's 'The quaint courtly language / Of wingbones and talons.' In my mother's mouth it was nearly always an oblique disapproval. 'You do have some quaint notions!' would cut short any attempt to discuss the then taboo subjects of spirituality, gender politics or popular music. In the gently damning 'she has a rather quaint sense of responsibility', the word would mean skewed, inappropriate.

My mother would not have recognised 'queynte', which, apart from being an industrial/techno band from Norwich, is a rude pun (you can order a T-shirt with the 'how queynte!' motif). Several words beginning with the qu- sound have had sexual designations – 'quim', 'quiff', 'quondam', 'quean', 'quoit' – and much has been made of the fact that Chaucer used 'queynte' in the fourteenth century for the female pudendum, but the connection between the two words and meanings – if there is any – remains obscure. The standard term was imported from French in the thirteenth century with the meanings 'clever' and 'finely wrought'. Its original form 'cointe' derives from Latin *cognitus*, 'known'. The sense of 'old-fashioned but charming' was first recorded at the end of the eighteenth century. Between 1950 and 1970, quaint was used just over 1,000 times in *The Times*, but it was used nearly 10,000 times in the same paper between 1870 and 1919, attesting to the Victorian and Edwardian fascination with the antique and kitsch. Like many of the charged keywords of Englishness, quaint is almost impossible to translate exactly into neighbouring languages: Spanish has *pintoresco*; Italian *bizzarro*, *antiquato*; German *malerisch*, *urig* and *kurios*; and French, depending on context, *pittoresque*, *desuet*, *au charme veillot*, but none of these captures exactly the nuances of the English word.

Queer

'They must have thought me, a Townie from York, a queer fish, so innocent of all things rural but apart from some initial teasing we got on very well together and I soon became one of the gang . . .' reminisces former master mariner Richard Crow (born 1915). V. S. Naipaul, up at Oxford in 1950, wrote to his family in Trinidad, 'The English are a queer people . . . the longer you live in England, the more queer they appear . . . so orderly and yet so adventurous . . . so ruttish, so courageous.' I have noticed recently that middle-class English 'natives', even of the *bien pensant* liberal tendency, are starting once again to use the word queer as it used to be understood – to mean odd, unsettling, as in 'a queer sensation', 'queer notion', etc. This comes after three decades during which the term has been appropriated by the gay community, first ironically, then assertively as a positive synonym for homosexual. It had of course been previously a euphemism or code word, like gay itself ('Something quick in his eye and ear / Gave a hint that he might be queer' – John Masefield in a poem from 1946), but often employed pityingly or simply pejoratively. 'Perhaps he's queer?' wondered the bumbling hero of the suburban eco-comedy *The Good Life* when his cockerel was reluctant to mate: surely the last time (it was 1975) a scriptwriter could get away with the usage. As currently deployed by progressives and **diversity** proponents, queer is defined in their words as 'an inclusive, unifying sociopolitical umbrella term for people who are gay, lesbian, bisexual, transgendered, transsexual, intersexual, genderqueer [feeling neither female nor male], or of any other non-heterosexual sexuality, sexual anatomy, or gender identity: it can also include asexual and autosexual people, as well as gender normative heterosexuals whose sexual orientations or activities place them outside the heterosexual-defined mainstream'. Queer Theory or Queer Studies, which takes its cues from Judith Butler's 1990 book *Gender Trouble*, is currently highly influential in academic circles. This set of ideas challenges traditional notions of fixed, gender-based identity and re-reads historical texts from radically new viewpoints.

Queer appears in the written records, like so many charged, resonant words, in the early modern period when the language was flooded with new coinages, many of them borrowings or alterations of foreign terms. It may, although this is not proven, derive from German *quer*, meaning 'oblique'. Its sense then was something like 'across the grain' or 'athwart', hence potentially puzzling or discomfiting. The word seems to exemplify the sound symbolism that applies also to **quaint**, quirk, queasy, quizzical, quiddity, all terms with faint connotations of destabilising, disquiet or mild perversity but seemingly unrelated etymologically. Linguistic conservatives and staunch opponents of politically correct usage (and presumably the simply unsophisticated, too) have of course never abandoned the original usage, and in an age when 'cripes' and 'crikey' are making a comeback, a retro, Enid Blyton-esque vocabulary shows signs of becoming fashionable. Certainly, queer played a prominent role in nineteenth-century literature, evoking as it did the curious, the whimsical or sublime. Charlotte Brontë, in *The Professor*, wrote, 'Just as I laid my hand on the handle of the dining-room door, a queer idea glanced across my mind. "Surely she's not going to make love to me," said I.'

By the nineteenth century, the phrases 'a queer fish' (an unfathomable individual) and 'in queer street' (in financial difficulties or otherwise in trouble) were in use. The extended colloquial sense of giddy, faint or unwell, as in 'feeling a bit queer', is more than two hundred years old, and in the early nineteenth century queer was a euphemism for drunk. In underworld slang of the sixteenth century it denoted worthless or counterfeit, and by the eighteenth century was being used in low-life milieux as a verb with the senses cheat, ridicule, upset or spoil. Of these, only the phrase 'to queer someone's pitch' survives. The specifically sexual sense of queer was not recorded before the Edwardian era, but may be older: by the end of the 1950s, elaborated phrases like 'as queer as a nine-bob note/two-bob watch' were applied to anyone or anything thought deviant or suspect (only a 'ten-bob', or ten-shilling, note existed before the 1971 decimalisation of currency, and a watch costing only two shillings would be exceptional and unreliable).

Queue

Big-city anti-congestion strategies are nothing new. In 1936, London Transport placed a full-page advertisement in *The Times* under the heading 'Courtesies of the Queue'. The text exhorted Londoners to 'form a queue wherever desirable', contrasting the practice at Parisian bus stops, where the passenger 'waits where he [*sic*] likes. So far from putting his own word "queue" into practice, he is content to present it to us English.' Rather plaintively, the advert appealed to 'the good sense of passengers', given the impossibility of supervising the 2,000 bus stops within fifteen miles of Charing Cross and the 274 trams an hour leaving Blackfriars. 'The national quality of order and fairness finds public form in the queue,' the anonymous copywriter insisted, and it's a safe bet that few would then have disagreed. (S)he risks bathos by finishing with the justification that 'there seems to have been a queue for Noah's Ark'. In 1988, Wendy Cope could still write, 'Standing at the bus stop / In a big, long queue. / Here's my mum and this is me / With nothing much to do.' I can't tell you the exact day on which it happened, but I know roughly when the orderly bus queue for the first time broke down – irretrievably – in central

London. The tipping point was in 1991, when the non-English and the un-English finally overwhelmed the English at the bus stops in the Strand and the queue became a continental-type cluster. Turn-taking is still sporadically observed, but the single-file line, a symbolic staple of Englishness since the days of **austerity**, has gone.

Queue is an Old French word meaning 'tail', derived from Latin *cauda*, first borrowed by the English in the late sixteenth century for the tail of an animal. In the eighteenth century it usually denoted a long pigtail. The figurative sense of 'waiting in line' (always the preferred formulation in American English) crossed over in the nineteenth century, first unsurprisingly in reports from Paris: 'At the moment when the doors of the Academie Royal were opened, scarcely a dozen people were *en queue*' (*The Times*, 18 November 1836). Its first appearance as a nativised 'English' word, not a French term in italics, was again in *The Times*, in 1856, in a reference to American voters 'falling into the queue' at the ballot boxes, while as a verb, often with 'up', it dates from 1893. On VJ Day in 1945 diaries noted: 'The queue for bread . . . stretched round to the Prince Albert'; '. . . women grumbling and arguing in the queues'. A little later, in a letter, 'we did think that once Japan was beaten we should do away with queues, but it doesn't seem like it'. In the 1949 cinema hit *The Huggetts Abroad*, starring Jack Warner and Kathleen Harrison, a cheery working-class English family set out by road for South Africa and are disappointed to find that there are no queues. Only in Russia would they have been able to feel fully at home, with the word *очередь* symbolising the same mix of dignified resignation and humiliation in the face of perennial shortages. *Time* magazine reported in January 1950 that the new welfare state implanted by Attlee's Labour government, 'the regime of queues and 40% taxes and womb-to-tomb security', had 'come to judgement', scorned by Winston Churchill, who dismissed the 'fair shares for all' experiment as 'Queuetopia'. The bathos of everyday life post-rationing was evoked by John Betjeman four years later: 'But her place is empty in the queue at the International, / The greengrocer's queue lacks one, / So does the crowd at MacFisheries. There's no one to go on to Freeman's / To ask if the shoes are done.' The queue continued through the 1960s to be a visible symbol of the 'British disease' of badly trained, poorly motivated employees, mediocre management and a disregard for the hapless consumer. In the 1970s, 'dole queue', a phrase dating from the depressions of the 1930s, was a key component in what historians and sociologists have called the 'politicised mythology of decline'.

The psychology of the queue has been studied, notably by an American psychologist, Stanley Milgram, who treated the queue as a classic example of how groups of people automatically create social order out of chaos. One estimate claims, astonishingly, that the average 'western' person spends four years of their life standing in line, while reactions to queue-jumpers ('line-cutters' in American) vary predictably between passive Japan and volatile India, with the UK somewhere in the middle. Years of technologised market-led innovation haven't seen the disappearance of the gaggle of strangers snaking out of the post office. Academic Joe Moran has observed that attempts by the service culture to end the need to queue were applied unevenly. 'In low-status public spaces, such as bus stops, people were still left to improvise their own queue discipline; [while] organisations like banks used queueless services to focus on valued clientele.' Meanwhile, a posting by 'Alice' in an online discussion of queueing etiquette points out that at open-air pop festivals 'people are so conditioned to get in a queue to get what they want, that huge queues tend to form at the toilets, food stalls or whatever else right near the most crowded areas e.g. the main stage'. The English these days are less placid when the line doesn't shuffle forward as expected – tantrums and scuffles at the supermarket checkout go by the name of 'aisle rage' or 'trolley rage'; at the budget airline check-in or the security screening (or at Gatwick airport's 'shoe repatriation zone') they mark the early onset of that twenty-first-century British (not only English) speciality, 'air rage'.

Quite

O f her fictional creation Little Lord Fauntleroy, Frances Hodgson Burnett wrote (in 1886), 'In the first place, he was always well, and so never gave any one trouble; in the second place he had so sweet a temper and ways so charming that he was a pleasure to every one; and in the third place he was so beautiful to look at that he was quite a picture.' The little predeterminer 'quite' (it is also an adverb of degree) is key to two essential quirks of Englishness: first the tendency to hedge and qualify, as with its neighbours 'fairly' and 'rather', and secondly the expression of utter certainty, the magisterial judgement, lofty and abrupt, and the whole-hearted agreement, albeit sometimes condescending. In the case of a phrase like 'quite charming', there is a possibility of outsiders misunderstanding: only intonation will differenti-ate the two possible interpretations. It was the second sense – that of 'perfectly', 'exactly' or 'completely' – dating from Chaucer's time, that prevailed in the nineteenth cen-tury, as evidenced by Mrs Gaskell ('quite silent'), Trollope ('quite in earnest'), Dickens ('quite awful'), Samuel Butler ('quite ready'), Lewis Carroll ('quite plainly'), etc.

Today the same word can mean 'wholly', 'to a considerable

254

extent' ('Quite the little madam, aren't we?') or '(only) to some extent', 'partially' or 'somewhat' ('feeling quite tired'), though theoretical linguists explain this slightly differently: 'At the micro-level the lexical unit represents a case for contronymy of antonymy type if it can be subjected to gradation and if it comprises at least two senses which are contradictory within one aspect.' Hearing a declaration like 'the meal was quite nice, but the waiter was quite impossible' poses quite a conundrum for foreign learners of English; they frequently complain that only English has a word that has two quite different meanings (English English, that is: US usage favours the emphatic alternative, thereby confusing Brits). EFL students, of course, just don't use it; for them things are absolute – either 'nice' or 'nasty'. They are thrown, too, by the assertion that 'she's quite something', and quite honestly, I'm not surprised. I think even a native speaker, whatever that is these days, can sometimes be baffled by the word's ambiguity, as in 'she's quite hairy'; is she fairly hairy for a woman, or is she covered all over with hair? And – think about it – how do we quantify the 'few' in the formulation 'quite a few people'?

Foreigners, when they want to agree, tend to say 'I agree', not 'Quite!' But for us, as brisk expressions of emphatic agreement or assent, 'quite' or 'quite so' date from the 1890s. At first their tone was informal, but by the 1940s they sounded a bit superior. In a curious case reported in 1916, the owner of a boarding house was arrested for failing to keep a register of aliens staying with him, one of whom was a German munitions worker. The court record shows that the police confirmed that the German was a registered enemy alien, then followed this exchange: 'Magistrate (to the defendant): You speak with an accent yourself. Are you English? Householder: Oh, quite.' The magistrate suggested that he must have caught the accent from the German lodger, and fined him forty shillings with costs. Was the defendant saying that he concurred with the judge's suggestion, or that he was entirely English? In the circumstances the nuance hardly mattered, but one wonders how far the man's command of his native language had deteriorated. For today's tabloid journalists, 'yes, quite' or 'well, quite' can be used in written imitation of a conversational style, allowing them to be snippy, sarcastic, patronising or huffy, as when someone states the obvious: 'The government have announced that the public must be protected from crime.' 'Well, quite.' In the online banter of some younger speakers, 'quite' or 'quite likely' can be a deadpan or facetious affirmative as in 'These are the most advanced sports shoes you can buy.' 'Quite.' 'It was quite' means 'it was excellent', and 'they were quite possibly' is a truncated euphemism meaning they were under the influence of drugs or alcohol (or, only now that I come to think of it, quite possibly both).

This multifaceted word began as an alternative form of 'quit', meaning 'released from obligation', 'free' or 'clear', from the late Latin verb *quietare* via French *quitter*. By some reckonings it is the 204th most common word in the global English word stock.

Rum

In October 2006, the *Daily Mail* was in full flight: 'Labour MP Eric Joyce . . . is a rum cove. He was twice expelled from school . . . [and] was thrown out of the Army for disobedience before finding his true vocation: Tony Blair's most fawning backbench cheerleader.' The dated public-school colloquialism, 'rum cove', which has been applied over the years to, among many others, the DJ Jimmy Savile, Labour Prime Minister Harold Wilson and Hollywood star Johnny Depp, harks back more than a century to Charles Dickens' 'rum customer', D. H. Lawrence's 'rum 'un', Conan Doyle's 'a rum crowd' and Thomas Hardy's 'a rum life for a married couple'. The phrase '(a bit of a) rum do' is another perennial favourite with modern journalists affecting an antique jauntiness: it can function as a coded **understatement** with the real sense of 'extremely worrying development', just as 'rum cove' can be a disguising of 'dangerous deviant', but more often rum describes something or someone just slightly suspect, unfathomable, a little intriguing, with qualities as yet undiscerned. The word's brevity is balanced by its ambivalence, mingling hostility and suspicion with curiosity and the potential for amused tolerance, evoking either the image of the plain-dealing, **sensible** English **yeoman** scratching his head and trying to puzzle out the **queer** ways of folk, or the upper-class silly ass: 'a dashed rum piece of music', frets P. G. Wodehouse's Bertie Wooster.

Behind this little adjective, however, lurks a long and complex cultural history, and a host of other couplings in which the 'rum' component can mean sometimes one thing, sometimes quite another and sometimes something in between. The slang dictionaries complied in the eighteenth and nineteenth centuries contain between them around a hundred rum-based combinations. Although the early record is very sparse, it seems that, from the sixteenth century, in the jargon of thieves, vagrants and frequenters of low taverns, rum meant 'excellent', 'clever', 'powerful' or 'daring' ('rum blowen/doxy/duchess' was a 'handsome (kept) woman'; 'rum tilter' a 'splendid sword'), but came by the mid-nineteenth century (when the variant form 'rummy' was also recorded) to denote also 'disreputable', 'dubious' and/or 'odd' (as in 'rum Ned', a silly fellow; or 'rum gagger', an impostor). 'Rum cove' was first defined in the late eighteenth century as a 'clever and dexterous [*sic*] rogue', while 'rum do' is a Victorian variant of the earlier 'rum go', a puzzling or unfortunate occurrence. This is presumably not so much a shift in meaning, but in perspective, as the terms came to be used as much by victims, or by witnesses to wrongdoing for whom the connotations were negative, as by perpetrators, for whom they were positive. In the eighteenth century, rum was part of the slang of pugilists and their upper-class patrons, and by the twentieth century had passed into the raffish slang of the services and public schools, thence to the City and Fleet Street.

The origin of rum is usually taken to be *rom*, the Romany or Gypsy word for a man, so again an appreciative term for

TV for the past thirty years. This is true not only of fiction-alised speech; if you listen in on the conversations of educated teenagers, university students and young adults, it quickly becomes apparent that sarcasm is also an essential component of the banter that the English indulge in without thinking – and which is not the case in most European languages, or in the US, though the Irish and Australians do share our predilection. Perhaps to some extent under Brit influence, younger North Americans have begun to incorp-orate sarcasm into their entertainments, with the result that my nine-year-old son can claim to have, in his words, 'learned to speak fluent sarcasm' from Cartoon Network TV shows.

Sarcasm is said to be the lowest form of wit, presumably because 'sarky comments/remarks' are both easy, sometimes involving no more than a change in intonation, and hurtful. (The source for this common observation, though, is obscure: Thomas Carlyle wrote in 1834 that sarcasm was the language of the devil, whereas the standard contention since Dryden's day was that punning was the lowest form of wit.) Along with its sometimes indistinguishable relative, **irony**, sarcasm does have some claim to be the most popular form of wit, at least according to a survey of humour types carried out in 2007. This revealed that stand-up comedians would do better to dispense with 'gags' in favour of the sort of wither-ing diatribes delivered by such as Jack Dee. Seven out of ten respondents found sarcasm funny, while 63 per cent admit-ted laughing at 'silly' jokes. Just over a third confessed to being entertained by slapstick, or the sort of real-life mishaps collected on television shows such as *You've Been Framed*. Humour in general, and mockery, scorn and humiliation in particular, play complex roles in rituals of social bonding and negotiations of identity. They may also be deployed less self-consciously as part of displays of aggression and power plays, leading counselling services and anger-management specialists to single out sarcasm as a tactic – or trait – to be deplored.

In June 2008, the *Sun* began to use 'Sarky' as a nickname for the French president, Nicolas Sarkozy, rhyming it with 'narky', which supposedly described the way *les anglais* were feeling after his interventions. Narky is another venerable playground and family colloquialism, widespread in the 1950s and 1960s in its earlier form, 'narked' (meaning irritable and/or irritated and probably deriving from Romany *nak*, 'nose', via a now forgotten metaphorical route). Sarcasm on the other hand comes to us, via French *sarcasme* and late Latin *sarcasmus*, from ancient Greek, in which *sarkazein* meant 'to tear flesh', 'bite the lips in rage', or sneer. Adopted for rhetorical and literary usage in the sixteenth century, the anglicised term similarly denoted biting or cutting wit. The form sarky is credited by the *OED* to the school playground, and its first citation is from D. H. Lawrence (a former teacher), dated 1912. Confusingly, internet geeks have recently taken to using the word 'snarky', once a synonym of narky (it occurs in *The Railway Children*) as an alternative for sarky, even inventing a new phrasal verb 'to snark on (someone/something)', meaning to taunt or mockingly disparage. Fellow geeks have suggested to me that these may be new coinages, blending sarky with 'snide'.

Sensible

Captain Sensible, aka Ray Burns of Balham, rejoined punk icons the Damned in 1996 and still tours with them. His nickname is ironic. Sensible English ladies (as opposed to flighty continental sirens) traditionally wore, according to style guides of the 1940s, 'stockings with seams, in a colour described . . . as "medium beige" . . . and brown court shoes of good leather with a sensible heel'. Recommendations for a school hike today exhort parents to 'make sure your child is wearing sensible clothing, like non-slip shoes, not **wellies**, and that he isn't too tightly wrapped up in colder weather so that his movements are hindered'.

In the British National Corpus word bank there are 2,684 instances of sensible, while 'sensual' and 'sensuous' languish with 331 and 193 respectively. It must be a reflection on us as a people that a word that started out meaning sensitive has ended up meaning unimaginative, down-to-earth, reasonable and – another loaded, acutely English endorsement – 'sound'. Too often its unspoken corollary is 'joyless', 'safe'; it is implicitly contrasted with continental flamboyance, wildly speculative philosophising and the striking of attitudes in general. One of our most frequent commendations both in conversational ('a sensible lad – very level-headed') and more formal ('an eminently sensible and practical solution') mode, and useful in official or political discourse: 'we must do more to promote sensible drinking', sensible is unspectacular, unassuming, only very slightly sniffily or stuffily judgemental in the mouths, for instance, of the earnest or sanctimonious. Several times in my life I have heard the suggestion 'try and be sensible about it' put forward in the context of devastating personal tragedy.

Sensible came to us in the fourteenth century via French, in which it preserves its original definition, from Latin *sensibilis*. Although its older sub-senses are still in the dictionary, it's a long time since sensible could denote 'capable of being felt or perceived', 'large enough to be considered' or 'aware, conscious or cognisant' in any form of discourse other than the ruminations of High Court judges. What, then, is the opposite of sensible? Not 'insensible', which is a fancy word for dead drunk, and neither will 'senseless' do, as a 'senseless loss of life' can't be contrasted with a sensible one. Our keyword's real antonyms are at one extreme 'having taken leave of one's senses', at the other the unacknowledged key to all that is jovial and genial about us: 'silly'. And of course our sensibleness can be considered a thing of the past, part of that old, stolid, slightly puritanical mindset that promoted pragmatism and insisted on a balanced view. Writing in the American *National Review* in 2000, Florence King noted of the English that for as long as she could remember, 'Despite their dotty vicars, unleashed doggy ladies, and the residual feyness evident in their pub hours, when all was said and done, the world called them "sensible".' She went on to cite the furore surrounding Princess Diana's death and New Labour's attempts to impose ethnic quotas on museum attendance as evidence that the term can no longer apply.

Despite this jaundiced transatlantic view, the evidence from UK agony aunts, student union websites ('Be safe, be sensible: if you think your drink may have been spiked, seek help') and overheard conversations is that sensibleness is still valued highly in our culture. (It was the author Guy Browning who pointed out in the *Guardian* that when asked to rate how sensible they are, sensible people usually mark themselves a seven or eight out of ten. Nine or ten wouldn't be sensible.)

Serious

If ever a single word reflected a profound change in social attitudes, it must be 'serious' as used by the English. As I used to explain to my French, German and Spanish business students back at the beginning of the 1980s, in their languages serious (*sérieux*, *seriös*, *serio*) was invariably an appreciative term. In day-to-day conversation it defined someone as respectable, dependable, in professional use it denoted a reputable, well-established organisation. In English, however, although it could occasionally be used – Victorian-style – to commend someone as solid and solemn, serious was more likely to be a criticism of an individual as lacking humour (see **GSOH**) – a very serious flaw in Anglo-Saxon eyes.

At the time, I didn't suspect that the same word would not only shift subtly in its connotations, but become a vogue term, symbolising the attitudes of the 1980s and the decades that followed. In fact serious was already being used in a special way by those engaged in trying to make a quick profit: gamblers and art dealers in particular habitually employed it in a stock phrase. As *The Times* reported in 1974, of a sale of paintings by English impressionist Fredrick Brown, 'Brown had not until yesterday been known to make

266

serious money at auction'; the same paper in its horse-racing section noted in 1978 that 'All the serious money in the ante post market has been for Nusantara and Rimosa's Pet.' Serious was a – the – keyword in the vocabulary of the new breed of youngish, overconfident, aspirational, unashamedly materialist Brits, and to become seriously rich (these days almost a category, like 'super-rich', in its own right: the phrase features in the titles of hundreds of self-help books) was their collective objective. The first, if belated, drama-tisation of the yuppie ethos in its English incarnation was entitled *Serious Money*, a play in verse by Caryl Churchill staged in London in 1987, a satirical take on the London stock market in which all the characters are eventually cor-rupted by the financial rewards offered to them. Its first run at the Royal Court Theatre proved to be so successful that it then transferred to the West End and Broadway. In that more innocent time, the commercial success of a subversive satire still attracted ironic comment.

Serious entered English in the fifteenth century as a nativising of the Latin *serius*. The term's ultimate origin is lost in antiquity, though it may share a common Indo-European ancestor with German *schwer*, which means weighty or difficult. By the mid-noughties, our word had become firmly established in the pop-culture vocabulary with a sense not easily conveyed by any other single term. *Serious Ocean*, for instance, was the title of a 2008 TV docu-mentary: here it meant awesome, not to be underestimated, testing of one's resolve and one's limits, not to mention urgently modish, all at the same time. Just like 'radical' (as in radical chic) and 'extreme' (as in extreme ironing – a faddish dangerous sport), serious has been appropriated (in plain English hijacked) by the media and commercialism and turned into an enduring cliché. Such mutations are a natural part of the evolution of a language, but at a deeper level what this transformation marks is something more profound: it signals the end of English amateurism, the end of cherished self-delusion, of dilettantism and a gentlemanly pose of never taking oneself too . . . seriously.

See also **dosh**

Slag

In August 2002, the UK press reported that a TV advertisement hailing Pot Noodle as the 'slag of all snacks' had been banned from the airwaves. More than 300 people had complained, and the Independent TV Commission ruled it offensive. Earlier complaints had led to the commercial, featuring a man in a red-light area facing temptation by the wicked ready-meal, being moved to after the nine p.m. watershed. Now the ITC had decided that the word 'slag' should not appear in ads at any time. In purely commercial terms the decision was unfortunate: the ad seemed to have boosted sales of the iconic dish dramatically.

In October 2004, press headlines revealed that the infamous Fat Slags 'have been consigned to the slag heap. Sandra and Tracey, the corpulent, cackling, sex-crazed cartoon stars of *Viz* comic, have been killed off . . .' (it wasn't true – Sandra Burke and Tracey Tunstall, and their hapless suitor, Baz, are still there at the time of writing).

Journalist Julie Burchill wrote in 1987 that 'self-conscious and self-adoring parodists of slagdom, such as Madonna and Samantha Fox, understand this: that a man who calls a woman a slag isn't saying anything about her, but a lot about his condom-size'. Feminists and proponents of girl-power have fastened on the word as an emblem of continuing dis-crimination, pointing out that while female slag (along with 'slut', which dates from the fifteenth century, and 'slapper', which may be of Irish or Yiddish origin) is always pejorative, its masculine counterparts ('stud', 'stallion', 'swordsman') are all complimentary. Even the unfeminist *Daily Express* added its voice in 2002: 'Trollop, slut, slag, tramp, whore, etc. The nastiest names still only apply to women – mostly to Edwina Currie. Men are jolly studs, stallions, knicker grip-pers. Even "groper" is upmarket from trollop, dammit. Can't think of equally awful names for nookie-men. Can you? Maybe we should have equality, such as "Britain welcomed the distinguished trollop Bill Clinton to the Labour party conference. The slutty old slag got a standing ovation."'

This monosyllable, typically used to convey real contempt and distaste, has a fairly complex etymology. Slagge first appears in the records in 1552, said to be imported from Middle Low German; it originally denoted refuse matter, a by-product of smelting or welding: western Germanic lan-guages have a word of this root meaning 'hit', hence the dross or debris separated from (an object or mass). Strangely, the similar word 'slack', meaning coal refuse, is labelled 'origin obscure' in old dictionaries as if it may be unrelated. Slack in the sense of lax or remiss used to be applied to loose morals (it still means promiscuous in Caribbean patois and black British slang); fictional schoolboy hero of the 1950s Nigel Molesworth applied it to the French, but officially at least it has no historical connection with its near-homonyms. A number of 'sl' words with distasteful connotations (sloven and slattern, for example) are found in Germanic and Celtic languages: they probably arose as imitations of the sounds of sloshing, slithering and slapping.

Slag in the sense of a contemptible male, a staple of crime movies and TV cop series (and incidentally another *Viz* comic strip, featuring the cockney psychopath gangster Big Vern), was first noted in 1943. Twenty years later 'The Trigger Man', a London criminal on remand for murder, wrote in a letter from Brixton prison, 'As you said it is better to be around to be called a slag than dangling from some hangman's rope.'

'Slaggy' meaning sluttish was also recorded in 1943, and the noun slag applied to a female dates from 1958, but both usages are probably much older. The verb 'to slag' (alternative forms being 'slag off' and, specifically in prison slang, 'slag down') meaning to denigrate, is from 1971. In this sense the word is sometimes heard in the USA, where lexicographers have tried to derive it from the German verb *schlagen*, to beat or lash, but this is unlikely to be the source of the UK's term. Slagging both in the sense of a dressing-down and in the sense of behaving promiscuously ('slagging it' for 'sleeping around' is currently part of London street-gang slang) seems to be comparatively recent. In 2005, the National Union of Teachers warned that playground insults such as 'slag', 'prozzie' and 'whore' can legitimise domestic violence and must not be tolerated. 'Schools should try to stamp out sexist banter so children do not grow up thinking these attitudes are acceptable.' Slag is still part of the English teenage vocabulary, but has been joined by newer slang synonyms, as Michele Kirsch reported from Islington Green School in 2006: 'To slag them off you call them, as one girl reels off with great relish, "Oh, a sket, a waste girl, an apple, a what-up girl, a tramp, a ho."'

Less obviously insulting, though this may be a matter of opinion, and reflecting the new embracing of celebrity in place of class or refinement – or marital fidelity – is the acronym WAGs (for 'wives-and-girlfriends'), invented as shorthand for the females escorting the English football team to the World Cup in Germany in 2006. This kind of abbreviation recalls the earlier and less flattering US designation MAW, standing for 'model/actress/whatever', often applied to women otherwise dubbed 'bimbos'. The un-cerebral WAG typically shops, parties and is snapped by paparazzi. Following the weddings of four England players in a single weekend in 2007, *Private Eye* magazine's fictional tabloid gossip columnist, Glenda Slagg, offered her readers the acronym 'SLAGS: that's "Stupid Lazy and Grasping Slappers" – Geddit?!?' Finally, it's interesting to note that no appreciative or flattering terms, colloquial or otherwise, have been coined for women in the last three decades or so, unless the media formulations 'yummy mummy' or 'kitchen goddess' count – but they do not seem to me to be unambiguously positive: 'slutty' meanwhile is this year's buzz term of approval in fashion circles.

Society

In his 1976 title *Keywords*, subtitled 'a vocabulary of culture and society', the Marxist academic Raymond Williams analysed the word society itself in terms of two essential, but sometimes overlapping meanings. They are in his words 'our most general term for the body of institutions and relationships within which a relatively large group of people live', and 'our most abstract term for the condition in which such institutions and relationships are formed'. When in 1987 Margaret Thatcher famously rejected the term – and despite a mysterious rewriting of the transcript for publication, she emphatically did – she seemed to be referring to both senses simultaneously. What she actually said, in an interview with *Women's Own* magazine, was 'I think we have gone through a period when too many children and people have been given to understand "I have a problem, it is the Government's job to cope with it!" or "I have a problem, I will go and get a grant to cope with it!" "I am homeless, the Government must house me!" and so they are casting their problems on society and who is society? There is no such thing! There are individual men and women and there are families and no government can do anything except through people and people look to themselves first.' Later she added, 'If children have a problem, it is society that is at fault. There is no such thing as society. There is a living tapestry of men and women and people and the beauty of that tapestry and the quality of our lives will depend upon how much each of us is prepared to take responsibility for ourselves and each of us prepared to turn round and help by our own efforts those who are unfortunate.'

She was of course 'problematising', as the terminology of critical theory has it, the notion of an ordered, coherent community, with identifiable institutions, values and behaviours, whose interests transcend those of the members it sustains, the new idea that ironically underpins phrases she might actually accept, like 'a debt to society' or 'a sad reflection on society', and, indirectly, words she might question, like 'social contract', or reject, like 'socialism'. Her demotic take on the deep division between 'organicist' as against individualist views of . . . er . . . society has stuck in the memory and continues to provoke the *Guardian* reader just as it comforts the reader of the *Daily Mail*. Perhaps what is significant about the word society as it is bandied about in England today is precisely that everyone understands it, yet, like its neighbours 'culture' and 'community', or trendier alternatives, 'collectivity' and 'commonality', its borders are permeable and its denotation fuzzy. The very latest academic theories, incidentally, have begun to reconsider society as a necessary effect of biology and evolution, as 'a process of symbiogenetic cooperative communication' that can't be eclipsed by 'liberal possessive individualism'.

Raymond Williams's more orthodox definitions, and the rather convoluted ruminations that follow, do underline the word's interesting ambiguities and complexities (the more you examine it, the less graspable it seems), but don't do it full justice. Society can also, since the sixteenth century, denote a group working together for a particular purpose (as in learned or cooperative society), and sometimes it is still used with its very first meaning of company or fellowship. Our word was adopted in the fifteenth century via French from Latin *societas*, the state of companionship, from earlier *socius*, a companion or ally. 'I do not think there is anything deserving the name of society to be found out of London,' wrote William Hazlitt in his *Table-Talk*, published in 1822. From the later eighteenth century 'Society' began to be referred to when the influential, fashionable elite was meant, and it became possible to talk of 'entering' or 'being accepted into society', or of 'a society wedding'. It is only this sense of society ('high society' is a twentieth-century elaboration) that is distinctly English, and even here, there is some ambiguity: when a writer laments the loss of 'my position in Society', exactly which circles has he or she been excluded from? Oscar Wilde knew, and warned, in *The Importance of Being Earnest*, 'Never speak disrespectfully of Society . . . only people who can't get into it do that.' The formulation 'polite society' has been applied to the period from the 1660s to the end of the 1700s, describing the refined manners then thought appropriate to the English nobility, gentry and, to use an anachronism, intelligentsia. A sincerely held code that evolved into a national affectation resulted in, firstly, the fop, and arguably, later, the Victorian cult of prissiness that persisted until very recently. In the current climate of in-yer-face social intercourse and media permissiveness, though, it hardly makes sense to talk of polite society, except facetiously, which is probably why the Polite Society, a UK pressure group promoting good manners founded by Ian Gregory in 1986, subsequently changed its name to the Campaign for Courtesy. There is a Polite

Society in the USA, but this exists to promote skills with the handgun, on the basis that, as the science fiction author Robert A. Heinlein wrote in 1942, 'an armed society is a polite society'.

Sorry

'The thief is sorry that he is to be hanged, not that he is a thief,' runs the old proverb. In 1976 a far, far trimmer, but hugely bespectacled and flared, Elton John sang 'Sorry seems to be the hardest word', yet in our everyday life this seems to be the opposite of the truth. In those works of his that have survived, Chaucer said sorry only eighteen times, Shakespeare has ninety instances, while indications are that, although deference and politeness may have receded, the word is still used a staggering 368 million times a day in the UK.

The standard view is that sorry is an important mainstay of a world view based on deference, tentativeness and social unease, shared by members of a society riven by acutely felt differences of power, wealth and sophistication; based in other words on 'class'. Accordingly, although the tendency to excuse oneself may have been there as long as the middle classes (there are examples in that supremely bourgeois Victorian novel, *Barchester Towers*, while satirist George Mikes noted its genteel use in the 1940s), it seems to have reached its apogee just as our society's uncertainties and contradictions reached a head, in the late 1950s and early 1960s.

This was when saying sorry for imagined transgressions, in trying to pre-empt criticism, or simply when recoiling after bumping into a fellow Brit became a reflex action, a momentary ritual on a national scale. (It was also acceptably 'U' – i.e. in use among the upper classes – to say 'Sorry?', or even 'What?' when asking for clarification, unlike the unforgivably non-U 'pardon'.)

As befits such an elemental word, sorry's origins are almost unreachably ancient. Surprisingly the two words sorry and sorrow have different origins, but their spelling was made to harmonise in the fourteenth century. Sorrow comes from *sorg*, a word that existed in almost all prehistoric Germanic languages as well as Old English and meant 'regret' or 'grief'; sorry is from *sarig*, an adjective formed from the noun sar, the archaic form of 'sore' in the sense of a source of nagging pain. When Chaucer used sorry (and he had to begin by apologising to the upper class of his day for writing in English instead of French or Latin), its meaning was restricted to 'pitiful', but by Shakespeare's time most of its modern connotations were already in place.

Academic linguists assert that saying sorry is what they call a 'speech-act universal', existing in all languages and cultures. They admit, though, that the 'realisations' of this act – which words are chosen and how often they are said – in practice vary greatly from community to community. It's unarguably true that apologising as a conversation strategy or verbal tic is very much a British speciality. Teachers of English to foreigners help their students to understand that the word has multiple uses, including interrupting, indicating that one hasn't heard, requesting repetition, disagreeing, as well as the ones they may be familiar with: showing regret or sympathy. For real expressions of regret, remorse or contrition, they rightly recommend adding the words 'really/so/very' – perhaps another 'very' to be absolutely sure. Among other European nations, only the Czechs, often regarded by their neighbours as a sensitive and reticent people, will sprinkle their conversation with their equivalent, *prominte*, though nothing like as frequently as the British do 'sorry'. So useful is our short alternative (unlike the cumbersome German *es tut mir Leid*, or Spanish *lo siento mucho*) and so much a part of global currency that 'sorry' is regularly used nowadays by, for example, the Germans, Swiss, Dutch, Finns and Slovenes when speaking their own languages to one another: stuck behind an old German camper-van on the autobahn, I noticed a handwritten notice in its rear window that said 'Sorry. Es geht nicht schneller' ('It doesn't go any faster').

On home territory the habit of apologising is so ingrained that some – curmudgeons, contrarians – have defined themselves by not doing it, hence the title of playwright John Osborne's autobiography *Never Explain, Never Apologise*. This dictum and the other versions of it are not Osborne's; it has been ascribed to the Duke of Wellington (expressing aristocratic and autocratic hauteur), Disraeli (political expediency), Edwardian Admiral John Fisher (sheer British intransigence) and Noel Coward (snobbishness). P. G. Wodehouse observed in 1914 that it's 'a good rule in life never to apologise. The right sort of people do not want apologies, and the wrong sort take a mean advantage of them.'

The comedy of embarrassment is a favourite British genre, and several dimensions of 'sorry' were present in the BBC TV sitcom of the same name, which was broadcast from 1981 to 1988. Its hero, Timothy Lumsden, played by Ronnie Corbett, was a forty-one-year-old unmarried librarian, still living at home with his domineering mother and henpecked father. Timothy's existence is mired in banality and frustration, his search for a partner and escape from the household constantly thwarted by his oppressive parents. Watching these forty-two episodes was – is even more so today – itself a harrowing experience for the sensitive, or the cynical, given the picture of Britain it paints: the cloying pettiness and prissiness, the suburban claustrophobia, the upsetting mismatch of the physical characteristics on display with the thought of actual sex.

Although it is overused, though it may have been debased, trivialised and emptied of real meaning, sorry is often nonetheless the only word that will do. A semi-apology or seeming apology that avoids the actual word is precisely what politicians and service-sector workers are trained to deliver, and it is precisely what many of us find infuriating and unacceptable. Mealy-mouthed mea culpas designed only to excuse and/or aggrandise the speaker, half-hearted mumbled regrets, not to mention the famous 'non-apology apology' ('I'm sorry if you feel I may have offended you') will not placate a media-savvy public conditioned to demand satisfaction even if that means sincerity. British royalty and British politicians (former London Mayor Ken Livingstone excepted, though his apology for slavery hardly cost him dear) have doggedly avoided public acts of contrition, clinging to the dated notion that they are undignified. Ironically Australians, not noted for effusive apologies, nevertheless have National Sorry Day, an event celebrated unofficially since 1998 in commemoration of and collective repentance for the state's abduction of aboriginal children.

In January 2007, a survey by insurance company esure claimed to reveal the ways in which ordinary Brits say sorry and how they react to the various uses of the word. The top five reasons for saying sorry were telling somebody we haven't time to speak to them or do something; apologising on someone else's behalf, for instance when a child or dog has misbehaved; telling someone we didn't hear what they said; asking someone to explain something, and only in fifth place, apologising for having let someone down, lied to them or otherwise wronged them. Thirty-seven per cent of 'sorrys' were aimed at partners, 19 per cent at strangers, 14 per cent at one's children, 14 per cent at colleagues, 8 per cent at friends, 5 per cent at parents, 3 per cent at siblings and 1 per cent at the boss. Eighty-six per cent of respondents thought that people use the s-word too lightly, as a 'cheap excuse' or convenient explanation of antisocial or inappropriate behaviour. Typically a woman told me, 'for some reason I always feel compelled to say sorry when someone has walked into me, even when it's the other person's fault', adding perceptively, 'maybe what I'm actually apologising for is my inner rage at their not apologising. Either way it's probably safe to say I have some self-esteem issues that need addressing.'

I'm a prime example myself of someone who constantly says sorry, but is almost never sorry. I use it not out of modesty or self-doubt but wholly hypocritically, indiscriminately, either to fend off other people, or in sarcastic self-abasement – sorry I spoke, sorry for existing . . . terribly sorry, but I couldn't care less.

Stodgy

Oh the Englishman could not be called
    romantic
His technique is not particularly good
All the French and the Italians chase their
    women round like stallions
But the Englishman's a suet pud.

(From a 1959 song by South African 'Paddy
Roberts', nom de plume of John Godfrey Owen)

O n 31 December 1875, Sir William Harcourt addressed
an audience at Oxford University: 'Well, I have no
objection to suet pudding when it appears as the garnish of
boiled beef; but as a sole article of diet – especially when the
dough is abundant and the suet scanty – it is perhaps a trifle
stodgy.' Stodgy also tellingly describes the texture of our
corner of the planet, for centuries mired in mire. It was once
the consistency of the battlefield, too. In verses ironically
entitled 'In the Pink', the war poet Siegfried Sassoon wrote,
'Five miles of stodgy clay and freezing sludge, / And everything but wretchedness forgotten.' Used figuratively, the
same word epitomised the attitudes of an older England,
from 'stodgy notions', a popular formulation in Victorian and

Edwardian times, to the 'stodgy old-fashioned approaches' and 'stodgy brands' excoriated in the go-ahead noughties.

Stodge – the ill-defined, suet-based school-dinner 'afters' of awful memory – along with abominations like tapioca ('frogspawn'), tepid, congealing rice pudding and semolina, has left me, for one, permanently scarred. The collocation 'stodgy fare' has been applied to typical English food in hundreds of articles, coming nowadays in two varieties: either a wallow in collective guilt at our insipid-tasting, glutinous and farinaceous diet, or perversely defiant, even urging the rehabilitation of much-loved comfort foods, the revival of retro-meals for a damp, chilly climate. It's not just beery, beefy yeomen and overgrown English boarding-school boys who love the stuff; unreconstructed Czech machismo is also measured by how many *knedliky*, their savoury dumplings, can be eaten at a sitting.

One of a concert of st words – stuffy, stiff, stifled, stilted, starchy, stuck-up – stodgy looks like, but isn't, a blend of 'stolid' and 'fudgy' – forcefully conveying the idea of being stuck fast, hampered, hobbled, immobilised, or, metaphorically, of embracing smug complacency, all notions applicable to England and Englishness at any time from the early Victorian to the end of the 1970s ('Why is the middle-class so stodgy – so utterly without a sense of humour!' wrote Katherine Mansfield, thinking probably of provincial New Zealand as well as pre-World War II England). In the same way those dates more or less delimit the popularity of said suet pudding, along with spotted dick, plum duff, dumplings and their more obscure local variants. No more is our word a portmanteau composed of 'stultified' and 'podgy', though it does indeed evoke the formal and conventional; the unadventurous, the inert and the constipated, the 'wanting in gaiety' as the *OED* used to define it. The early nineteenth-century adjective stodgy, popular among Regency bucks, post-dates the humbler, rustic noun stodge, first recorded in the seventeenth century and of obscure provenance. Some authorities derive all these parts of speech from an original verb that may once have existed in northern English and Lowland Scots dialect. In archaic slang, 'stodging' could mean stuffing oneself, while a 'stodger' could denote a glutton, a dullard or a school bun. In current US youthspeak, a stodge is a grouch or a bore, and stodgy is a fashionable pejorative with such senses as disappointing, inferior, unfair, unfashionable, etc., derived perhaps fancifully by some of its users from the phrase 'it's dodgy' rather than from the standard adjective. 'Stodgified' is occasionally used as a synonym for 'stoned'. In the latest London street slang, in a characteristic ironic reversal, stodgy actually means 'cool', typically intensified as 'bare stodgy or 'well stodgy'.

Compare, **chippy**, **crumpet**, **cuppa**, **sensible**

Suburbia

Whatever must they think of us? At the time of writing, the anarchic English black comedy *Suburban Shootout* is showing on TV networks across Europe, a successor to the less disturbing – superficially at least – *The Good Life*, *Ever Decreasing Circles*, *As Time Goes By*, *Sorry* and *Keeping Up Appearances*. Few probably realise that *Keeping Up Appearances* did not originate as a long-running TV satire of suburban snobbery, but as a 1928 novel by Rose Macaulay, of which *The Times* wrote at the time, 'The parable of Daisy and Daphne Simpson, trying to appear what they were not in a society of "high brows" and to conceal what they were – namely, the product of a suburban, and honestly vulgar, upbringing – is deliciously funny.'

'Suburbia' suggests an exotic state (or state of being, state of mind) like Slovenia, Slavonia, Ruritania or Utopia, yet is used as a term of derision or dismissal for a limbo, a something-and-nothing liminal zone where mediocrity holds sway. 'Suburb' (via French, from the Latin *sub*, below, and *urbs*, city: in modern French suburb is *banlieue* or *faubourg*) first appeared in English, according to the *OED*, in the late sixteenth century: by the 1600s its derived adjective 'suburban' had already taken on negative connotations, being applied to the supposedly dissolute inhabitants of outlying districts of London. 'Suburbian' was coined for the same purpose, the noun form 'suburbia' appearing at the beginning of the nineteenth century.

The long-drawn-out migration from the cities to their outskirts during the later nineteenth and twentieth centuries was well described in a reader's letter to *The Times* in 1895: '. . . the occupants of small residences who now find quiet comfort, and good air on the verge of the metropolis, the artisans who exchange a room or two in a town lodging for a small house in a suburban street, as plants circle outwards to take possession of fresh and healthy soil'. A subdivision of suburbia, 'Metroland', was the marketing label coined in 1915 by the Metropolitan Railway to encapsulate the parts of Middlesex, Buckinghamshire and Hertfordshire served when it expanded its network to the north-west of London. From the 1930s to the 1970s, the suburbs were the object of condemnation, or at the very least pity and condescension on the part of pundits and the literati. Of Dr Stephen Taylor's 'The Suburban Neurosis', an article published in the *Lancet* in 1938, a sentence will give the flavour: 'Existence in the suburbs is such that the self-preserving, race-preserving and herd instincts can neither be adequately satisfied nor sublimated.' In 1955, amateur critic and topographer Ian Nairn invented the term 'subtopia' to describe the areas around cities that had in his view been failed by urban planning, losing their individuality and spirit of place: the less exotic expressions 'ribbon development' and '(sub)urban sprawl' referred similarly to poorly planned expansion into the 'green belt'.

As revisionist historian Dominic Sandbrook has noted of the fifties and early sixties, 'to novelists like Angus Wilson or

Penelope Mortimer, or to the playwright John Osborne, "suburban" meant base, cheap, commercial, venal, heartless, mediocre, materialistic, unimaginative and banal'. Serious surveys, notably Willmott and Young's *Family and Class in a London Suburb* of 1959, confounded expectations by revealing that those living in suburbia were cheerful, sociable and well adjusted. Suburbia's treatment at the hands of critics has been one of consistent contradiction, or contradictoriness: excoriated in the 1980s by architecture correspondent Jonathan Glancey, its curiosities were celebrated by the cultural commentator Jonathan Meades. John Betjeman, having once referred to pre-World War II suburban sprawl as 'red-brick rashes', spoke up in 1948 for 'a new beauty – the beauty of the despised, patronised suburb, the open heart of the nation'. When in 1993 Tory leader John Major predicted the survival of 'the country of long shadows on cricket grounds, warm beer [and] invincible green suburbs', he was ridiculed even by members of his own party. It's true that the then prime minister went over the top by quoting George Orwell's 'old maids bicycling to Holy Communion through the morning mist'. Popular culture, too, has had a love/hate relationship with suburbia (with hate probably coming out on top). As inspiration for a televisual tradition, in the words of critic Michael Bracewell, 'Suburbia bred a mock-heroic comedy, in which lost dogs, eccentric vicars, embarrassing neighbours and unexpected dinner guests could be seen as the alpha and omega of the human condition.' Manfred Mann's jaunty lament in the 1966 single 'Semi-detached Suburban Mr James' ('I can see you in the morning time, washing clean, the weather's fine / Hanging things upon the line, as your love slips away') prefigured suburban hippies' rejection of their own *Heimat*. Punk described itself, in the words of the Members' 1978 hit, as 'the sound of the suburbs' and bands like the Lurkers only half-ironically romanticised outer London's districts in *Fulham Fallout* and 'In Richmond'.

The real *rus in urbe* (as opposed to the garden cities to which the phrase was originally applied) is, it seems, in many ways exactly what it is thought to be: the bucolic setting for all that is average. In 2006, in an attempt to understand more about its customers, the AA motoring organisation carried out a survey of those who lived in streets called 'Acacia Avenue', of which there are fifteen in England, from Liverpool and Port Talbot to Hove in Sussex and Verwood in Dorset. They found, just as the series of earlier post-war studies had found, that despite the assumptions of intellectuals, suburbanites are more than averagely happy, proud and self-reliant – yet neighbourly. New concepts in planning and development and ideas of 'third spaces' and 'brownfield sites' – neither home nor office, neither city nor country – may mean that the old notion of suburbia, like the inflections of class and tradition that it represented – eventually becomes subsumed in something much more complex. But as long as the lower-middle- and middle-class heartlands stay standing, net curtains will continue to twitch, there will be rustlings in the privet hedges, lawns will be mown and cars washed – and in the words of the Pet Shop Boys, '. . . a siren screams / There in the distance, like a roll call / Of all the suburban dreams.'

See also **cottage**, **doily**

The Establishment

A term would not qualify for inclusion here if it was simply a piece of 'journalese', the shorthand favoured by the print media, nor if it was political or sociological jargon. But if a phrase is picked up by what used to be called 'the man in the street' and if it is held to define a defining characteristic of English life and becomes a long-established part of the national conversation at all levels, eventually a carping cliché, then it must be treated in passing. 'The Establishment' was coined by the historian A. J. P. Taylor in 1953 to describe the unacknowledged, both official and unofficial but essentially opaque power structure, the hidden 'old-boy network', which not only ran the country but dictated (by implication, never overtly) the rules of social conformity.

Establishment comes ultimately from Latin *stabilire*, to fix or construct, via Old French *establissement*, whence it was adopted at the end of the fifteenth century. By the end of the eighteenth century the word often signified a stable condition or a governing system, either political or more often ecclesiastical; the sense of a business or a household is early Victorian.

289

The mid-twentieth-century notion of an insider elite, operating in concert, based to a large extent on 'the old school tie' and a London–Oxbridge matrix, came generally to be identified by the early 1960s with the stagnation, the amateurism at the top and the lack of social mobility that beset Britain, with its lack of what since the 1990s has been termed 'transparency'. 'Establishment cover-up' was a formulation bandied about in connection with the defection of spies Burgess and Maclean and the subsequent kid-glove treatment of fellow conspirator Anthony Blunt, as well as by outsiders and the disaffected from all walks of life.

In neatly conceptualising a whole culture, the expression (Dominic Sandbrook in his *Never Had It So Good* tracks its development in detail) was a boon to satirists, and in 1959 *Queen* magazine printed a spoof school magazine (resembling the *Eton Chronicle*) entitled *The Establishment Chronicle and Nepotist's Gazette*. It listed the Establishment's 'club rules', which included 'power may discreetly be misused'; 'power must only be exercised . . . through front-men . . . by glimpses of social advancement'. In 1961, *Private Eye* contributor and backer Peter Cook opened the Establishment Club, a private nightclub and café-theatre in London's Soho, where fashionable satirists could mock the Establishment beyond the reach of censorship.

Creeping meritocracy and a globalised service culture have rendered the original idea of a relatively small, coherent, partly class-based Establishment obsolete, although there are of course still islands of influence in politics, the media, the business community. The idea of a smug, misguided, even malign consensus working against our best interests hasn't gone away – witness the many disapproving references to 'Establishment figure(s)' in pamphlets and polemics – but it's highly significant that in New Britain most of the railing comes from the right rather than the left, frequently targeting subsets labelled 'the liberal establishment', 'the intellectual establishment' or 'the educational establishment'. It still came as a shock to think that, as a linguist specialising in non-standard language, I might have become part of such a collective. An article in the *Sunday Telegraph* in July 2008 reporting that a secondary school had banned slang among its pupils and was subsequently performing well was followed by an online discussion, in which one posting read, 'I am sick of the liberal left establishment "celebrating the richness" of kids' mumbling.'

The Few

I n August 2006, under the headline 'History's a mystery', the *Sun* reminded its readers that 'Sixty-six years ago this month the Battle of Britain was fought out over southern England. Victory by "The Few" saved us from Hitler. It was the most crucial battle in our history. Five hundred of our brave airmen died. Yet few kids seem to be taught about it today. A thousand children aged 15 to 16 were asked what they knew by the Battle of Britain Historical Society. Eighty per cent said the battle had never been mentioned in their lessons. Only one per cent understood the terrible consequences if we'd lost.' Six years earlier, the *Swindon Advertiser* had reported with some bitterness a prime ministerial speech proposing a memorial to Australians who gave their lives for the Mother Country during World War II. 'This suggestion is in marked contrast to his, and the government's refusal to support the appeal by the Battle of Britain Historical Society for a permanent memorial to The Few, as the event is not considered part of our national heritage.' In September 2005, the Battle of Britain monument *was* duly unveiled, sited on London's Victoria Embankment and funded by public donations. Another memorial is at Capel-le-Ferne on the cliffs above the English Channel, where many of the aerial engagements took place.

Along with the evacuation from Dunkirk one of the most inspiring narratives of World War II, the struggle between predominantly young, mainly British airmen and the German air force for mastery of the skies has been seen as pivotal in preventing invasion and 'subjugation, the fate of most of our continental neighbours', to quote a school history text. Churchill's famous encomium delivered on 20 August 1940 included the ringing assertion that 'Never in the field of human conflict was so much owed by so many to so few.' In his 'Salute to the Gallant Few' in the BBC archive of World War II memories, 1st Airborne Division veteran Alexander Barr applied the now familiar formulation to the doomed 'Operation Market Garden' to capture a bridge in occupied Holland in 1944. It opens, 'Heroes of Arnhem, "Gallant Few" / You showed what British grit can do / Through each succeeding day and night / You battled on without respite.' The notion of the brave individual defying overwhelming odds, of the few standing firm against the many (which of course goes back as far as the Spartan stand at Thermopylae), allied with the idea of a small elite bringing order to a disordered world, was already lodged in the national psyche by World War I. The enduring phrase 'the gallant few' was virtually a nineteenth-century cliché, appearing in poems such as Thomas Campbell's 1799 'The Pleasures of Hope' ('in vain, alas, in vain, ye gallant few!' – referring to a massacre of Polish patriots) and applied to the Texan heroes of the Alamo siege among others. In a 1915 speech, Ramsay MacDonald warned that 'foreign affairs must no longer be left to the few'. 'The few' also echoed passages from icons of Englishness. The King James Bible has '. . . for many be called, but few chosen' (Matthew

20:16), and Shakespeare's *Henry V* 'We few, we happy few, we band of brothers / For he to-day that sheds his blood with me / Shall be my brother.'

Few is from Old English *feawa*, from an ancient Germanic word that could mean 'little' and 'silent', distantly related to Latin *paucus*, from which we get 'paucity'. Of secondary significance but telling nonetheless is the use of the word 'gallant' which often accompanies it. The adjective and its noun, gallantry, have a ring of the forties and fifties, and of course an echo of earlier, if imaginary, notions of chivalry, and neither is often heard today. Gallant combines the appreciation of dashing courage and of attentiveness to women, though in the French, from which we adopted it five hundred years ago, the second sense dominates; in that language it can also mean 'flirtatious' or 'racy'. Many ladies of a certain age used to pronounce gallant as if it were French ('gah-LONT'), either just for fun or because they found the idea excitingly exotic (and presumably uncharacteristic of their English spouses). Gallant is interesting in that it was formerly applied, a little condescendingly, to other nations. In particular, 'Gallant Little Belgium' has become a catch-phrase referring to support for that country that led to the 1914 declaration of war against its occupier, Germany. In fact the *Sunday Times* headline on 13 December that year was simply 'Gallant Belgium'.

Yet another concept that keys into the same notion of heroic defiance is that of the 'little man', which was popular between the world wars and was visualised in the cartoons of Sidney Strube in the *Daily Express*. It is an **irony** or perhaps a hypocrisy that a long-time imperial superpower could construct such a self-effacing – but also charmingly Chaplinesque – image for itself (Strube portrayed a bowler-hatted everyman helplessly buffeted by monstrous vested interests) and get away with it. A less attractive version of the embattled, heroic few, an idea rarely articulated but lurking beneath the surface in a class-conscious society, is where it denotes an alpha group without whom the vulgar crowd is leaderless and lost. In 1948 the diarist James Lees-Milne recorded a dinner in the company of the novelist Ivy Compton-Burnett during which she asserted that hitherto England had 'come out on top because she had been pushed along by the educated few'. Lees-Milne and his companion agreed that the nation would inevitably lose its edge, now that 'the educated few were being pushed around by the uneducated many'.

See also **pluck, the Hun**

The Hun

On 12 June 1917, a reader wrote to the editor of *The Times*, which published the letter under the heading 'No peace with Kaiserism'. It read: 'In various ways we can hammer into the Hun mind the solid determination of the whole civilized world to have a final settlement with that evil spirit of lies, murder, robbery, and wanton destruction which has lowered Germany from the level of a civilized nation to that of a herd of man-eating tigers.' On 16 February 1918, the same paper reported the views of Mr Rudyard Kipling on the dangers of negotiating a peace treaty on terms favourable to the enemy: 'Under the Hun dispensation man will become once more the natural prey of his better-armed neighbours, women will be the mere instrument for continuing the breed, the vessel of man's lust and man's cruelty, and labour will become a thing to be knocked on the head if it dares to give trouble and worked to death if it does not.' On 27 March 1944, Winston Churchill delivered a speech preparing the nation for the final offensive in a second conflict: 'Since I spoke to you last not only have the Hun invaders been driven from the lands they had ravaged but the guts of the German Army have been largely torn out by Russian valour and generalship.'

The Hun

It was Kaiser Wilhelm II himself who had given his ene-
mies the label by which to damn his militarism, and, as
cultural theory now terms it, to 'otherise' his people for the
century to come. In 1900 he had publicly urged the German
army to fight 'as the Huns of 1000 years ago', evoking the
enduring legends of Attila's Turkic-Mongoloid barbarian
hordes laying waste to Eurasia in the fourth and fifth centuries. In the English language 'Hun' had, by the dawn of
the nineteenth century, been transformed from a descriptive for the Hun-yü nomads to a metaphor for 'reckless and
barbarous destroyers of beauty'. It was at first an 'educated'
colloquialism, therefore more likely to be used by officers
than men, but once endorsed by the press it became a universal epithet.

Later to morph into the 'Bo(s)che' (from nineteenth-
century French slang *tête de bôche* for an obstinate person), the
'Krauts' (from the popular *sauerkraut* cabbage dish), Jerry
(probably a familiarising alteration of 'German', though it
used to be slang for a chamber pot) and occasionally 'Fritz' (a
supposedly stereotypical given name, also used collectively
of the Germans in Polish and Russian), for most of the twentieth century the Hun represented not only an actual
opponent, but *the* symbolic enemy. When T. S. Eliot wrote in
1936, 'I'll tell the world we got the Hun on the run', he was
probably repeating an already widespread catchphrase, one
that was recycled in World War II. A decade before Eliot, the
public had thrilled to the Ampthill divorce case, during
which Christabel, wife of John 'Stilts' Russell, heir to the
Ampthill baronetcy, claimed to be a virgin despite giving
birth to a son. She accused her cross-dressing husband, with
whom she had apparently spent only one night, of engaging
in 'Hunnish practices', the exact nature of which has
engaged the curious ever since. He accused her of adultery

with at least one of her thirty reputed lovers, and she was found guilty but was cleared on appeal. It is likely that Christabel did not coin the expression and that 'Hunnish' was slang for barbarous in her high-society circle. Nowadays there are no longer any 'unnameable acts' and the phrase lives on only in comic banter; another proverbial formula, 'The Hun is always either at your throat or your feet', was quoted by James Bond in Ian Fleming's fiction, but was used and perhaps coined by Churchill.

The Germans are now our friends, though after her death in 2002 it was revealed that the Queen Mother had gone on referring to them as the Hun since 1937 – so much for the royals' supposed affinities. But the designation is still resurrected for 'amusing' journalese provocations, as when motoring-journalist-turned-populist-pundit Jeremy Clarkson opined in the *Sun* in 2003, 'Some say we cannot possibly join the single currency because we'll wake up next morning with the Hun in charge and a baguette on the kitchen table.'

It is a feature of twenty-first-century British English that it is relatively poor in racial slurs compared with some other languages, despite Salman Rushdie claiming the opposite in his Channel 4 polemic of 1982: 'British thought, British society has never been cleansed of the filth of imperialism. It's still there, breeding lice and vermin, waiting for unscrupulous people to exploit it for their own ends . . .' Xenophobia of course still surfaces, in extremist publications, and here, again, is the *Sun* in 2002: 'Britain's military and emergency services are on full alert for a terrorist attack on the UK tomorrow – the anniversary of September 11 . . . today Tony Blair will tell the Hun that it must act to topple Iraqi madman Saddam Hussein.'

Toast

There are dozens of toast-inspired internet sites, all in English. One discussion group typical of the genre was established in 2000, in its moderator's words, to promote 'a better understanding and enjoyment' of the frugal, wholly unpretentious, made-in-a-moment snack. On its pages British and North American contributors swap toast-related reminiscences and culinary tips, but levity is discouraged: posting jokes 'is flippant and belittles toast. It's not funny and I don't intent to litter our list with this sort of stuff: just a warning.'

The most recent reports on the subject of toast make interesting reading, in that they are quite contradictory: on the one hand the industry magazine *The Grocer* reported a 7 per cent decrease in toast-munching in 2007. On the other, UK fast-food outlets and some continental-style pavement cafés have started to add toast to their menus, and to advertise it as if it were the latest thing. A 2009 study revealed toast to be a favourite food of UK students, whether by force or by choice it didn't say. It was *Observer* food critic Nigel Slater who confirmed toast as an icon of Englishness in his 2003 memoir of the same name. As the *Guardian* noted, 'The story begins with burnt toast and ends with profiteroles and hot chocolate sauce. Between lies a universe bounded by Caramac, grilled grapefruit, Terry's All Gold, Bisto, crab-and-watercress sandwiches, cheese-and-onion crisps, Campbell's meatballs in gravy and lemon meringue, hostess trolleys, Hush Puppies, Pyrex plates, driving gloves of string and leather, books from the Folio Society, winceyette sheets, salmon pink begonias, Dreft, *The Golden Shot* and *Randall & Hopkirk (Deceased)*.'

Although other cultures must have grilled – and burned – bread (and cheese) since hunter-gatherers began to settle, it is England that has contributed the result to the global menu, and given the world – what exactly is it? Not a delicacy, not a dish, scarcely even a foodstuff or a culinary footnote. Just a name that also evokes the old comforts of the hearth – warming our feet by the fireside or waving a toasting-fork (formerly a toasting-iron, both terms were once slang for a rapier). The word toast itself is not originally native, though: it was imported in the fourteenth century from the French verb *toster*, itself derived from Latin *tostus*, meaning baked, parched or dried. The French then borrowed our word – *un toast* is a piece of the same – in the nineteenth century and use it still, though the Académie Française prefers *pain grillé*. Toast incidentally rhymes with 'roast' – another emblematic word from the culinary repertoire of Englishness. The resemblance is from the French stage of their evolution; roast is not ultimately from Latin but from a west Germanic root.

Toasting in the sense of raising one's glass in tribute comes from the seventeenth-century conceit that a lady to whom one might drink will flavour the company just as spiced toast does a drink (it was the habit to dunk it in a bumper – a large glass or tankard – of wine or port). In eighteenth-century English slang, a toast was, in the words of the

OED, a 'brisk old fellow fond of his glass'. Significantly perhaps, for something so taken-for-granted yet so ubiquitous, in rhyming slang it's 'Holy Ghost'; 'Mickey Most' (a 1960s record producer) a rarer alternative. In modern American slang, now used by English youth too, it's a negative concept: 'you're toast' means you are defeated, confounded, foiled, caught out – even dead (recalling the archaic 'to have someone in toast', a nineteenth-century Britishism meaning to render helpless): 'toasted' is slang for drunk, intoxicated by drugs or hung-over. For the rest of us it's still toast and marmalade, tea and toast, beans on toast (as likely as not from the chrome-finish four-slice Dualit in the kitchen) as usual, as we snuggle up, as warm as toast (next to our flueless gas fire).

See also **crumpet, cuppa**

Tosh

Making a comeback, along with other rather dated posh-sounding terms, 'tosh(!)' is a usefully inoffensive alternative to the equally English 'b****cks!', or 'b*lls!', while more expressive than 'rubbish!' or 'nonsense!', and not quite as silly as 'pants!' or as childish as 'knickers!' 'Hogwash' is a little more specific, 'balderdash' harrumph-ing, 'piffle' lightweight. 'Bosh', of course, is both a coincidental rhyme and a virtual synonym, but sounds snootier and has yet to enjoy a revival: it is thought to be the Turkish word for 'empty', *boş*, first recorded in English in 1834. (Also in the formulation 'bish-bash-bosh': it can also be used as a verbal gesture, rather like slapping one's palms together to signify 'all finished' or 'job well done'.) **Dosh** is unrelated.

Typically, tosh is used to rubbish portentous or misleading rhetoric, and to dismiss palpably false claims – especially in the last few years in the context of medicine and health (homeopathy was declared to be tosh, for instance, on its 250th anniversary in 2005; 'life-enhancing drink, or load of tosh?' was the rhetorical question on a website reviewing the claims of modish health foods the following year). 'Most economic forecasting is little more than tosh,' announced the *Guardian* in 2005. For me this little word epitomises a very English, very robust impatience with pretence and pretension of all kinds, and a readiness summarily to reject and ridicule that may once have been patrician, but which we all now enjoy.

Very often intensified by adding 'unmitigated', 'pure', 'utter', 'absolute' or just 'complete', and occasionally elaborated into 'tosh and twaddle' or 'tosh and taradiddle' – even into the old formula 'tish and tosh, and old wet fish!' – the term is appropriately brusque without sounding ugly. My edition of the *Oxford English Dictionary* doesn't seem to know where the word comes from, but dates its first written use to 1892 and defines it nicely as 'bosh' or 'twaddle'. It is often assumed that it is a blend or portmanteau word made up of two pre-existing terms such as 'trash' and 'bosh', but there is no firm evidence for this. It could just be an imitation of a snort of derision, although – and it seems unlikely to be coincidental – in the later nineteenth century, 'toshers' were scavengers who searched the London sewers for objects of value. Tosh was obsolescent, except for affected usage, during the 1960s and 1970s, but began to be heard again from the eighties, used by all classes. In the 1990s, being short, sharp and conveying superior judgement, it became popular among press commentators and would-be pundits.

Very rarely heard these days, tosh used also to be a matey – or deliberately over-familiar – form of address between males, used to strangers typically by spivs and toughs. The word's last gasp was probably the Toshiba commercial of 1990 in which a cockney voice intones, "Ello Tosh, got a Toshiba?' in imitation of comedian Alexei Sayle's novelty song, "Allo John, got a new motor?' In this sense the word seems to be of Scottish origin: in Scots and Cornish dialect tosh could mean neat, trim or clean. In the slang of the more exclusive boarding schools, a tosh was a bath; in low-life milieux it meant cash, while 'tosheroon' (probably a mis-hearing of the Romany 'posh-koroona', 'half-crown') was the slang nickname for both a half-crown and a sixpence in pre-decimal currency.

Trade

In February 1997, Tory MP Elizabeth Peacock rebuked Conservative activists in London's Kensington and Chelsea constituency for selecting Alan Clark, a 'self-confessed philanderer, reprobate and adulterer', to represent the party in parliament. Mrs Peacock noted that he was 'not a very nice character, but an arrogant man who has been extremely rude about the north and people in trade – yet he is no aristocrat himself: his family made their money in the cotton business'. She was alluding to, among other provocations, Clark's definition of his social inferiors as people 'who have to buy their own furniture'. A year earlier, speaking of the Roxburgh Club, a book club for those who have their own libraries, the Duke of Buccleuch insisted, 'We don't allow people in trade to join.' Members at that time included a number of dukes, some earls, Tory minister William Waldegrave and American billionaire arts patrons John Paul Getty and Paul Mellon. It is an irony that the word that describes the very foundation of our nation's wealth has routinely been used to denigrate and damn.

The ominous words 'in trade' echo faintly in my own childhood memories. The story was often told of how a great-uncle, a captain in the colonial army, met and fell in love with his colonel's daughter aboard the ship bringing them back from India. He succeeded in marrying her, but his wife's family never spoke to him again on the grounds that his own father was a mere proprietor of a drapery store. In rather different circles, particularly in the pre-liberation homosexual underground, 'the trade' has functioned as a euphemism for those providing sex for money, as in Joe Orton's diary reference to a queen of his acquaintance, 'she has the trade in'.

The word itself comes from Middle Low German *trada*, 'track', one of several similar terms in west Germanic languages that also gave English 'tread'. The sense of the practice of an occupation appeared in the mid-sixteenth century and was a narrowing of a more general notion of activity or action. In the slang of the later seventeenth century, trade could refer to prostitution in general, coming in the nineteenth century to refer mainly to homosexual 'rent boys', with 'rough trade' denoting violent or extremely uncouth partners.

From the late eighteenth century, the phrases 'a person in trade' or 'people in trade' were frequently employed in documents and in the press as categorisations, distinguishing from farmers, soldiers and those in service, but generally without pejorative overtones. It was in Victorian times that 'in trade' also became a snobbish put-down, reflecting the resentment – and jealousy and fear – provoked by parvenus operating independently of the land-holdings and social networks that sustained the traditional ruling classes. This English prejudice against commerce (despite the jibe – attributed to Napoleon but originating with Adam Smith – that we were 'a nation of shopkeepers') was in fact part of a wider but unacknowledged discrimination by a small elite against anyone – artists, engineers or, to use a foreign term, 'intellectuals' among them – who did not subscribe to their own allegiances and modes of existence. Another memory from long ago – from the early 1970s – is of a girlfriend's father ushering me into his study, which was festooned with regimental banners and memorabilia. After asking what my intentions were towards his daughter, he ignored my mumbled, scarcely audible attempt at a noncommittal response and continued: '. . . my father was in the Church, I was in the army, one of my sons farms and the other is in the City – now what are you going into?' It is ironic but unsurprising that banking, together with the other **posh** person's occupation of choice, publishing, not to mention cultivating the land for profit, was exempted from the taint of 'trade'. In fact the story is even more complicated, as prejudice was not solely top-down. Many poorer people too, especially country folk, felt misgivings if not shame at engaging in trade rather than pursuits that harked back to an imagined pre-industrial heritage in which pious **yeomen** flourished. Until well into the 1960s, the 'tradesman's entrance' was literally – and in slang anatomically too – the back passage.

Since even the snobbiest representatives of Old England succumbed to the free market, the word trade (in this sense abandoned along with 'arriviste' and 'nouveau riche') no longer forms part of the discourses of Little Englanders. In the first world 'trader' now means a finance or commodity specialist – trading bizarrely complex 'instruments' or virtualised products, while the polemical debate has moved to the global context and hinges on whether the t-word is preceded by 'free' (the right's preference for *sauve qui peut* and the devil take the hindmost) or 'fair' (the left's promotion of subsidies for disadvantaged – and sometimes underperforming – producers).

See also **gentle**

Twee

On 2 February 1980, *The Times* delivered a withering ad hominem dismissal under the heading 'James Bond: from action man to a slapstick puppet hero'. 'The moment Roger Moore stepped into the graceless *Live and Let Die*,' it went on, 'Bond became flabby and harmless, a square guffaw at the expense of a decade now past. With his twee cigars, smart sporting blazers and cosy features Moore threw out Connery's insolent cool and replaced it with an awful pink geniality.' Of all the terms used – graceless, flabby, harmless, cosy – perhaps the most striking – and the least likely (apart perhaps from 'pink') to be associated with Bond in normal circumstances – is twee; the evocation, even if strictly speaking inaccurate, of slim panatellas, cigarillos, mini-cheroots in flat tins, is truly hurtful.

The first use of the word in *The Times* was in 1934, in analysing the qualities of the 'magic voices' required for broadcasting during the Children's Hour: 'The "twee", "talk-down-to-kiddies" type of story-teller is worth only a self-estimated value, and that is nothing at all.' In 1940, the editor implicitly contrasted the context of war with '. . . the threshold of the Easter holidays, it is scarcely necessary to

308

mention the utterly twee spring frocks, the absolutely eat-able little hats, the natty spring suitings and shirtings and shoeings that smile seductive in a thousand windows'. Twee has since been applied, often qualified by 'painfully', 'unbearably' or more recently 'terminally', to all things cloy-ingly English, from inglenooks, Laura Ashley fabrics and middle-class sitcoms to Mrs Gaskell, Dorset and Fortnum & Mason. In 2006, the *Daily Mail* rather disloyally complained that there was no English word 'somewhere between naff and twee' that exactly evoked the special flavour of royal celebrations. Twee is one of the keywords in the lexicon of English self-laceration, and not surprisingly it's difficult to render its flavour exactly into other languages. In neigh-bouring French, for example, *mignard* or *chichiteux* come close but suggest rather 'pretty-pretty' and 'fussy' respectively. Spanish has no real equivalent, perhaps significantly, though one suggested word is *cursi*, which, however, carries louder, more vulgar connotations.

Twee originated around the turn of the twentieth cen-tury and is said to be an adult imitation of a childish mispronunciation of 'sweet'. Such usages, which include pet names and other kinds of 'baby talk' are technically known as 'hypocorisms', from Greek *hypo* ('under the heading of') and *koros* or *kore* ('boy' or 'girl child'). The very sound of the word seems to reinforce its sense: saying it physically involves a pouting of the mouth and a dimpling of the cheeks and it whistlingly chimes with 'teeny', 'wee', 'weedy'. Hardcore academic linguists are wary of so-called sound symbolism, the idea that particular sounds necessarily evoke particular meanings, and it's certainly true that such associations almost never apply across more than one lan-guage, but the pioneering linguist Otto Jespersen remarked a hundred years ago on the association of the high front vowel sound that occurs in twee with the notion of 'diminutive' in English.

The words used by lexicographers in trying to define twee – 'dainty', 'fey', 'precious', 'cute', 'prettified', sometimes 'mawkish' – are all themselves complex enough in their connotations to tax the abilities of translators. The word is known in the USA but usually labelled 'chiefly British' in dictionaries; it has taken on a new significance there since the 1990s as the name of a sub-genre of pop music. Twee, also known as 'cuddlecore', is a kind of self-consciously lightweight indie pop dismissed by detractors as insipid, but celebrated by devotees as 'delicious and sweet'.

What, then, is the real core of the concept 'twee'? Certainly the notions of diminutive and saccharine are there, but isn't the essential component an idea of cosiness, of reassurance by way of kitsch? Of something innately English that is reinforced by other words examined in this book: by **quaint**, by **cuppa** and **crumpet** and **chat** and by **doily**, too. It's also a useful little dagger in our armoury of spitefulness: in 2007, the *Sun* commented waspishly on the then PM: 'giving a speech to members of Stonewall, the gay rights organisation, Tony Blair said the first civil partnership made him "skip with joy". How twee!'

Twit

His wife called him near-paralytic
His mum and his dad, parasitic
His sister, a git
His vicar, a twit
He brings out the worst in a critic.

Coming across this limerick, courtesy of the collection at Speedysnail.com, I realised that although this book contains many disapproving and discriminatory terms, it lists only very few of our extensive national gallery of insults. I would like to rectify this by the insertion of 'twit'. One of my father's characteristically withering put-downs (I still remember him more than forty years ago describing an uppity neighbour as 'a tuppeny-ha'penny little twit'), it conjures up a hapless nonentity, an insignificant, foolish though probably harmless irritant. Coming as it did long after 'dolt' and 'clodpoll' and the Edwardian 'nitwit' entered the language, shortly after that quintessentially 1950s epithet 'nit' (literally a louse larva), it was less shocking than its coevals 'twat' and 'tit', and not as harsh as the wonderfully demotic 'git', but like them very much home-grown, unlike the later imports from America, 'wimp', 'nerd' and 'geek'. Perhaps only 'twerp', first attested in 1874, of obscure origin and like twit

311

more usually applied to males, and 'wally' – that seemingly now defunct vogue word of the late 1970s – together with portmanteau variants 'twilly' and 'twonk' come close to epitomising the same negative qualities while sounding equally silly. It was the silliness of 'twit' that appealed to the writers of *The Goon Show* radio comedy, who included it in almost every script.

Despite the citation, it has always seemed to me that only the English and possibly the Welsh can qualify as twits; whatever the Scots and Irish deserve in terms of mild contempt, it is something subtly different. The noun began to be heard in the UK in the 1920s and remained in widespread circulation, in Australia, too, until the end of the seventies. North Americans were introduced to it via British TV comedies such as *Monty Python's Flying Circus* (with their memorable 'upper-class twit of the year' sketch) and have sometimes employed it subsequently, along with the adjective 'twittish' and noun 'twittishness', as a gentle, WASPish slight. Twit's inherent silliness is pointed up by Ken Dodd's 1965 novelty song hit 'Where's Me Shirt?', which featured the lines (delivered in a strong Liverpool accent) 'I feel a proper twit without me shirt / I've lost me ticklin'-tackle and me nicky-nocky-nee . . .' Considering the word's uncoolness, it's surprising that, according to Marianne Faithfull, when she answered her lover Mick Jagger's doorbell in 1969, he roared, 'Shut the door, you silly twit, it's the police.' (He was right: it was the drug squad.) Oddly, too, in Roald Dahl's 1979 children's fantasy *The Twits* (the Spanish translation is entitled *Los Cretinos*), the eponymous couple are in fact not harmless, hapless twits but malevolent, smelly and dirty.

Before its demise, *Punch* magazine invented a benchmark of English ineptitude and buffoonery, which it called the 'twit factor' with which to assess public figures, 'calculated by multiplying a Breeding Quotient (BQ), marked between 1 and 5, by the Outrage Index (OI), based upon observed behaviour, marked between 1 and 10, and then dividing the result by the Agreed Mitigator (AM), a mark between 1 and 10 assessed on the basis of redeeming features such as intelligence, professional merit etc.'. The *Daily Mirror* ran a more straightforward 'Twit of the Week' column in 1992, rewarding readers' nominations with a tenner, while internet postings frequently use the label as a non-libellous insult for such as Oliver Letwin, Tory promoter of the poll tax, Hollywood star Keira Knightley for claiming that fame is a bore, most Englishmen played by Hugh Laurie and Hugh Grant, and any non-techie who asks a silly question in a techie user group.

Used in preference to a much stronger epithet (after a complaint from a nine-year-old reader's mum, publisher Random House agreed to replace twat with twit in Jacqueline Wilson's novel *My Sister Jodie*) or as an affectionate rebuke, twit can serve as the verbal equivalent of a pulled punch, as when comedienne Caroline Quentin accused her pal Amanda Holden of behaving 'like a twit' by having a doomed fling with actor Neil Morrissey in 2001. Hence in twenty-first-century England the word can sound a little old-fashioned, or perhaps just not robust enough: my nine-year-old son tells me that 'double-headed twitboy' is one of the very mildest insults in his schoolfriends' repertoire.

There is also the verb to twit – to tease and provoke in a cheeky, impertinent, **chippy** English manner – which was recorded in this form as long ago as the sixteenth century. It is treated by dictionaries as standard English rather than as a colloquialism, probably due to its ancient lineage. It comes via Middle English *atwite* from Old English *aetwitan*, composed of *aet*, 'against', and *witan*, 'to accuse or reproach'.

Although some reference sources assume that the more modern noun derives from the old verb, reasoning that a twit is someone who is twitted, this is unproven: twit might be a contraction of 'nitwit', might have some metaphorical link with 'twitter' or could be a quite separate, perhaps arbitrary coinage.

As a final footnote, there have been claims, argued over in pubs and refracted across the internet at the time of writing, that twit is actually an obscure technical term denoting a pregnant goldfish. It isn't so, but like most urban legends, this one resists all gainsaying.

Understatement

Not-for-profit website ICONSonline currently lists 'understatement' at number 738 in its 'Icons of England' (Christmas panto is at number one, Rupert Bear at number eight), commenting, 'Not only does understatement prevent us from being reduced to hysteria in the face of the unexpected and the outrageous, but it also helps us not to get too big-headed in the event of some outstanding achievement.' It's nothing new. Deliberate understatement for effect, with the labels 'meiosis' (from *meioun*, to diminish) and 'litotes' (from *litos*, simple), were part of the repertoire of Ancient Greek rhetoric. But it's something we, the English, are said (not least by ourselves, with quiet pride) to be particularly prone to, and something so English that French has no word for it (a few worldly intellectuals might employ *l'understatement*; others would have to cobble together something like the clunkily literal *affirmation en dessous de la vérité*).

The concept relates to those other key aspects of Englishness, restraint, reticence, moderation and humour (see **GSOH**), and is a form of hypocrisy. Understatings issue from below the unflappable stiff upper lips of the heroically unperturbed – or the callously indifferent. But the word is usually appreciative: 'a talent for . . .' 'a master of . . .' 'a nice line in . . .'. It is of course the opposite of the bombast, exaggeration and overdramatising that we expect foreigners (and that includes fellow members of the **Anglosphere**) to exhibit. In 1799, when it was first recorded, 'understatement' had a different sense or at least emphasis; it meant deliberately underestimating or stating falsely (in which sense it still occurs in financial jargon). During the nineteenth century, the word came to characterise an English habit of deliberately, later perhaps unconsciously, underemphasising in order to turn an encounter to one's advantage, instil confidence, create humour, etc. It enabled mealy-mouthed Victorians to avoid calling a spade a spade, let alone a 'bloody shovel', and gave rise to a host of clichés of the 'slight unpleasantness', 'minor inconvenience' variety. In *Watching the English*, anthropologist Kate Fox lists the typical examples of understatement in everyday conversation: 'not bad' (meaning outstandingly brilliant); 'a bit of a nuisance' (meaning disastrous, traumatic, horrible); 'not very friendly' (meaning abominably cruel). She ascribes the compulsion to play down to two 'default' characteristics of the English: their deep-seated moderation and their avoidance of seriousness. 'Moderation' doesn't quite do justice to the upper-class code whereby English males resisted any display of feelings or voicing of opinions, and in their own minds at least, shrugged off misfortune and stared down danger.

Some examples have passed into folklore: Vice-Admiral Collingwood's dispatch from Trafalgar after a hand-to-hand battle to the death across the decks of the *Temeraire*: 'the contest was vigorous'. Scott's companion Captain Lawrence Oates leaving his tent in the Antarctic blizzard with the words, 'I am just going outside and may be some time.'

'Things are a bit sticky,' reported Brigadier General Tom Brodie, his men surrounded by 300,000 Chinese troops in Korea in 1951.

Understatement has never been restricted to the officer class; members of the middle and lower-middle classes have striven to appear imperturbable and unfussed, and the lower orders too have favoured a man-of-few-words machismo that relies on euphemism ('have a word with him' or 'sort him out' could mean beat him to within an inch of his life) or facetious understatement ('a bit out of order', i.e. shockingly unacceptable). Of course the compulsion to understate has become embedded, institutionalised like **eccentricity** (even women do it): so, of a helpless sot, 'he likes a drop or two'; 'a slight spot of bother' is substituted for 'a horrendous calamity'. Understatement may be commendable when it is self-deprecating – 'I was just doing my job' – or seeking to avoid offence: 'She's not the most highly qualified in the field', or conflict: 'We seem to have come up against a difference of opinion.' But the danger is that people who do not know the quirks of the culture – in other words, nearly all foreigners – will take these statements at their face value and fail to grasp their real import. A closely related quirk, and one that bemuses 'non-natives', is what some ethnolinguists have called 'one-downmanship', the opposite of boasting, whereby speakers denigrate themselves, minimise their talents and wallow in false modesty ('I'm absolutely hopeless at public speaking/DIY/balancing my books'), sometimes competing to appear less competent than others in a ritual known as 'capping', from the implicit 'You may be poor, but I can cap that . . .'. Language teachers usually illustrate this by reference to the comic 'Four Yorkshiremen' sketch from *At Last the 1948 Show* and *Monty Python's Flying Circus*, in which the principals try to outdo one another with increasingly absurd accounts of their deprived childhoods. Like most of the traits we find so appealing in ourselves, understatement, when it becomes ingrained, can grate on the nerves after a while. When it involves transparently misrepresenting the facts – politicians downplaying yet another fiasco ('things didn't go quite as we expected' is a favourite) – it's rightly derided, and in private conversations fatuous attempts to de-emphasise ('I think Lucy was rather disappointed to lose her job') invite the **sarky** put-down, 'that's the understatement of the year/decade'.

The alternative approach is still distasteful to many of us if it means gushing (first attested in this sense in the 1860s) and – another figure of speech – hyperbole (Greek for 'excess') or 'hype'. But therapy, coaching and training specialists now encourage us to jettison false humility in favour of 'bigging oneself up': to quote Helen Whitten, MD of Positiveworks Ltd, 'I am continually dismayed that whenever one suggests to anyone young or old that they need to learn to . . . articulate their strengths in order to succeed that they reject the idea as something too "American"'. New Britain is not Old England, however, and writing of supposed English reticence, *Times* columnist Philip Howard noted in 1990 that 'Foreigners never believed in this strong, silent stereotype for a moment. They have met our tourists and seen our tabloid press. They know that the national characteristics of English speech are hyperbole, obscenity, bigotry and repetition.' This is not the whole story either; the truth is that, in the contradictory, paradoxically complex England of today, ritual modesty and a traditional refusal to over-react can coexist with their opposites: high fives, hugging and kissing on the playing field, the emotional incontinence of celebrity worship, the in-yer-face, effing-and-blinding, anything-goes hysteria of **yoof** broadcasting and fly-on-the-wall TV. As regards the word itself, it's interesting to see exactly how we deploy it: a scan of thousands of recent examples shows that in 90 per cent of cases, it forms part of the formulaic pattern 'to say . . . would be an understatement', proving at least that we use our rhetorical devices and our clichés knowingly. 'Understated', typically applied to clothing, accessories or decor, is, significantly, still uniquely an appreciative term.

See also **fusspot, handbag, irony**

Wellie

If the horticultural charity Garden Organic has its way, the third week in April will become known as National Wellie Week: families and companies are urged to wear their boots for the duration and undertake wellie-themed activities to raise money. The wellington boot, once symbolising England's military grandeur, has since the 1970s been appropriated, under its nickname, as a household word, now a symbol of homely, hearty enthusiasm, native vigour and/or outdoor living. The boot began as an early nineteenth-century aristocratic fashion statement – the Duke of Wellington's personal adaptation of the high-fronted, tasselled Hessian boot (around 1818 the Iron Duke's name was briefly attached to a style of coat, hat and trousers too); by the 1850s, the first waterproof rubber versions of a calf-height boot began to be mass-produced, to be worn by women and children as well as haughty males. A mac(kintosh) and wellingtons (and umbrella too) were staples of the fashion-free English wardrobe from the thirties to the seventies, and have lived on, though the preferred colour has changed from black to green to multicoloured and even patterned.

The domesticated diminutive form of the name ('welly-bobs' and 'wellygogs' are baby-talk alternatives) was popularised by Scots comedian Billy Connolly in 1974 and subsequently by radio announcers and DJs: this ageless, classless item of footwear became a sort of cosy national joke. The light-hearted 'give it some wellie' urged the hearer to apply more force, acceleration or aggression (the image evoked, according to word-buff Nigel Rees, may be a gardening boot applied to a spade rather than the act of kicking), while more recently, and rather oddly, the words 'pasty' or 'beans' can be substituted with the same sense. As used in 1989 by Liverpool legend Ron Yates commenting on Wimbledon Football Club's style, 'It was just wellie, wellie, wellie. The ball must have been crying for mercy' – the implication, though, is certainly of brute strength rather than skill. In the phrases 'get the wellie' or 'the order of the wellie', the word is substituting for 'the boot' as a colloquialism for dismissal. As a verb (common in military slang at the time of the Falklands conflict), it means attack, bully or defeat. From the 1980s, the noun, here probably a shortening of the silly euphemism 'willie-wellie', could also refer to a condom.

Wellie-wanging is a competitive sport probably originating as an improvisation by campers or rural revellers, now typically practised at village fetes and in pub gardens, that consists of tossing a rubber wellington boot as far as possible. The 'wanging' presumably echoes the sound of the boot hitting turf or concrete, or else is analogous to 'fling' and 'wing'. A so-called world championship is held annually in the village of Upper Thong in Yorkshire. A different aspect of countryside Englishness is conjured up by 'green wellie', used to characterise either county-set hoorays, young farmers, showjumpers and their ilk, or alternatively (often labelled pejoratively 'the green-wellie brigade') *bien-pensant Guardian*-reading ramblers and exponents of environmental issues, or well-heeled owners of rural second homes. Penultimately and inevitably, since the millennium, 'wellied', like almost every other synonym for damaged, defeated or destroyed, is used to mean drunk. Last of all, I've just learned that **slag** wellies is provincial English town-centre slang for thigh-high or otherwise provocative boots, worn by females.

It's worth remembering, after all these reflections on the wellie as a symbol, that it's really much more crucial than that. The wellie is what makes the English climate manage-able, makes the puddles and waterlogged ditches of our rain-lashed island negotiable – makes a **wet** and **windy** Saturday a potential time of play, rather than misery . . .

Wet

'Wet' ('he is a wet and a weed' – the fictional public schoolboy Nigel Molesworth in 1954) came to notice as a vogue term in the political and media lexicon from 1980, when PM Margaret Thatcher first applied the public-school term of derision to members of her party she considered indecisive, lacking in resolve and/or unreliable. 'Tory wets' became a recognised relatively liberal sub-variety. Of then Foreign Secretary Francis Pym, for example, a 1982 profile noted, 'his doubts about the speed and direction of the Government's economic policies arise not from the fact that he is a "wet" whatever that might mean, but because he . . . shares that scepticism of fashionable dogma which is the hallmark of the traditional Tory'.

Wet is an ancient word, occuring in Old English and other north Germanic languages, and is related to Slavonic *voda* and Greek *hudor*, water. Either as noun or adjective it has been used figuratively, derisively, of people since the 1930s, sometimes twinned with 'weedy'. Since the 1990s it is often coupled with 'wimp' or 'wimpy' ('he sounds merely a wet wimp' – *The Times*, on Stephen Fry's reading of his own story *The Hippopotamus*), but often occurs straightforwardly in the admonition, still typically by a female to an irresolute male, 'Don't be so wet!'

Someone miserable can be described as being like, or having a face like 'a wet weekend', an expression popular from the 1980s but probably older (the apotheosis of boredom, apparently, is 'a wet weekend in Wigan', recorded from 1991), and there is a long association between water(iness) and weakness or insipidity. Although the association is now taken for granted, it is not entirely clear which metaphor it derives from. Wet of course (along with **windy**) characterises English weather, with the gloom, torpidity and irritation that results. In 1967, *The Times* expatiated on the problems of dressing for a rainy summer in the fashions of the day: 'What happens in practice is that you leave the house smothered from head to toe in flower-printed plastic, and twenty minutes later the sun is blazing down from a cloudless sky and you are crackling along getting more and more sticky and cross.' Wet can also describe a sorry-looking individual – or dog – after being drenched, or a once-rigid material after immersion.

'Drip' has been employed since at least the 1930s (in US usage, too) to describe an ineffectual, disappointing character, and 'dripping' ('her husband is absolutely dripping') was a favourite term of dismissal by Sloane Rangers and other upper-class speakers from the later 1970s. In earlier decades, 'sopping', 'wringing' and more rarely 'soaking' were public-school and varsity synonyms. 'Damp' may also mean feeble in (usually middle- or upper-class) colloquial speech, and 'moist' occurs today as both a middle-class colloquialism and, much more abusively, a vogue term in street slang.

See also **windy**

Whimsy

T he old word 'whim' and its derivatives are among those (like 'humour' – see **GSOH**) that pedants and eccentrics like to deliver in an antique pronunciation, in this instance with an aspirated 'wh' (whistled through pursed lips) instead of the standard 'w'. Whim, then meaning a play on words, is first attested in 1641; by the end of the century, it could also denote a caprice or eccentric notion. The word was probably a shortening of 'whimsy', itself recorded in 1605 in the sense of a sudden fancy. The origin of both seems to be a nonsense word of obscure derivation that among other things was a nickname for the female pudendum. 'Whim-wam', dating from 1529, could also signify, like its later synonym 'knick-knack', an amusing decoration or ornament, or a fanciful idea. No one is sure whether this is an arbitrary, i.e. meaningless, invention or if it is an alteration of an older term such as Norwegian *kvimma*, meaning 'to flutter'. It was thought to be obsolete, but word-buff Nigel Rees records a number of folksy formulae ('a whim-wam to wind the sun up/for ducks to perch on for a goose's bridle', etc.) still used by parents to fend off inquisitive children.

In the eighteenth and early nineteenth centuries, whim

and its derivatives were often employed disapprovingly, as in William Cowper's lines, 'Wearing out life in his religious whim, / Till his religious whimsy wears out him', or in Samuel Richardson's *Clarissa*, '. . . to proceed in such a shocking and solemn whimsy', and the straiter-laced Victorians continued in this usage, but by the last two decades of the nineteenth century, collocations like 'charming whimsy' and 'inspired whimsy' began to appear, describing works of popular fiction and the humour exemplified by *Punch* magazine. The semantic components of the words bring together a clutch of English tendencies: indulgence in the fanciful and fantastical, facetiousness and levity, the complicating of responses to nature. The seemingly **gentle** and harmless counterpoint to cruel satire and habitual sarcasm, whimsy, which taps into a cult of childhood, or what crueller commentators have labelled English infantilism, is often tinged with erudition and poignancy – exponents who come to mind are Victorians Edward Lear and Lewis Carroll; in the nineteen-forties and -fifties Heath Robinson and Roland Emmett with their displays of childlike ingenuity, and the more acerbic Ronald Searle. For some, whimsy reached an apogee in the Edwardian era with publication of Kenneth Grahame's *The Wind in the Willows* in 1908, a work now recognised by many as genuine home-grown English mysticism, such that extracts are read at weddings in lieu of religious discourses or prayers. The bittersweet Englishness of rural arcadia was also reflected in A. A. Milne's stories and verses and re-imagined with an admixture of faerie and the help of hallucinogens in the flower-power era in the songs of Donovan, Syd Barrett and lesser practitioners of psychedelia like Tyrannosaurus Rex. By the 1990s, the mood has changed to 'some whimsy by a liberal do-gooder' (the *Sun*); 'a byword for woolly thinking whimsy and knit-your-own naffness' (*The Times*) – and Prince Philip, too, is said to disapprove of what he calls his son's 'indulgence in whimsy'.

So the wh-words have travelled in a sort of arc, from dismissive (disapproval of the facetious, the eccentric) to commending (exaltation of childhood, childishness and childlike-ness) to dismissing (impatience with the unnecessary) again. With the advent of the hard-edged 'me generation(s)' of the last two decades, have we lost our taste for whimsy, or our ability to evoke it? Certainly in 1998 an edict went out from executives at the BBC ordering programme-makers to develop sitcoms with 'more bite and less whimsy'. For a while it seemed that whimsy's last gasp might be Douglas Adams's *Hitchhiker's Guide to the Galaxy* (in the radio and TV versions, not the unwatchable movie), but English stand-up Eddie Izzard and the Irish *Father Ted* comedies kept the flame alight, and in the noughties a new inflection was provided by the duo the Mighty Boosh. Beyond the mass media, whimsy flourishes in domestic contexts in one of its earliest forms, that of ornaments and curios. The best known examples are porcelain animal figurines called Whimsies, manufactured by George Wade Pottery and eagerly collected, though the adjective whimsy is applied equally to awful fey folk art, and so-called 'nucraft' indulgences, as often as not home-made in the US or Canada. In the end, whimsy is an ambivalent thing, antique and antic, equally something to treasure and something to be embarrassed by.

'Mimsy' is an odd coinage that may or may not be related to the wh-words. It was either invented or borrowed from northern dialect by Lewis Carroll for his nonsense verse (Carroll's Humpty Dumpty declared it to be a blend of 'miserable' and 'flimsy') but has been used since as an adjective to mean 'prim', 'fey' or **twee**. It can also be a playful euphemism for the female pudendum, as in gossip website Popbitch's 2008 report that blonde model Agyness Deyn 'dyes her mimsy the same shade of platinum as her hair', so we seem indeed to have come full circle.

Wicked

Long before its slang sense caught on, this was an emblematic word for a particular kind of English behaviour, epitomised by such folk devils as the wicked squire (some legends, like those surrounding Sir Rowland Alston of Odell Castle in Bedfordshire, were the stuff of quasi-documentary histories, others provided fictional melodramas with a stock figure), the wicked uncle (from *Hamlet* through to modern children's stories) and, shared with pan-European folklore, the wicked stepmother or witch. Lord Byron referred to himself as 'wicked' George, recalling his own late father who was widely known by the epithet, and in ironic contrast to the supposedly 'good George' of the day, the King.

Although wicked had been used since the beginning of the twentieth century as a folksy or literary colloquialism in North America, in the form of a figurative intensifier ('wicked cold', for example) or synonym for 'daring and successful' ('to play a wicked hand'), it was probably adopted independently by British youngsters at the end of the 1970s, by analogy with the American slang use of 'bad' to mean excellent, an example of what is technically known as 'ironic reversal'. When part of UK '**yoof**-speak' it can be spelled 'wikkid', elaborated to 'well wicked' or shortened to 'wick', and is an interesting example of what linguists call a vogue term of appreciation (like 'ace', 'brill', 'mint', 'fit', etc. in their day) that hasn't fallen quickly out of use as such terms usually do. Although it may be cutting edge only in the primary school playground these days (and in the mouth of Ron Weasley in the Harry Potter books or 'wigga' parody Ali G), wicked shows no sign of disappearing from the slang lexicon and has been picked up by adult speakers – among them the homeless, drug-dealers and users, and chavs, as well as more respectable parents aping their childrens' speech-patterns, fashion designer John Galliano – 'Fabrics that are softer and stretchier are being invented all the time and new machinery, it's wicked' – and footballer David Beckham (when he shaved his head in imitation of Robert de Niro in *Taxi Driver*): 'I watched it the other night and thought, "That's wicked".' Fellow footballer Rio Ferdinand pronounced that meeting Nelson Mandela was wicked . . . and, of course, mockney chef Jamie Oliver on his Aga cooker: 'It's wicked for toasting teacakes and **crumpet**s.' Tabloid and **yoof** journalists routinely use the word to express, simultaneously, breathless enthusiasm and a phoney, patronising mateyness.

The standard adjective, first recorded in the thirteenth century, comes from the Old English nouns *wicca*, 'wizard', and *wicce*, 'witch'. In addition to meaning 'of evil character and/or behaviour' (editions of the Bible in English abound in the adjective, while the 1485 Geneva Bible has the archaic 'Let the Wicked forsake his waies'), from around 1600 the word had the secondary senses of roguish, sly or mischievous (Shakespeare uses it as a synonym for 'rascally'). From Victorian times this extra dimension, this connotation of 'naughtiness', began to oust the earlier literal denotations, resulting in the word being used to castigate badly behaved children. Playing on its ambiguity was one of Oscar Wilde's rhetorical tricks; in a moment of near-seriousness he wrote, 'As long as war is regarded as wicked, it will always have its fascination. When it is looked upon as vulgar, it will cease to be popular.' There then followed a descent into cliché in the form of books and articles entitled 'The Wicked Wit of . . .' Sir Winston/Jane Austen/ Charles Dickens – and Oscar himself.

See also **fab**, **nang**

Windy

'**W**et and windy' used to be the stock phrase heard in almost every forecast of English weather, conveying as it did the key components of our marine climate; conditions likely to obtain somewhere across the island on almost any day of the year. Windy alone in earlier times could also mean long-winded, bombastic, voluble, garrulous ('another windy speech from the honourable gentleman'), while in the old phrase 'like the barber's cat, all wind and water' (used contemptuously of someone opinionated or boastful), water is probably a euphemism for 'piss'.

'Get' or 'have the wind up', later 'put the wind up (someone)', dates from the early twentieth century, punning on the phraseology of sailors and denoting the onset of fear. As part of the hearty slang of the public schools and armed forces, recorded from World War I, windy could mean either momentarily fearful, or habitually nervous or cowardly, and frequently conveyed deep contempt for those breaching the codes of acceptably heroic behaviour. As used to dismiss empty talk, the idea is of wind as insubstantial, yet expansive, inflationary. Referring to cowardice, the association is with physiological panic reactions: heavy breathing and the release of intestinal gas (the correct term for the latter is 'flatus'). Nowadays, if heard at all, windy is more likely to denote the literal 'breaking of wind', as in a 2007 vignette from the *Guardian*: under the heading 'Better out than in: club tells windy member to go outside', it was reported that seventy-seven-year-old retired bus driver Maurice Fox had been censured by Kirkham Street Sports and Social Club in Paignton, Devon, for breaking wind too often, too loudly and, frankly, too pungently. Fox was quoted as saying, 'I sit by the door anyway and try to get out when I can . . . but sometimes it takes me by surprise and just pops out. They can be a bit loud at times: if I've got time and know they are coming I go into the porch inside the door – and there is no smell at all since I gave up the cider and started on the Bass.' 'Windypops' is jocular family slang for flatulence, alternatively expressed as 'Daisy's done a windy'. In contemporary rhyming slang, 'a bit Mork' can refer to the literal and to the figurative senses of windy: still used more than two decades on, it's short for *Mork and Mindy*, the name of the insipid US comedy shown between 1978 and 1982.

When not used literally but metaphorically, then, this seemingly straightforward adjective manages to incorporate three key aspects of Englishness simultaneously – **understatement,** euphemism and facetiousness. Maurice Fox, by the way, now visits the Palace Place club, where his wind does not seem to cause so much of a stir. 'I think it's because the Palace is men-only.'

See also **foggy**, **wet**

Wizard

An obsolescent expression of breathless, ingenuous English enthusiasm may after all be making a comeback, or at least clinging to life in these less innocent times. For most of us emphatically dated (but see below) and forever associated with hearty upper-class enthusiasms, 'wizard' – the adjective and exclamation – was first recorded in the slang sense of 'excellent' in 1922. It brings to mind the breathless adventuring of Buchan's **plucky** protagonists, of Biggles and Algy and Ginger, a lost world of unquestioning loyalties and public-school bonhomie. Regularly uttered by the boy heroes (but not the girls) of Enid Blyton's *Famous Five* stories from the 1950s, it featured unsurprisingly in Craig Brown's 2006 parody in which the **chums** metamorphose into contestants on the TV reality show *Big Brother*: '"It's absolutely wizard! I can't wait to explore that secret underground smuggler's passage!" exclaimed Julian, who was tall and strong for his age.'

The Wizard was a long-running boys' comic, first published in 1922; during its first thirty years it featured heroes such as 'Wilson the Wonder Athlete', who came from the Yorkshire moors to break the four-minute-mile barrier long before Roger

Bannister; Bill Samson, 'The Wolf of Kabul', and his native servant Chung; 'Limp-along Leslie', a lame sheep-farming footballer with a lame dog, winners at international sheep dog trials and at Wembley, and Smith of the Lower Third. In 1963, *Wizard* was amalgamated with its rival *Rover*, then was revived from 1970 to 1978, when 'Cast Iron Bill', Britain's toughest goalkeeper, hung up his boots for the last time.

The enduring cliché of RAF slang 'wizard prang', translatable as 'a fun crash' ('prang', first written down in 1941, mimics the sound of metal in collision), defines cool insouciance – or hare-brained recklessness – in the face of death, and was in use among all ranks during the Second World War, as a humble navigator's log records. Among comments such as 'no picnic' and 'intense flak' is the entry for '8/8/44 Bremen', which reads: 'Wizard prang, area devistated [*sic*] 2000x4000 yeards [*sic*] bang on bombing. Hordes of searchlights flak pretty accurate.' From 1966 to 1971, *Smash* comic ran a half-page strip called 'Wiz War' devoted to the feud between two wizards: the white-robed Wizard Prang and his black-clad enemy Demon Druid, and for completists it should be noted that in *Whoops Baghdad*, the unlamented Frankie Howerd vehicle, the 1973 successor to *Up Pompeii*, the character of Wizard Prang was played by Bill Fraser.

The word wizard in its original sense of male sorcerer is from Old English *wys*, 'wise', with the ending '-ard': 'one' or 'male person'; it was first recorded in writing in 1550. By the seventeenth century, it had come to mean not only an expert in magic (a Mr Anderson, the 'Wizard of the North', performed conjuring tricks at Prince Albert's birthday celebrations at Balmoral in 1849), but a brilliant practitioner of literature (Thomas Hardy was dubbed 'the Wessex Wizard' by the poet Siegfried Sassoon), political strategy (Lloyd George was known, not always affectionately, as 'the Welsh wizard', while

Dylan Thomas was 'the Welsh wizard of words'), art, sport, etc. The uninitiated may still refer to a maker of electronic magic as a 'computer wizard' or the abbreviated 'whiz(z)'.

In the print media, the adjective and, more rarely, the exclamation survive in the overexcited, parodic code of tabloid journalists. Under the headline 'A wizard name!', the *Daily Mail* reported in 2006 on the latest fads in baby names, which that year included Gandalf and Superman. 'According to a trawl of British birth certificates, there are six Lord of the Ring wizards growing up in Britain, along with two little boys who apparently like to wear their underpants on the outside.' A year later, the same paper revealed that J. K. Rowling's magician, Harry Potter, had helped standards at Robert Mellors Primary and Nursery School in Arnold, Nottinghamshire, to rise dramatically after pupils picked him as the inspiration for their classes: the headline this time was 'Just wizard!'

'Wizard wheeze', in the sense of a brilliant and cunning scheme or trick, though it sounds old-fashioned and arch, turns up a surprising number of references in a contemporary internet search. Formerly part of a Molesworthian schoolboy repertoire, but these days used by private individuals as well as bloggers and journalists, it nearly always refers ironically to creative accounting practices or government attempts to hoodwink the public. In fact wizard *tout court* is still part of the slang lexicon. A posting on the CBBC website in 2002 by thirteen-year-old Chester from Reading declared, 'My fave slang is "cosmic" and I say it when something is just totally "minted". My crew also likes to say "wizard" which means out of this world!!!!!!!!!!!!!!!!!!!' More recently I have recorded young people using 'w(h)izzy', and 'w(h)izzo' (possibly from wizard, or else an imitation of the sound of speed) in the same sense of outstanding, thrilling, dazzling, etc.

Yeoman

I can still remember from my youth a well-spoken elderly lady upbraiding someone who had suggested that she was 'upper class': 'We are of pure yeoman stock!' In 'Harvest Home' (1865), Sebastian Evans described his rustic hero as 'Thewed like Adam, with a stride / Proud, yet with a noble pride— / Pride that hateth, scorneth no man: / Just, in truth, a brave young yeoman.' His fellow minor poet Alfred Austin declared in 'A Point of Honour' in 1897, 'We have never been either rich or poor, but a proud, stiff yeoman stock.'

The word, its designation and the enduring clichés it represents, nurtured in particular by the Victorians, have all but disappeared, but for centuries represented an important social category and embodied qualities thought to be especially English.

Yeoman probably began as an alteration of 'young-man', in the sense of servant or attendant, and this was its pre-sixteenth-century meaning; in 1420, the noble household included, in descending order, 'Knygt, squiere, yomon and page'. From the Reformation onwards, it was increasingly used to denote a freeholder below the rank of gentleman (see **gentle**), owner and cultivator of a small landholding;

more loosely the term described a respectable countryman, as opposed to a poor cottager or mere labourer. From the later sixteenth century, it often carried appreciative overtones, commending an upright, hard-working rural ethos; the expressions 'yeomanly' and 'yeoman('s) service' (more rarely 'yeoman's duty', 'yeoman effort') emphasising bluff, staunch loyalty. Since the nineteenth century, 'stout' is a frequent collocation, with its own connotations of well-built, unyielding to the point of immovableness, even bumptious: though unusual 'doughty' (from Old English *dohtig*, 'worthy and strong') is a word that I also associate with the yeoman.

There has been a certain fuzziness about the exact definition of the yeomanry – Latimer wrote, 'My father was a Yoman, and had no landes of his own, onlye he had a farme ...' while Cobbett says, 'Those only who rent are, properly speaking, farmers. Those who till their own land are yeomen.' Perhaps this reflects a social and linguistic ambivalence in the absence of a simple division between peasant (with its implications of feudal primitive, hence reserved for describing foreigners) and lord, and the complexities of landownership and status that obtained between the end of feudalism and the agrarian and industrial revolutions.

The core attribute, more crucial even than sturdiness and homeliness, was the yeoman's freedom and independence. There has never been a feminine counterpart to the yeoman; though 'yeowoman' was coined around 1850, it did not catch on. He represented a true nobility, derived from character and identification with the countryside, rather than from an accident of birth, at odds, too, with the modern, essentially urban notion of a deracinated, self-interested 'middle class'. The yeoman's alter ego is the rustic simpleton, since the early nineteenth century derided as yokel – an English dialect word for a green woodpecker or yellowhammer – or bumpkin, possibly from Dutch *boomken*, 'small tree' or *boomkijn*, 'squat barrel'.

The yeoman also, of course, has a military heritage, in the form of the Yeomen of the Guard, the bodyguard of the monarch founded in 1485 and still in existence with a ceremonial function, and the Yeomanry, a volunteer civil defence force of cavalry, first mustered in 1761 and merged with the Territorial Army in 1907. Nowadays the yeoman's successor, the farmer, is less likely to be seen, at least by townies, as the guardian of natural heritage, and more likely as its despoiler, and this once charged and evocative bi-syllabic mainly survives as a brand name of various robust outdoorsy items such as protective walling, drainage systems, garden tools, camping equipment, navigation aids, etc.

Yob

In December 1976, a Labour party political broadcast featured a character called 'Algernon', a stereotypically snooty upper-class male. He appeared to be free of worries, quite indifferent to the welfare of others, first attending a boarding school to avoid mixing with 'ordinary children' and afterwards not working, just avoiding being taxed. One commentator wondered (in both senses of the word), 'As I sat stunned by the blatancy of this pandering to Every(English)man's lowest political instincts I asked myself: What if the Tory press office were to devise an equivalent programme, taking as their prototype Labour voter the caricature of a scrounger, a layabout, a red agitator or a yob?'

Brutal in significance and in sound, yob is the only example of backslang – a venerable form of language disguise that has its French equivalent in *verlan* – to be adopted into mainstream speech. Originally simply the word 'boy' reversed, it soon came to be used pejoratively, taking on the more specialised sense of troublesome, uncouth youth. There is no precise female equivalent, 'hoyden' (an ill-mannered tomboy, possibly from Dutch *heidijn*, 'heathen') having (regrettably in my view) fallen out of use, but there

Yob

are plenty of predecessors in the rogue's gallery of male villains, among them my late mother's favourite, the hobbledehoy (sixteenth century, perhaps from 'hob' – a rustic dolt, 'of the hedge'), as well as the thug (nineteenth century, from *thag*, Hindi for 'thief'), the lout (defined in the mid-Victorian era as a 'heavy, idle fellow'), riff-raff (originally fifteenth-century French *rif et raf*, 'plunder and sweepings') in general, the rough and the tough, and the **oik**.

The first recorded use of yob dates from 1859. In July 1897, the *Penny Illustrated Paper* ran a report on a shooting competition written in a faux-plebeian style as if by a Little Englander deploring a victory by South Africans: '. . . what I'm cribbin' about is the blessed cheek o' some yob from a place which ain't even marked on the map'. George Edward Dyson attempted the same ventriloquism in a late war poem from 1919: 'If I was in a hurry, mate, to finish up this war / I'd lay out every Fritz on earth, but, strike me, what a yob / A man would be to work himself out of a flamin' job!' After years as a low-life colloquialism, heard in England and Ireland, (joined by 'yobo' in 1922, 'yobbo' from 1938), in 1960 the word suddenly became popular with the middle classes and the press, and since then has featured strongly (with spin-offs 'yobbery' and 'yobbishness') in our armoury of disapproval, deployed in conversational spluttering and journalistic 'why, oh why?' pieces. 'Soccer yob' became synonymous with 'football hooligan' (hooligan is the Irish surname Houlihan). The prominence, and usefulness, of the y-word is illustrated by its recent history. In February 1984, Derek Jameson, the former Fleet Street editor who inspired *Private Eye* magazine's oafish 'Sid Yobbo', was suing the BBC for libel. He publicly protested that he was 'not a yob', telling the High Court in London that during his tenure at

341

the *Daily Express*, 'I did what editors do all over the world – I used pictures of pretty girls.' In June 1988, a 1962 Rolls-Royce Silver Cloud with the number plate YOB 1 went on sale at Sotheby's, its value increased by an estimated £5,000 by the plate and the fact that it had been owned since 1974 by Dave Hill of the boisterous pop group Slade. In September 1994, the then Prime Minister, John Major, declared war on what he termed British 'yob culture', promising a 'blitz' on petty crime and urging courts to take tougher action against wrongdoers. In May 2005, the Labour government's chief adviser on youth crime called upon politicians and the media to stop calling children 'yobs' and warned that Britain risked demonising a whole generation of young people by doing so. Nonetheless, in January 2006, premier Tony Blair took part in a podcast organised by the *Sun* newspaper and urged its readers to 'shop a yob' – inform on a miscreant – as part of a campaign begun by the paper three years earlier 'to crack down on thugs who make **decent** people's lives a misery . . . to help YOU declare war on anti-social behaviour'. In October 2006, Scotland Yard banned police officers from using the word yob in official reports to describe troublemakers after Cindy Butts, the deputy chairwoman of the Metropolitan Police Authority, said it was alienating. The move did not succeed in banishing the word, the press and public still use it, and in the meantime the lexicon of loutishness continues to expand, taking in the latest folk devils, the hoodie, named after the hooded top favoured by street gang members and knife-carriers, and the ASBO, whose nickname is formed from the initials of the 'anti-social behaviour orders' imposed to restrict the movement of potential or actual law-breakers.

See also **bovver, cad, oi, slag, yoof**

Yoof

A buzzword for broadcasters and marketing specialists, a bugbear for conservatives, 'yoof' imitates the gormless pronunciation of young people themselves and the adults who seek to commodify or emulate them. It also not insignificantly imitates the strong London accent of one-time TV presenter Janet Street-Porter, who in the 1980s pioneered the genre that became known as 'yoof broadcasting'. It began with Channel 4's *Network 7*, a teen programme mixing music with chat, followed by *Def II*, *Rapido* and *The Word*. By the start of the noughties, much of the schedules was taken up with programming consciously aimed at older pre-teens, teens and twenties. As Vanessa Thorpe pointed out in the *Observer* in 2002, 'It has always been easy to poke fun at youth television, or more popularly, at "yoof TV" . . . a team of older, suited executives sitting around a table together, trying to work out what might make "hip" and "exciting" programming for young adults and adolescents is an inherently risible idea.' Six years later in the *Guardian*, Barbara Ellen wrote that 'It may not be the young who have changed for the worse so much as the not-so-young; the fake youth generation who can't and won't let go and are probably so far beyond help now that we actually consider ourselves to be better at being young than genuine yoof, with their unfortunate complexions and happy-slapping shenanigans.' It has become common to take broadcasters to task for pandering to a younger audience, and since 1994, when it enjoyed a burst of popularity, 'yoof' has been the keyword around which virtually all of such polemics are constructed. Typical is an opinion piece by Tory politician Michael Gove from 1997 in which, describing himself as a 'thirty-something Young Aberdonian', he lambasts the right-wing Centre for Policy Studies for suggesting that his own party use the media and technology to project a younger image. 'One does not need to be a nonagenarian Old Etonian like Anthony Powell to find this clumsy genuflection to Yoof hideously politically misjudged . . . embarrassing . . . potentially harmful to the Tory cause.' Occasionally the buzzword becomes a countable noun: 'The harshness of the new culture doesn't seem to have made people any happier, not even the yoofs whose presumed tastes reign supreme' (Jonathan Foreman why-oh-why-ing in the *Daily Mail* in 2005).

What some call 'yoofspeak' was promoted by then Mayor of London Ken Livingstone in 2006 in the form of free crash courses for tourists in what linguists refer to as multi-ethnic youth dialect (MEYD), also known as multicultural London English. Open-air tutorials were offered in five languages or dialects: Bengali, Spanish, sign language, cockney and teen slang. As a constituency, however, young people are not easy to reach, even via their own modes of communication: in 2007, in an attempt to engage with what was referred to as 'Generation TXT', the Hansard Society, a charity promoting political education, invited sixteen-to-twenty-five-year-olds to send evidence to parliamentary committees by mobile phone. After contacting 500 schools and 200 community youth projects, 101 young people registered to take part in the Citizen Calling Project. Sadly, just eight bothered to send a message. Shortly after this, the Frontier Youth Trust, a Christian group, set up a phone line for young people to leave text messages for God. Its chief executive, Dave Wiles, toured youth clubs and schools across the country dressed as a Franciscan monk to promote the project, but it is not known how many messages were sent or what they said – or if any received a reply.

In fact a consciously non-standard pronunciation of 'youth' in the form of 'yout' or 'yut' was noted in the USA as long ago as 1949. In the UK, the late lexicographer Paul Beale cited researchers D. and R. McPheely, who recorded teenagers in Leicestershire using 'yoof' as a term of address and a synonym for 'person' in 1977. The modern usage is almost certainly unconnected to these earlier instances and seems to have originated in sarcastic banter by music journalists witnessing the efforts of the broadcasters. 'The yoof' is now used lightheartedly in Australia and occasionally in the USA, but in the UK those who really belong to the category – street gang members, schoolkids, younger clubbers, devotees of social networking internet sites, etc. – refer to themselves as 'youth', or in MEYD, with its Afro-Caribbean-Asian inflections, as 'the yout'. In a final shift, marketing agencies and trend-spotters routinely use 'yoof' quite without irony or humour as the 'official' designation of what they like to term a target 'meganiche'. A cynic might point out three things: that 39 per cent of users of social networking sites are actually over thirty-five; that the youth market is no longer a coherent 'demographic' but a myriad 'microniches'; and that the under-twenty-five sector doesn't even punch its weight economically. In a mature economy, it's the baby-boomers who wield 80 per cent of the spending power.